THE THEORY AND PRACTICE OF SYSTEMATIC
PERSONNEL SELECTION

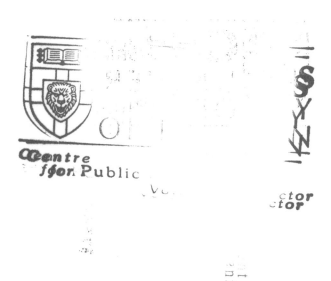

The Theory and Practice of Systematic Personnel Selection

Second Edition

Mike Smith
Senior Lecturer in Occupational Psychology
Manchester School of Management, University of Manchester
Institute of Science and Technology

and

Ivan T. Robertson
Professor of Occupational Psychology
Manchester School of Management, University of Manchester
Institute of Science and Technology

MACMILLAN

First edition (*The Theory and Practice of Systematic
Staff Selection*) 1986
Reprinted once
Second edition (*The Theory and Practice of Systematic
Personnel Selection*) 1993

Published by
MACMILLAN PRESS LTD
Houndmills, Basingstoke, Hampshire RG21 6XS
and London
Companies and representatives
throughout the world

ISBN 0–333–58651–4 hardcover
ISBN 0–333–58652–2 paperback

A catalogue record for this book is available
from the British Library.

10   9   8   7   6   5   4   3
03   02   01   00   99   98   97   96

Printed in Great Britain by
Antony Rowe Ltd
Chippenham, Wiltshire

Contents

PART II PSYCHOMETRICS

PART III SELECTION METHODS

List of Tables and Figures

Tables

Figures

Preface

We were delighted when *The Theory and Practice of Systematic Staff [Personnel] Selection* became an established advanced text, particularly when we heard of it being referred to as 'The Bible of Selection'! However, even then we were conscious that there had been developments which had come too late to be included in the book and since that time there have been even more. Consequently, we were delighted when Macmillan asked us to produce a second edition.

Our aim has been to retain much of the structure and tone of the original book while at the same time undertaking a complete revision and introducing new topics of ethics, meta-analysis and the psychological impact of selection and assessment procedures. Another change was to alter the title so that it was clear that the book was relevant to all categories of personnel. We sincerely hope that our readers approve of our efforts.

MIKE SMITH
IVAN ROBERTSON

Acknowledgements

We would like to offer our grateful thanks to the following colleagues who proofread draft chapters:

Amar Cherchar, UMIST
Dominic Cooper, UMIST
Dee Cullen, British Telecom
Ian Enzer, UMIST
Kjersti Larsen, UMIST
Tim Marsh, UMIST
Karen McAllister, British Telecom
Nanette McDougall, British Telecom
Paul Ryder, UMIST

We would also like to thank Janet Denny and Sangita Patel for the seemingly endless task of word processing the typescript, Gordon Lengden for producing many of the figures and diagrams, and Julie Smith and Kathleen Robertson for copy-editing and help with the index.

Part I
Preparation

1 Introduction and Ethical Issues

THE CONTEXT OF SELECTION

Next time you are on a long-haul flight, take a good look at your 300 or so fellow passengers. Without doubt they will differ in all sorts of ways: some will be tall and some will be short. Some will be thin, and some, probably those in the seat next to you, will be very large indeed. It is not only their physical characteristics which will differ: their personalities will vary, too. Jobs differ. The cabin staff need qualities to enable them to deal with demanding passengers. The navigator needs precise spatial reasoning. It is clear that selecting the right person for some jobs can be literally a matter of life or death.

Even in less hazardous situations, selecting the right person for the job can be of enormous importance. A company can be dragged to its knees by the weight of ineffective staff which decades of ineffectual selection methods have allowed to accumulate.

Subsequent chapters will show that vast sums of money are involved. It is fairly easy to use selection to improve productivity by 6 per cent. Under very favourable circumstances selection can bring about gains of 20 per cent or more. Applied to whole economies, the huge potential of proper selection is apparent. Six per cent of the USA's Gross National Product (GNP) is over $300 billion, 6 per cent of the UK's GNP is over £28 000 million and 6 per cent of Australia's GNP is over A$22 000 million.

Effective selection also brings benefits to the employing organisation and its employees. Companies who are able to ensure a match between job requirements and people's characteristics will obtain a competitive advantage. Good selection procedures should reduce the worry and pressure on employees in jobs where they are out of their depth.

THE ESSENTIALS OF A SELECTION SYSTEM

The need for selection arises from two indisputable facts: first, people differ in their characteristics; second, jobs differ in the demands they

3

make on workers. In essence, selection involves systematically matching people to jobs. The stages can be divided into four (see Figure 1.1).

First the *preparation stage*. Preparation involves analysing the job to determine what is involved and what is needed from workers. Two things flow from the job analysis: a specification of the characteristics of the people who are best equipped to meet the demands of the job, and criteria which can be used to assess work performance. The development of the personnel specification and the development of criteria often take place simultaneously. The third aspect of preparation is to attract a reasonable number of people who might have the characteristics the job requires and to deal with the candidates.

The *selection stage* follows preparation. The first and crucial decision is to decide upon the most appropriate method of selection. The choice of methods is wide and ranges from tests and interviews to graphology and astrology. In recent years several investigations have tried to assess the usages of different selection methods. J. M. Smith and Abrahamsen (1992) have collated the data and the results are shown in Table 1.1. Each methods has advantages and disadvantages. Comparing their rival claims involves comparing each method's merit and *psychometric properties*, such as reliability and validity.

The final stage of a selection system concerns *evaluation*. Evaluation also involves aspects such as the absence of bias.

This book follows the basic selection process which has just been outlined. In each chapter both the practical and theoretical aspects are described.

Selection and Other Areas of Organisational and Occupational Psychology

Selection is one of the main methods an organisation can use to ensure it has an effective work force. Certainly it is fairly easy to obtain a 6 per cent increase in productivity by using better ways of choosing among candidates. However, the contribution of better selection must be assessed in perspective. Figure 1.2 shows the relationship of selection to other methods of ensuring an efficient work force.

Producing an efficient worker starts with a careful analysis of the job and then producing a personnel specification of the person who is suited to the job. Next the process can take three routes or a combination of three routes. Suppose the personnel specification calls for operatives whose hand–eye co-ordination is good enough to allow them accurately to position the protective layer of a laser video disc.

Figure 1.1   The stages of systematic selection

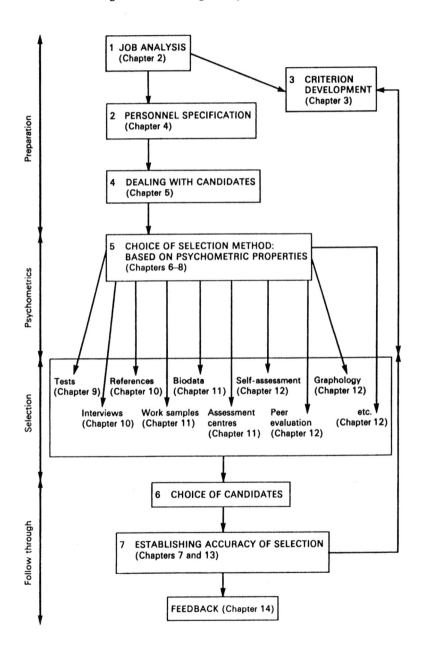

Table 1.1   The use of various methods of selection in six countries

	Country						
Method of Selection	UK	*France*	*Germany*	*Israel*	*Norway*	*Netherlands*	*All*
Interviews	92	97	95	84	93	93	93
CV/application letter	86	89	92	72		63*	80*
Medial examination			50			71	61
Experience			40			63	52
References/recommendations	74	39	23	30		49	43
Diplomas and certificates			44			28	36
Cognitive tests	11	33	21		25	21	22
Peformance evaluation			19				19
Preliminary test						19	19
Personality tests	13	38	6		16		18
Discussion groups		15					15
Trainability tests	14						14
Graphology	3	52	2	2	2	4	13
Work sample	18	16	13		13	5	13
Assessment centres	14	8	10	3	10		8
Biodata	4	1	8	1	8		4
Astrology	0	6		1			2

Notes: Numbers refer to the percentage of maximum possible usage: *indicates minimum value.

The company could try to select appropriate people or it could try the ergonomic approach. It could redesign the protective layers with a series of lugs which will fit together only when they are aligned correctly. Instead of trying to identify the top 10 per cent of applicants in terms of their hand–eye co-ordination, the company can employ a wider range of applicants and save upon costs. Generally, it is better to redesign equipment or other aspects of the job rather than try to select appropriate individuals: the result will be more precise and will last longer. However, there are many jobs which cannot be redesigned or where restructuring can only be achieved at inordinate expense.

Alternatively, the company could accept most applications and provide a training course in hand-eye co-ordination. Whilst this solution might be feasible, it is probably less effective than selecting applicants with the appropriate capabilities. The output of a training course can be uncertain, and most training schemes cost far more than appropriate selection methods. Consequently the best general advice is that a company should first design a job so that it demands as few requirements as possible. Next, it should select workers on the

Figure 1.2　Organisational psychology paradigm

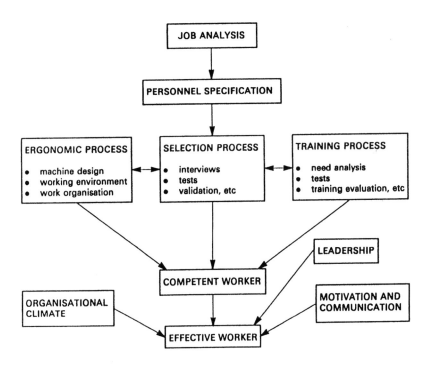

remaining requirements. When it is impossible to select workers with the right abilities the company should invest in training facilities.

Of course, in practice the situation is rarely this clear cut. Ergonomics, selection and training interact and complement each other to produce a competent worker. To be effective, the organisation must also provide motivation, communication and an appropriate organisational climate and structure.

ETHICAL ISSUES IN SELECTION AND ASSESSMENT

The ethical issues of staff selection seem to be ignored by most texts. However, we make no apology for including ethical issues in our first chapter. Ethical issues are important aspects which should permeate the whole selection process. Many ethical codes (for example, British Psychological Society (BPS, 1974) can be subsumed under five principles.

The *Principle of Positive Self Regard* maintains that human dignity should be upheld and that except in quite exceptional circumstances, at the end of the selection process *candidates should have as high an opinion of themselves and their human worth as they did at the start.* This principle was probably first enunciated in counselling. It is particularly relevant to selection because selection situations have a high potential for adverse personal impact (see Chapter 14). Candidates should not be subjected to degrading or embarrassing situations. In this context, degradation and embarrassment must be seen through the eyes of the candidates, and not through the eyes of the selectors whose sensitivities may have been dulled by years of exposure to selection situations. The principle of positive self regard is also relevant to the way that candidates are received and treated during the selection process and the way any feedback is provided.

The *Principle of Informed Consent* maintains that *candidates have a right to know what they are letting themselves in for before they make any significant commitment to take part.* Candidates should have a clear idea of the process that is used, the way that decisions will be made and the uses to which any information they provide will be put. They should also be clear about who will own the information and the relationship between the selector and the organisation involved. This information to candidates should be given without misrepresentation and in a way which can be understood easily: long-winded, academic but technically correct explanations often make it more difficult to exercise the principle of informed consent. The principle of informed consent can also be violated by exaggeration, sensationalism and superficiality.

In the selection context, the principle of informed consent also applies to the relationship between the selector and the organisation for whom he or she performs work. The main issues are:

(a) information about the selector's qualifications and affiliations should be accurate;
(b) false claims about experience, capabilities and characteristics should not be made. Announcements of services and brochures should be descriptive only. Any claims about the efficiency of the service should be limited to those which he or she would be willing to submit to professional scrutiny.

Sometimes the principle of informed consent involves moderating exaggerated beliefs which are already held by others. For example, if an organisation believed that graphology was a perfect method of selection, there would be an ethical obligation to attempt to change the organisation's view. In some cases, the principle of informed consent also means preventing others using one's professional name and reputation in connection with services or products in such a way as to misrepresent one's responsibility for them. Any free trials given to organisations and individuals should be representative of the work which would be done and should not be atypical. For example, it would be wrong to give a free trial of personality assessment using both form A and form B of the 16PF and then, when awarded a contract, to conduct routine personality assessments on the basis of form C. In many ways, selectors are spared some of the really difficult issues which the principle of informed consent may raise. In most cases we deal with adults who are able to exercise their own proper judgement. We are rarely on the rack of deciding to over-ride a person's own judgement with our own judgements or the judgements of a guardian or trustee.

The principle of informed consent also applies to situations where a conflict of interest may arise between unions, management, subordinates, superiors, candidates and prospective employer. In eventualities like this it is important, at an early stage, to define the nature and the direction of obligations and to make sure that they are clear to those concerned.

The *Principle of Competence* means that *selectors should give a high quality service which meets high technical and professional standards.* Observing the principle of competence probably starts by recognising the limits of one's own competence and also recognising the limits of the techniques which are used. Once these limits are recognised, it is then easier to ensure that work is only undertaken within the area of competence and that work lying outside this area can be referred to others. Work which is undertaken should be done to high standards of integrity and objectivity. Often these standards, such as the use of tests, are defined by the appropriate professional body (such as the American Psychological Association (APA) or the Australian Psychological Society).

In a changing world, the principle of competence also imposes the need to extend competence. This extension of competence has two main parts: personal competence and the competence of one's discipline. It is relatively easy to extend one's own competence by training or self-development. The main difficulty is obtaining experience in a way which cannot bring harm or distress to others, and avoiding the danger of believing that one has reached a state of competence when one has not. An example of the latter would be when a new graduate attempts to apply his or her theoretical learning without supervision from an experienced selector. The extension of the discipline's body of knowledge about selection is more difficult, and is often a long-term and cumulative aim. The authors of this present book have certainly benefitted from the body of knowledge of others. We hope that the readers of this book will in turn help to extend what is known beyond the present state of the art.

The *Principle of Confidentiality* is important because selection often involves information which could be used to the detriment of the persons or organisations who give the information. In essence, the principle of confidentiality means *guarding information so it cannot be misused in a way detrimental to those who give it*. In this context, detrimental should be defined in the eyes of the person who owns the information. Observance of the principle of confidentiality therefore starts by defining who owns the information (it is often the person who imparts it) and clarifying with the owner his or her views about its dissemination. In the absence of any specific agreement to the contrary, it must be assumed that information obtained during selection is confidential to a small number of people who need to have that information in order to arrive at an accurate and equitable decision.

At the level of the *candidate*, the principle of confidentiality means taking the following into account.

1. Unless there is specific agreement (preferably written) to the contrary, documents identifying specific individuals should have very strictly controlled circulation. It should be noted that personal identification can be overt (ie a name) or implicit – for example a series of tabulations can identify an individual because, say, they are the only college educated, male, 45 year old, working as a psychologist in a firm in Wollongong! To avoid difficulties of this type (and for statistical reasons) publication of tables where there are fewer than about five entries per cell should be avoided.
2. Data and information should be stored in a safe place. If the data is stored on a computer any relevant data protection legislation should be observed. Proper arrangements should be made for the ultimate destruction or confinement of confidential material.
3. Personal information which is irrelevant to selection should not be reported – even though it may be sensational, lurid and dramatic!

4. Before taking up references, the express permission of the candidate should be obtained.

5. The candidate's ownership and copyright of personal documents should be respected. These documents should not be photocopied without specific consent.

The principle of confidentiality involves more than safeguarding the information given by candidates: it also involves the issue of *what information can be requested*. The candidates' right to privacy means that they should not be asked to divulge information irrelevant to the selection decision. This often involves personal privacy; it may also involve information about present or previous employers which would have commercial value. In most circumstances asking a candidate for specific information about the sales figures, operating procedures and product development activities of their present employer is quite unethical. It is also clearly unethical to use the selection situation to obtain ideas or work for free. It may be reasonable to ask candidates for their ideas about how a project should be handled, but it is wrong then to use the ideas of rejected candidates without their permission or without paying them.

The duty of *confidentiality to the organisation* employing the selector is also important. Good selection invariably means that the selector obtains commercial, and often valuable information about the organisation. This information should be safeguarded too. It should not be divulged either gratuitously in social conversation or as a ploy to obtain work from another organisation.

Finally, there is a duty of *confidentiality to the owners of the materials* used during selection; often this boils down to those who produce tests. Confidentiality of the material should be maintained and not divulged to prospective candidates or those who are not registered test users. A scenario where the principle of confidentiality is often broken is at the stage when tests are being introduced to the company for the first time. The Chief Executive may wish to be given tests so that he can judge their suitability. The danger is that they will be photocopied and subsequently handed to someone applying for a job where that test will be used as a part of the selection process.

One issue provides an exception to the principle of confidentiality. Where there is good reason to believe that there is a clear *danger to the individual or society* then confidential information may be given to other people. In cases of this kind, a first step is probably to discuss the case, in confidence, with a colleague of equal or senior experience. The colleague chosen should have no connection with the individual and no interest in the point at issue.

The *Principle of Client Welfare* is more nebulous than the other four but it is equally important. It does not involve many technical issues but rather a civilised and fair way of relating to clients. A simple point is that a selector should *terminate a consulting relationship* when it is clear that the client is no longer benefiting from it. In selection, these situations are much rarer than in, say, psychotherapy where individual clients can develop a strong dependency on an adviser. However, they can still occur in selection if an organisation continues to call on the services of an external selector because it does not realise that the expertise and resources are available within the organisation.

Sometimes, selectors and psychologists recognise that a situation is beyond their domain of competence and, sensibly, refer the organisation to a colleague who has relevant expertise. An important point is that the psychologist must *maintain responsibility*, as best he or she can, until referral has been taken up. This is important because an occupational psychologist is often the only psychologist with whom an organisation has any contact. Consequently, there is a tendency for any kind of behavioural problem (clinical, forensic or psychiatric) to be referred to the occupational psychologist. One of the authors vividly remembers a dramatic case in an organisation for whom he had assessed several individuals. After a gap of several years, he received a telephone call to say that the firm was undergoing a great deal of pressure and one of the senior managers had taken to bringing a gun to the office: what should the organisation do? The situation was way beyond any previous experience. After initiating elementary action to safeguard the welfare of others, colleagues and authorities with relevant experience were contacted. Nevertheless a watching brief was maintained, giving the best advice available until colleagues and authorities had clearly taken over responsibility.

The final point under this heading is that the selector should show sensible regard to the *social codes and moral expectations* of the community in which he or she works. An atheist accepting a commission in a monastery should not engage in conversations or behaviour which would cause gratuitous offence!

There is a final set of ethical considerations. They govern the ways in which selectors relate to each other and are general principles which govern *relationships between most professionals*. In general they concern boundaries and roles. The issues are, perhaps, most difficult when working in a joint practice or on corporate activities. A guiding principle is the agreement of an orderly and explicit arrangement concerning roles and obligations. This agreement should also cover the termination of the arrangements. All partnerships and arrangements eventually dissolve. Dissolution will be much easier and less traumatic if the conditions for the dissolution are clearer from the start. A common principle governing the relationship between professionals is that a professional should avoid offering services to someone already receiving them from another professional unless the other professional has agreed. This common sense stipulation is meant to avoid confusing clients, preventing manipulation by clients and causing unwitting or damaging interference in a course of action already in train.

Finally, there is an obligation to refrain from comment and criticism on the views or conduct of professional colleagues unless those views and conduct clearly violate professional standards. Restraint of this kind helps promote a harmonious profession and prevents the diversion of energy into disruptive quarrelling. However, this does not, and should not, prevent proper scientific debate in conferences, seminars and journals. Indeed, if that were the case, this book would be much slimmer and probably less useful, in terms of both theory and in practice.

2 Job Analysis

The first stage of filling any vacancy can be completed long before the vacancy arises; it consists of analysing the job. However, the process of analysing a job is not solely concerned with selection. Accurate job analysis is an important part of the general management process and it can be used in many ways.

THE MANY USES OF JOB DESCRIPTIONS

One hosiery company maintains job descriptions for all its employees and ensures that they are kept up to date by a series of annual reviews. The job analysis was originally for selection but, once the job descriptions were available, the company found that they were useful for many other purposes. The job descriptions have helped:

(a) to reorganise the company workforce;
(b) to produce a more rational and acceptable salary structure;
(c) to identify training needs.

  A reorganisation of the company structure arose out of the existence of job descriptions. Once the company had a clear statement of contents of each job, it realised that it could structure its work force in a more efficient way. In the case of one employee, the job descriptions helped to bring to light the fact that, due to past history, he was reporting to a director who was not in a position to exercise effective control over his work. The job descriptions also helped remove animosity between the canteen staff by ensuring that all tasks were allocated to specific individuals, and reducing the possibilities for misunderstanding.
  In each of these instances, the nature of the problem and their solutions were apparent from clear, concise, *written* descriptions of the jobs involved. In theory, the improvements could have been achieved without written descriptions. In practice, they were not. In practice, selection without a written job description is usually muddle-headed, capricious and incomplete.

METHODS OF JOB ANALYSIS

Standard textbooks in such as Blum and Naylor (1968), E. H. McCormick and Tiffin (1974) and Landy and Trumbo (1980) list several methods of analysing jobs. The method which is adopted will depend upon the exact situation and the intended use. In a situation where there are limited resources a fairly common-sense approach is called for. The selection process often requires only a straightforward analysis which identifies the six or seven most salient points. In large organisations such as the armed forces, or a large organisation in the telecommunications industry where there are hundreds of recruits each year and where the consequences of mistake are high, it is worth undertaking a rigorous job analysis.

A Basic Six-Step Approach to Job Analysis

In most selection contexts a basic six-step approach is quite adequate and will bring about a notable improvement in efficiency:

1. Collect together documents such as the training manual, which give information concerning the job.
2. Ask the relevant manager about the job. Ask about the main purposes of the job, the activities involved and the personal relationships which must be maintained with others.
3. Ask job holders similar questions about their job. In some circumstances it may be possible to persuade job holders to keep a detailed record of their work activities over a period of one or two weeks.
4. Observe the job holders performing their work and make a note of the most important points. If possible, observe each job being performed on two separate days, at different times of the day.
5. Attempt to do the job yourself. (It will be impossible to follow this step for every job. It would be dangerous for anyone but a skilled worker to operate some types of machinery such as a drop forge and in other jobs, the main activities are mental work which cannot be directly observed.)
6. Write the job description. There is no single format which is better than others. However, the format described in Figure 2.1 has been found to be very useful and can be used with little prior knowledge. It assembles the information about the job under six headings. An example of a job description produced using the six-stage method is given in Figure 2.2.

Figure 2.1   Contents of job description

---

1 Job Identification

Covering job title, location of the job (for example, press-shop, Longbridge works), number of people in the job and the person to whom job holder is responsible. The job description *does not* include the name of the person holding the job. It is a description of the job which needs to be performed irrespective of the person who is currently doing the job.

2 Main Purpose of the Job

A brief and unambiguous statement is all that is required.

3 Responsibilities

Often this section contains a list of the key results which the job holder must achieve. It seeks to provide a record of the job holder's responsibilities for people, materials, money, tools and equipment. It is particularly important to identify the key results. Usually, the key results concern:

(a) a product produced to a previously agreed schedule (such as 300 word processors per month for production line C);
(b) a specified standard of quality (for example, customer complaints less than 5% within 1 year of purchase, and costs of 'warranty repairs' less than 15% sales turnover);
(c) the efficient utilisation of resources (for example, value added per employee over 20 000 ecus and return on capital of 11%);
(d) the development of personnel, especially the development of subordinates (for example, to ensure that staff are trained in at least two skills and to ensure that the department provides at least one person per year who has sufficient potential and experience to warrant promotion to middle management).

In management job descriptions, it may also be necessary to detail the control over subordinates: the number and level of people controlled, the responsibilities for their recruitment, supervision, development, discipline, dismissal and salary determination. Financial control is another area where detailed description may be necessary (for example, responsibilities for budgetary control and cost control: what assets or stock fall under his jurisdiction? What are the obligations for sales, purchasing or investment? What role does he need to play in forecasting and planning?). A final aspect which should be included in the responsibilities section is the amount of guidance and supervision that should be expected from the superior.

4 Relationships with People

In addition to identifying the people involved, it should also indicate the nature of the relationship (for example, liaison, consults, directs, notifies). If the job holder needs to work in a team or has to deal with different types of people, it is usually specified here.

5 Physical Conditions

In job descriptions for operatives, the *fifth* section concerning *physical conditions* may be the most important section. It specifies the place of work, the hours and the possibilities for overtime working. The fifth section should also state whether the work is active or sedentary and the physical demands which are made on the job holder's senses or the requirements for strength, physical endurance or skills. If the work involves any risks, they are normally recorded in this section.

6 Pay and Promotion

The salary, increments, commissions bonuses and perks (such as luncheon vouchers or company car) should be clearly stated. Pension schemes, absence and illness regulations and any bonus schemes should also be included. Finally the prospects for promotion or transfer should be included in appropriate situations.

Figure 2.2   Example of job description

JOB DESCRIPTION

1 Job Title   WOOD MACHINIST (Trencher)

2 Location   MILL SHOP

3 Number in Job   8

4 Purpose of Job
To take pre-cut and pre-planed wood and to cut trenches of specified
dimensions at specified positions.

5 Responsibilities
Responsible to Mill Shop Foreman.

6 Relationships
Works largely on own, but has some contact with the operatives performing
previous and subsequent operations. Sometimes required to train new
operatives.

7 Physical Conditions
The Mill Shop is dry, well lit and ventilated but there is no heating at any
time of year; noise levels can be high. Work is performed in standing
position. Some lifting and carrying is involved.

8 Outline of Job
8.1   Transport batch of wood from previous process by pulling along
       trolley.
8.2   Check with plan the position of the trenches, change cutters on
       trencher if necessary.
8.3   Take small batches of wood to bench, place in position under
       trenching machine using pre-set guides. Pull cutters of trencher
       forward, keeping hands clear of cutters.
8.4   Restack trenched wood neatly and safely.
8.5   When batch is completed, pull cart to next operative.
8.6   Complete simple forms.

9 Safety Aspects
The work involves a number of potential hazards:

9.1   Falling stacks of wood.
9.2   Injury from the cutters of the trenching machine.

10 Salary and Conditions of Service
Salary: Flat rate of 900 ecus per week plus monthly group bonus.
Holidays: Three weeks per year plus Bank Holidays.
Hours: Monday–Friday 9.00am–5.00pm.
Saturdays – 8.30am–12.30pm.
Breaks: Afternoon and morning breaks of 15 minutes. Lunch break of 1 hour.
Overtime: Usually available.

MORE INVOLVED APPROACHES TO JOB ANALYSIS

When to Use More Complex Methods

The basic six-step approach is well within the competence of an intelligent manager or personnel specialist. It is cost-effective and yields results which are quite adequate for most selection purposes. However, if the organisation intends to establish a complex and sophisticated selection system involving extended interviews, psychological tests and practical exercises, then the extra detail of a comprehensive job description can be usefully incorporated.

The circumstances where a complex method is justified usually involves three factors. First, more complex methods of jobs analysis are warranted when large numbers of recruits are involved. For example, if an electricity undertaking recruits more than 50 fitters per year and there is a good supply of candidates, the extra expense will be justified. A second circumstance justifying the use of a more complex method is when the consequences and costs of failure are very high. For example, the costs of training a policeman are over 100 000 ecus; the cost of employing an unsuitable refinery technician could, in an emergency, result in millions of ecus of damage; and the cost of employing a zany chief executive could spell disaster and bankruptcy. Third, the extra expense of sophisticated analysis may be acceptable if the job analysis can be used for some other purpose such as the design of training or a job salary grading exercise.

The Complex Methods of Job Analysis

Probably the most comprehensive list of job analysis techniques was that compiled by Blum and Naylor (1968), which itemised ten different methods. The main advantages and disadvantages of nine of the methods are set out in Figure 2.3.

Figure 2.3   Advantages and disadvantages of nine methods of job analysis

---

1 **Questionnaire Method**
   Advantages   Good for producing quantitative information and can produce objective and generalisable results; cheap.
   Disadvantages   Substantial sample needed; Substantial foreknowledge needed to be able to construct questionnaire; respondents must be able and willing to give accurate replies.

2 **Checklist Method**
   Similar to questionnaire method but, since responses are either YES or NO, the results may be 'cruder' or require larger sample. They tend to require fewer subjective judgements.

3 **Individual Interviews**
   Advantages   Very flexible; can provide in-depth information; easy to organise and prepare.
   Disadvantages   Time-consuming; expensive; difficult to analyse.

4 **Observation Interviews**
   Similar to individual interview but gives additional information, for example, visual or auditory information. These contextual cues make it more difficult for the analyst to be misled. The methods may expose both the analyst and the worker to increased safety hazards.

5 **Group Interviews**
   Similar to the individual interview but they are less time-consuming for analyst and some claim that richer information is obtained since interviewees stimulate each other's thoughts. They are more difficult to organise and there is the danger that a group is over-influenced by one individual.

6 **Expert Analysis**
   Advantages   Quick, cheap and can be used for jobs that do not yet exist. Can avoid restrictive practices.
   Disadvantages   The 'experts' may not be true experts and an unrealistic analysis may result.

7 **Diary Method**
   Advantages   Cheap, flexible and requires little advance preparation. Useful for non-manual tasks where observation is of limited value. Can also be used in jobs involving a wide variety of tasks.
   Disadvantages   Needs co-operation from respondents; tendency to keep incomplete logs, so frequent but minor items often omitted.

8 Work Participation Method
  Advantages   Can produce very realistic analyses.
  Disadvantages Expensive, time-consuming and can only be used for jobs
                   requiring short training and no safety hazards.

9 Critical Incident Method
  Advantages   Focuses on the aspects of a job that are crucial to success.
  Disadvantages Often produces incomplete data difficult to analyse.

Observation and Expert Analysis

The most frequently used methods are observation, diaries and questionnaires. An excellent example of the use of *observation method* is Mintzberg's study of *The Nature of Managerial Work* (1973). He observed each of five chief executives over a week. Providing the observers are well trained, the observation method can provide high quality information, but it is labour intensive and costly. The observation method is applicable to situations where there are a few people holding the jobs and where high quality information is needed. Job analysis using the observation method is easy to conduct. All that is needed is a timepiece (usually with a digit to show seconds) and sheets of paper with the volunteer's name and other identification data, plus appropriate column headings such as time, activity and place. In practice, job analysis by observation methods encounters three main difficulties. First, many jobs are not amenable to this type of analysis; some 'mental' jobs involve little observable activity, and some highly skilled manual jobs involve actions which are too speedy to analyse although slow motion and video techniques may be used to overcome this difficulty. Second, some 'volunteers' may not wish all their actions to be observed. This may arise when the job involves very confidential information or where work is done at non-traditional times in non-traditional settings (for example, when work is done in the evenings at home). Third, analysts may record their observations inaccurately, using words and concepts which are not in general use.

Functional job analysis was developed to mitigate the third problem (Fine and Wiley, 1977): it was designed to control the language used to describe a job. Functional job analysis (FJA) adopts the same conceptualisation of work as the US Training and Employment Service, which essentially maintains that work is done in relation to data, people or things. Figure 2.4 shows that each of these areas has a number of levels. FJA is relevant to many methods of job analysis, but

22

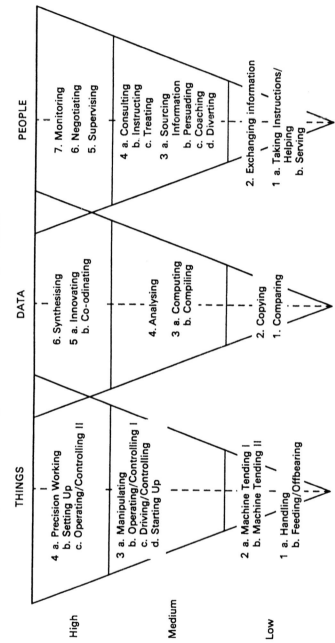

Figure 2.4 Fine's functional job analysis

THINGS

4 a. Precision Working
  b. Setting Up
  c. Operating/Controlling II

3 a. Manipulating
  b. Operating/Controlling I
  c. Driving/Controlling
  d. Starting Up

2 a. Machine Tending I
  b. Machine Tending II

1 a. Handling
  b. Feeding/Offbearing

DATA

6. Synthesising
5 a. Innovating
  b. Co-odinating

4. Analysing

3 a. Computing
  b. Compiling

2. Copying
1. Comparing

PEOPLE

7. Monitoring
6. Negotiating
5. Supervising

4 a. Consulting
  b. Instructing
  c. Treating

3 a. Sourcing
     Information
  b. Persuading
  c. Coaching
  d. Diverting

2. Exchanging information

1 a. Taking Instructions/
     Helping
  b. Serving

High

Medium

Low

Source Fine (1986).

it is particularly relevant to the observation method. However, it is a fairly complex system and a minimum of four or five days' training is needed for observers.

C JAM and *B JAM* are abbreviations of combination job analysis method, and brief job analysis method, and were developed by E. L. Levine (1983). A group of subject matter experts, usually called SMEs, generate a list of tasks which are involved in a job. Each task is then rated on its difficulty, criticality and the time needed. The importance of each task is derived by the formula.

Task Importance = Difficulty × Criticality + Time

The SMEs also generate a list of the knowledge, skills, abilities and other characteristics (KSAOs) which are needed by a job. Each KSAO is rated on four attributes: 'necessary for new workers', 'practical to expect', 'extent of trouble likely', and 'distinguishes superman from average worker'. By combining these ratings, KSAO importance is calculated.

Diaries

At first sight, nothing could be easier than analysing a job by the diary method. All that is needed is a sheet of paper headed with the date and the volunteer's name. In practice, difficulties arise in five ways. First, not all jobs are suitable: short cycle repetitive jobs, jobs involving speedy or delicate manual skills, and jobs occupied by employees unused to verbalising their activities present particular problems.

Second, there is the problem of controlling how and when the volunteers use the diary: some volunteers ignore the diary for weeks and rely on their memories to make their entries in the ten minutes before the actual deadline for handing in their diaries. One variation is for the job analyst to telephone the volunteer at a prearranged time (for example, 4.30 p.m.) every day and ask what activities have been undertaken in the preceding 24 hours.

Third, diaries are notoriously open to distortion according to the image the volunteer wishes to project. It is easy to claim longer hours on a wider variety of more important tasks than is objectively the case. Fourth, it is difficult to maintain consistent reporting standards: some volunteers report in tedious, excruciating detail while others hardly give any information at all. Fifth, there is the problem of analysis. Diary sheets have to be collated. Frequencies and duration of activities have to be extracted and tabulated. This time-consuming process is inherently inaccurate. In addition, there may be an element of subjectivity because different volunteers may use different words to refer to the same activity or, even more confusingly, they may use the same words to refer to different activities. The analyst is often left with the subjective task of deciding what the volunteer means and *then* allotting it to an appropriate category.

One way of mitigating these problems is to abandon the idea of a blank piece of paper for a system of headings to guide the diary entries. Better still, all the possible entries can be listed and the volunteer is merely required to tick the appropriate boxes. For example, Hinricks (1964) designed a log sheet for a study of the ways in which research staff communicate with each other. Each time there was communication, the volunteer ticked the appropriate boxes. This approach involves more preparation and there is the danger that something crucial is missed from the log sheet. However, it overcomes many problems and is much easier to analyse. An excellent example of the use of diaries is Rosemary Stewart's classic study, *Managers and their Jobs* (1967).

Questionnaire Methods

Many practitioners adopt the questionnaire method. The simplest type of job analysis questionnaire or, as they are sometimes called, a job inventory, is the checklist. Checklists usually contain over a hundred activities and job incumbents mark activities which are included in their jobs. A classic example is Morse and Archer's (1967) analysis of wire and antenna engineers in the US Air Force. A more recent example of a checklist is Youngman, Ostoby, Monk and Heywood's (1978) checklist for engineering occupations.

Checklists require thorough preparation which should include wide consultation and a 'field trial' in order to ensure that no important activities have been missed and that the instructions, wording, layout and method of responding are correct. A distinctive feature of checklists is that they can be only used in situations where a large sample is available. In essence, the analysis will be based upon the proportion of people giving positive answers to an item. If the sample is below 30, the results will be both erratic and insensitive.

Rating scales are an improvement upon the relatively crude and insensitive checklist. Like checklists, rating scales present the volunteer with a list of work activities but, instead of simply asking to mark those activities performed in the job, a scale would ask for ratings between one and, typically, seven, according to the amount of time it involves. The following scale is typical of the seven-point scales in use.

1. It rarely occurs (less than 11% of the job)
2. It occupies a small part of the job (between 11 and 24%)
3. It occupies rather less than half the job (between 25 and 39%)
4. It occupies about half the job (between 60 and 74%)
5. It occupies rather more than half the job (between 75 and 89%)
6. It occupies a large majority of the job (between 75 and 89%)
7. It occupies practically the whole of the job (more than 90% of the job)

The percentage bands need to be adjusted according to the complexity of the job, since jobs with many activities tend to produce lower percentage figures for each individual activity. Job rating scales are not necessarily restricted to asking about time. Morse and Archer's checklist also requested ratings of time spent and importance.

Often a checklist or rating scale will need to be designed for each type of job and guidelines for the development of checklists is given by E. J. McCormick (1976). However, several general purpose rating scales are available. The most widely used is the position analysis questionnaire (PAQ) developed by E. J. McCormick, Jeanneret and Mecham (1972). The development of the PAQ was particularly rigorous and scientific: the studies involved collecting data for 3700 jobs and then using the statistical procedure of principal components analysis to extract the recurrent trends in the data. There were six major trends concerning:

(a) the input of information (for example, perceptual interpretation);
(b) mental processes (for example, decision-making);
(c) work output (for example, use of foot controls);
(d) relationships with people (for example, serving/entertaining);
(e) work environment (for example, hazardous physical environment);
(f) other characteristics.

Within each of these headings, scales were developed to measure more specific requirements. For example, the heading 'mental processes' included items concerning decision-making and information processing. In total there are scales for almost 200 job elements. Most of the scales share a particular advantage; they start with a thorough description of the aspect to be rated and then each point on the rating scale is accompanied by a benchmark (a specific standard which can be used for comparison). Examples of two of the scales are given in Figure 2.5.

Thus the PAQ enjoys the advantages of being generally applicable, comprehensive and having benchmarks. However, it is time-consuming to administer and requires some specialist knowledge. The PAQ is a 'broad spectrum' job analysis questionnaire which is not particularly suited to the analysis of managerial or professional jobs. However, the professional and managerial position questionnaire is similar to the PAQ but contains 98 scales relevant to managerial work.

The occupational analysis inventory (OAI: Cunningham, Boese, Neeb and Pass, 1983) was designed for occupational education and guidance purposes. Its 602 items cover five main areas, information

Figure 2.5 Two examples of benchmarked scales similar to those used by McCormick

---

Near Visual Discrimination (visual discrimination of objects within arm's reach)

7 Inspects precision watch parts for defect
6 Proofreads newspaper articles for publishing
5 Reads electric house meters
4 Makes entries on sales tickets
3 Observes position of knife when carving beef
2 Paints house walls
1 Sweeps street with push broom
0 Makes no near visual discrimination

Finger Manipulation (Please check the activity below which involves about as much finger manipulation as the incumbent employs in his job)

7 Performs surgical operations on humans
6 Cuts ornamental designs in jewellery
5 Tunes auto engines
4 Adjusts camera settings to take commercial pictures
3 Packs cakes of soap in cardboard boxes
2 Pulls weeds by hand
1 Carries pieces of furniture
0 Job involves no finger manipulation

---

received, mental activities, work behaviour, work goals and work context. It is particularly good at capturing the technical content of jobs but can be used with most jobs. Unfortunately the OAI is time-consuming to use.

The job component inventory (JCI: Banks, Jackson, Stafford and Warr, 1983) was designed to identify the training needs of 16–17 year olds. It is a British scale and contains over 400 questions covering tools, equipment, perceptual and physical requirements, mathematics, communication, decision-making and responsibility. Administration of the JCI lasts about 45 minutes and can be achieved by trained administrators rather than job analysis experts. It is most suited to jobs requiring limited skill.

The work profiling system (WPS: Saville-Holdsworth Ltd, 1988) starts with a huge pool of over 800 items which take the form of three interlocking questionnaires suitable for:

(a) Managerial and professional workers;
(b) Service and administrative workers;
(c) Manual and technical workers.

After selecting the appropriate level of questionnaire there is a system for choosing the eight or so most appropriate sections for completion. In this way respondents are rarely confronted with more than 200 questions. The WPS takes less than 50 minutes to administer. It yields so much information that computer 'scoring' is virtually obligatory and the computer-generated report gives results in terms of 32 activities for 32 generic activities, such as 'planning', as well as the component activities, such as 'setting short-term objectives'.

Other Job Description inventories are:

● TI–CODAP (Christal, 1974)
● job element method (JEM) (Primoff, 1975)
● ability requirements scale (ARS) (Fleishman, 1975)
● management position description questionnaire (MPDQ) (Tornow and Pinto, 1976)
● threshold traits analysis systems (Lopez, 1988).

AGREEMENT AND RESTRUCTURING

When the job description has been prepared it should be discussed with either the job holder or the union representative. It most circumstances the job description is prepared by the job holder's superior, but where it is prepared by someone else, such as the Personnel Officer or Training Officer, the job description should be discussed with the job holder's superior. In the light of these discussions the job description is amended until it is accepted by both the job holder and the boss. In some organisations agreement is formalised to the point where both parties are required to sign the final version.

THEORETICAL ASPECTS OF JOB ANALYSIS

Previous sections of this chapter have carefully avoided the theoretical and academic issues of job descriptions, but there are five issues that deserve some consideration.

Task-Orientated versus Worker-Orientated Variables

Job analysis can focus on two related domains. The first, and probably the most traditional domain, focuses upon *tasks*, such as 'delivers lecture', 'counsels students', 'writes books'. The second focuses upon the *activities* a worker has to perform, such as oral communications, interpersonal empathy and written communication. Inventories use either approach, with a strong tendency for more recent inventories to concentrate upon the worker-orientated variables. In theory, the advantages of the two approaches are finely balanced. As Figure 2.6 shows, job analysis is itself an activity involving a number of stages. For both worker-orientated and task-orientated variables the process starts with the worker performing a job observed by the analyst, and in both cases the route leads to the same final output of attributes which are required to perform the job successfully. Furthermore, the two routes pass through the same three domains and involve equivalent sets of deductions and reports. The main difference lies in the positioning of the interim report. In the *task-orientated* route there is first only a small inferential leap between the observation and the report of the task variables. This is followed by a large inferential leap to obtain the attributes. In following the *worker-orientated* route there is first a large inferential leap followed by a small one. According to this analysis there should be little difference in terms of the functioning of a selection system. However, opinion is more polarised and partisan. E. J. McCormick, Cunningham and Gordon (1967) suggest that the worker-orientated questionnaires yield results which are less vulnerable

Figure 2.6 A schematic analysis of job analysis

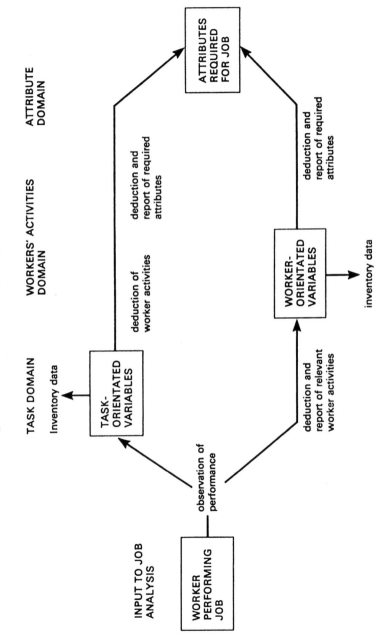

to technological constraints and include more areas. On the other hand, Prien (1977) concludes worker-orientated job analysis data are 'more vulnerable to contamination and . . . more insufficient than task oriented job analysis'. Spector, Brannick and Coovert (1989) suggest that that task-orientated methods might be more appropriate when hiring individuals expected to need little training, while ability-orientated methods are more appropriate for selection when extensive training is expected.

Reliability of Task Analyses

The concept of reliability is considered in detail in Chapter 6. For the present purposes, it is enough to note that it refers to the consistency of a measurement. If the same measures are taken on two occasions and the same answer is obtained, the measures are perfectly reliable. The question therefore arises 'How reliable are job analyses?' This question rather resembles the question 'How long is a piece of string?' and it evokes the same answer: 'It depends.' Clearly, a rushed analysis by an untrained person will not be reliable. So the question becomes 'How reliable can job analyses be?' Again, in reality, the question is more complex because there are three types of reliability. *Repeated measures reliability* is obtained by one analyst performing a job analysis and then, reanalysing it after a period of, say, a week. The two analyses are then compared for consistency (E. J. McCormick, 1976).

There is more specific evidence concerning the second type of reliability: *inter-rater reliability*. In essence, this is investigated by two analysts examining a job at the same time but arriving at independent conclusions. The conclusions are then compared. It is rare for the strict requirements of this method to be met, but a number of studies have approximated this design. For example, Wexley and Silverman (1978) administered an inventory to about 48 effective managers and to about 48 ineffective managers. The results indicated effective store managers did not differ significantly from one another in their ratings to work activities and worker characteristics.

Schmitt and Fine (1983) summarise a number of studies using FJA, which uses a controlled language for the reporting of job analysis, and they note: 'Data in unpublished technical reports do suggest high reliability. For example, in a Coast Guard study, Zepp, Belenky and Rosen (1977) reported that over 98% of 5754 FJA ratings made by independent raters were no more than one scale point different.' Schmitt and Fine go on to describe a study of graduate students who had attended only a four-day training programme. The six graduate students produced coefficients of 0.81, 0.97, 0.82, 0.97 and 0.79, depending upon the exact trait under analysis.

Palmer and McCormick (1961) report a correlation of 0.75 between raters applying a 130-item checklist. The median of the 13 inter-rater coefficients reported by Spector, Brannick and Coovert was 0.67. Thus the overwhelming balance of evidence indicated that with properly constructed inventories and with analysts who have received at least minimal training, the inter-rater reliability of job analyses can be good. However, much of this apparent agreement could be due to what is termed the DNA artefact. Many methods allow job analysts to tick a box saying that a question *does not apply*. In some analyses these replies have been counted as zero. If raters simply agree on those items which do not apply, correlations as high as 0.5 could be produced, irrespective of the fact that they disagreed in their replies to the other items (see R. J. Harvey and Hayes, 1986).

The third type of reliability concerns *inter-sample reliability*. In other words, do the results obtained from one sample correspond to the results obtained from another sample? The evidence on this question is relatively sparse and involves the assumptions that two samples who are said to be performing identical jobs are in fact performing identical jobs. The study by Christal (1969) provides direct evidence. He took 35 samples representing ten career fields: the median correlation for estimates of whether a task was performed in the course of the job was 0.98, and the median correlation for estimates of the time spent on the task was 0.96.

Validity of Task Analyses

Validity is a topic which is discussed in detail in Chapter 7. Here it is sufficient to note that validity is concerned with how well job analyses measure what they claim to measure. Ideally, validity is assessed by comparing the procedure in question against another procedure which is known to be perfect. If they yield similar results, the procedure in question is said to be valid. In practice, difficulties arise because it is hard to find any perfect measure against which to compare the job analysis. If the job analysis is compared against a suspect measure and there is disagreement, it is impossible to know whether the job analysis is at fault or whether the measure used for comparison is at fault.

Industrial psychologists have adopted four main approaches in attempts to establish the validity of job analyses. The first approach, involving comparisons with objective data, is particularly concerned with job inventories which are filled in by workers themselves. It raises the question whether replies are an accurate reflection of the true position. Hartley, Brecht, Weeks, Pagerey, Chapanis and Hoecker (1977) comment, 'we have been able to find only two studies relating to this question, and these have produced results that raise serious questions about the validity of self-report estimates'. They quote Burns's (1957) paper, in which a comparison of diary methods and questionnaire responses revealed that workers over-estimate time spent on important activities and underestimate time spent on 'personal' activities. Klemmer and Snyder (1972) found that workers' estimates vary greatly in accuracy and that time spent in face to face communication is underestimated, whereas time spent reading and writing is overestimated. McCall, Morrison and Hannan's (1978) review of studies of managerial work also concludes that managers do not know how they spend their time. Against this uncertain background, the Hartley *et al.* data is relatively definitive! The highest levels of respondent accuracy was recorded when incumbents were asked *simply to identify* the activities they undertook: here accuracies of 82 per cent and 95 per cent were recorded for two organisations. When individuals were asked to *rank the order* of their activities, correlations of 0.66 and 0.58 were obtained. When individuals were asked *estimate the absolute time spent*, a median correlation of only 0.31 was obtained.

The second approach to investigating the validity of job analyses, such as the PAQ and the TAS (Task Abilities Scale by Fleishman), uses comparisons with expert opinion. This involves the difficulty of ensuring that expert opinion is correct. There is very little empirical evidence available. However, Prien (1977) writes, 'In general, the research results are clear and convincing. The PAQ and the TAS measure what they are supposed to measure!'

The third approach relies upon the ability of the analysis to classify and differentiate between jobs. Here the evidence is more plentiful. Prien (1977) notes: 'Task oriented questionnaires do differentiate within the jobs intended and the differences are consistent within the criterion group characteristics (chief executive officers have higher scores on long-range planning' than do middle management).' This observation is supported by a study by J. M. Smith (1980), which used a novel 'Repertory Grid Technique' to analyse the jobs of a general manager, a factory manager and a product development manager, and found that the results indicated clear differences between the jobs. Prien (1977) refers specifically to the validity of the PAQ when he says,

'The validity of the PAQ ... has been established using ... an occupational classification criterion.' Presumably this refers to E. H. McCormick and Asquith's (1960) study of naval officers. They found that the PAQ responses varied much less when an individual filled out a form several times than when several different people responded to the PAQ. Meyerson, Prien and Vick (1965) also adopted this approach and found that Hemphill's executive position description questionnaire differentiated between company presidents, middle management and personnel department. Similar studies have been conducted by Meyer (1961), Marshall (1964) and Rusmore (1967).

The final approach to establishing the validity of job analyses involves using them to predict some other variable such as salary, job evaluation rankings or the average scores of incumbents as psychological tests, which could be expected to be related to job content. Typical studies are by Champagne and McCormick (1964), Prien, Barrett and Suwtlik (1965) and Mecham and McCormick (1969), who obtained correlations in the range of 0.83–0.90. Similarly, Boshoff (1969) founded that Hemphill's executive position description questionnaire correlated 0.65 with conventional job evaluations.

Sources of non-validity

Validity is often destroyed when other factors or biases contaminate the data. Consequently, in recent years, psychologists have spent considerable time trying to identify factors which might contaminate the rating given during a job analysis. The effort has been largely wasted. Spector *et al.* report that there is little evidence that the ratings are biased by sex, social cues (for example, statements that the job is interesting), experience, performance (for example, good or bad workers), tenure or personality.

Job Families

Job analysis is an essential first stage in the process of scientific selection of staff, yet it is a tedious, time-consuming and expensive process. It is also wasteful because some jobs are very similar to each other. If the jobs which are very similar could be identified they could be grouped into families. Then, when the situation arose, it would not be necessary to perform a comprehensive and separate job analysis since the generalised job analysis of the family could be used. Further, the jobs could be arranged in a hierarchical order which would help us understand the relationships between jobs and job families, and would provide a useful tool for selection, placement, career guidance and training. Orr (1960) obtained six job families which were:

(a) high-level technical supervisory and mechanical jobs;
(b) low-level unskilled jobs;
(c) high-level skilled mechanical jobs;
(d) very high-level jobs with respect to intelligence;
(e) clerical and supervisory level jobs;
(f) medium-level mechanical jobs.

Prien and Ronan (1971) offer a synthesis of this line of research by offering a three-level classification: manual jobs, white-collar jobs and supervisory/technical/managerial jobs.

Pearlman (1980a), in an excellent review of job families and their uses, points out that establishing job families would have three important benefits. First, it would help the development of better selection methods since it would be worth devoting resources to a system that could be used for a large number of vacancies. Second, the sizes of the samples used in validation studies could be increased because the occupants of several similar jobs could be aggregated. As a consequence of larger sample sizes, the results of these studies should be more accurate. Third, a classification of jobs and job families would help determine whether results of studies were generalisable to other jobs within the same organisation and other organisations.

Comparisons between Methods

A final issue for this chapter is a comparison of the effectiveness of the different methods of job analysis. In view of the many methods and many research reports, it is surprising to find that few direct comparisons between methods have been attempted. Boshoff (1969) compared three methods and, more recently, E. L. Levine, Ash and Bennett (1980) compared four methods. The methods were (1) Flanagan's (1954) critical incidents methods; (2) Primoff's (1975) job elements method; (3) McCormick's PAQ and, (4) the US Department of Labor's system of task analysis. The results indicated that the PAQ was the cheapest method of analysis, but some judges thought that it produced the poorest results. The critical incident technique received the highest ratings, but other differences were not large. Schuler (1989) cites a study by Cornelius, Schmidt and Carron which shows that simple procedures are not necessarily inferior to elaborate ones.

3 Criteria

Once a job description has been prepared, there is a very strong impetus to proceed directly to personnel specifications, placement of adverts and selection of candidates. However, *the stage which should follow the analysis of a job is the development of criteria.* To understand the reason it is necessary to look forward to the time when the selection system is in operation. Sooner or later someone will ask whether the selection system works and whether it is valid. To answer these questions it will be necessary to compare the predictions of the selection system against a standard, or perhaps several standards. These criteria *can* be produced at this later stage but there are two good reasons why they should be defined soon after the job analysis has been completed.

The first reason is very prosaic: it may be too late to collect the information if a decision is delayed until criteria are actually needed. An example is a company involved in making cellular telephones. It installed a selection system for the inspectors in charge of the probe cards that are a vital component of the integrated circuits. The new selection system was installed. At the end of the six-month experimental period, it was decided that the number of service calls to customers to replace faulty probe cards would be an appropriate criterion. Had this decision been taken six months earlier it would have been easy to devise a simple system to collect the information. In the event, many tedious hours were spent scanning engineers' reports and collating the data. This particular company was in a relatively fortunate position: with effort it *could* retrieve the data at a later date. In many companies it would have been lost forever.

The second reason concerns intellectual honesty and integrity. If the choice of criteria is delayed until the selection methods are in use, the decision stands a greater chance of being biased in a favourable way. At its worst, a selector may choose the criteria which support the methods in use. More subtly, it can mean that the choice can be distorted at a subconscious level by the absorption of subsequent decisions and events. Intellectually, there is greater integrity in deciding in advance the standards by which the system will be evaluated.

IMPORTANCE OF CRITERIA

Not only should criteria be chosen at the right time, but they should also be chosen with great care. This care and effort is justified by the fact that an unwise choice of criteria can lead to conclusions which are severely misleading. For example, Albright, Smith and Glennon (1959) give details of a selection system for salesmen developed by the Standard Oil Company. Initially, the opinions of supervisors were used as criteria. When compared against these opinions, the selection method seemed to make inaccurate predictions. However, at a later date, other criteria were obtained. When judged against actual promotion decisions it was clear that the same selection methods were able to discriminate between good and poor salesmen. In this example, poor choice of criteria led to a misleadingly pessimistic view of the selection methods involved. As a generalisation, it could be claimed that deficiencies in the criteria usually lead us to underestimate the value of our selection procedures. Fortunately, as shown by formulae in Appendix IV, in certain circumstances it is possible to apply statistical corrections in order to obtain more accurate estimates.

The vital importance of choosing criteria carefully is not always recognised. Jenkins (1946) wrote that inadequate criteria is at the heart of much poor prediction and that psychologists in general 'tended to accept the tacit assumption that criteria were either given of God or just to be found lying about'; he felt and that most textbooks and journal literature would lead to the conclusion that 'expediency dictated the choice of criteria and that convenient availability of criterion was more important than its adequacy'.

LEVELS OF CRITERIA

The most obvious starting place for a search for appropriate criteria is the job description, because it is almost certain to contain explanations of the behaviours and actions which a worker is expected to perform. These behaviours and actions are *immediate level criteria* and can be used to check whether the selection system is choosing the workers who do the expected things and behave in an appropriate way. However, the fact that a worker is smartly dressed, punctual and polite does not necessarily mean that he or she is a good worker.

So, perhaps a search for criteria should concentrate upon a second level: the *results which should be achieved*. A good job description should give clear clues of criteria at the results level. For example, it may refer to a sales objective or it may refer to production output. Often conceptual problems arise. Workers may be doing the right things but achieving poor results through no fault of their own. They may have been issued with outdated equipment, or may have been given the hard jobs with short production runs and frequent changes in methods and design. Under these circumstances the criterion has become contaminated by other influences and it would be unreasonable to expect any selection system to identify, with total accuracy, those workers who are most productive.

The search for criteria does not stop at this second level. A worker might obtain prodigious levels of production. He or she might sustain an output each day of assembling 80 onboard computers for an 'up market' car. If, however, the production line which then uses the computers can only cope with 50 cars per day, the extra effort is wasted. The point of this slightly trite example is that there is an organisational aspect of choosing criteria. In Thorndike's (1949) terms, the third level is the level of *ultimate criteria*: how much the person contributes to the organisational goals. Typical indices of ultimate criteria in industrial companies are productivity levels, net profit, organisational growth and satisfactory accomplishment of obligations placed on it by higher authority. To locate these criteria it is often necessary to refer to company policy documents, or even the policy documents, of government agencies. Bass (1952) points out:

> Instead of evaluating the success of programs for improving selection . . . in an industrial organisation solely in terms of the extent to which they serve to increase the company's productivity profits and efficiency, it has been proposed that they also be evaluated on the extent to which they increase the worth of the organisation to its members and society as a whole.

At this point the use of ultimate criteria becomes almost unbearably complex. Furthermore, there are several practical problems. First, data concerning ultimate criteria take a very long time to accumulate. By the time conclusive data are available the company will be bankrupt! In any event, there is a high probability that the data will emerge too late to influence a selection system. Second, many ultimate criteria are too nebulous and ill defined to be measured within reasonable cost limits. Third, there may be many contaminating influences caused by government policy, economic conditions or changes in the company's markets. Except perhaps at top executive level, it would be unreasonable to expect the results of a selection system to be strongly related to ultimate criteria.

TYPES OF CRITERIA

Guion (1965) provides a useful classification of the many different criteria by dividing them into three major types: production data, personnel data and judgemental data.

Production Data

Production data have many attractions as criteria, especially in manufacturing organisations where high levels of output are nearly always a part of the organisation's goals. Consequently, management is usually impressed when production data are used. Another advantage is that production data may be easy to quantify. For example, a pharmaceutical company can count the number of saline drips packaged by each operative for each shift, and an aerospace company can count the number of heat resistant ceramic tiles which a technician can instal each week. A final advantage of production data is, in many cases, their availability: often information already exists on time sheets or work schedules.

The exact nature of these criteria will vary from industry to industry and from occupation to occupation. Some general indices are listed in Table 3.1. With some ingenuity, output statistics can be evolved for many non-production jobs such as sales, clerical jobs and service jobs: for example, a comedian could be evaluated on the laughs per audience member he evokes per minute!

In spite of this allure, production data suffer a number of disadvantages as criteria. First, they are usually contaminated by factors outside the worker's control. There are few situations where all workers operate under exactly the same conditions. Even after heroic efforts, some workers will only produce a mediocre performance because they work on old machinery. Length of production run and product specification can also make a difference. For example, in one carpet-manufacturing company, it was accepted that the best workers were usually asked to make the 'one off' carpets of difficult design, carpets. This produced the paradox of higher output figures for the poorest workers. The work situation can also exert an influence: some

Table 3.1   Some production indices used as criteria?

Indices	Examples
Quantity indices	• units of output per hour, day, etc. • consistency of output • saleś per month • new customers per month • time to locate faults (in inspection and troubleshooting jobs) • enquiries dealt with per day • calls (salesmen) per day • commission earned • earnings based on piece rate
Quality indices	• percentage of rejects • percentage of waste materials • percentage of breakages • time required to detect and correct faults • complaints per week month, etc. • commendations per year • errors reported per day • average size of orders • response time to enquiry • customer satisfaction repeat orders, etc. • survey results
Cost indices (the money criterion)	• cost per unit of production • value added per unit • cost per order • cost per enquiry

good typists produce relatively little typescript because their desk is situated near a busy telephone or enquiry desk so that their work is subject to constant interruptions. The work situation is particularly important when assessing the output of salesmen: some have good territories and some have lousy territories. For example, Wietz and Nuckols (1953) illustrate that sales figures should be adjusted for the sales potential of the the territory.

   In addition to these difficulties, in many jobs it is either impossible or even dangerous to use production data as criteria. At operative and senior management level it is relatively easy to identify key ratios which can be used to judge performance. However, in many staff positions and in many professional jobs such indices are hard to identify or quantify. In some situations the use of production data as criteria can lead to a distortion of the organisation. For example, undue pressure for high monthly sales figures can lead to sales personnel pressuring customers, making false promises and impossible service commitments. In the short term these tactics can be successful and the salesperson is often promoted. In the long term, however, the rape of a sales territory in this way can lead to disaster. Similarly, pressure upon teachers for a high pass ratio can lead to a reduction in standards. Pressure on the courts to produce more decisions per day could lead to a collapse in the credibility of justice. Landy and Rastegary (1989) indicate that 11 per cent of validity studies use production data in 'real' settings and a further 11 per cent use productivity in simulated settings.

Personnel Data

Criteria can often be obtained from the records which a personnel department may maintain on an individual worker (See Table 3.2). They tend to be more global in nature than production data but they are still clearly linked to the objectives of an organisation. According to Landy and Rastegary, personnel data are used in about 20 per cent of validity studies. Again, they have the advantage of being fairly easy to collect, although it must always be remembered that some clerical errors are inevitable.

Several personnel criteria are concerned with job attendance. Lateness (or tardiness) is perhaps the most short-term aspect of job attendance and is difficult to measure unless mechanical 'clocking in' procedures are used; and even then, collusion by colleagues can introduce error. The advent of electronically recorded 'flexi-time' systems produces added coimplications in defining lateness but data collection is facilitated. Tardiness may also be influenced by short-term factors, such as the weather.

Absences are an important criteria. Unfortunately absenteeism is a fairly complex phenomenon. A major distinction lies between certified and uncertified absence, the presumption being that selectors should be particularly keen to reject candidates who are likely to be absent for no good cause. Another major distinction lies between the frequency and the duration of absences. Often there is a presumption that frequent, unpredicted absences are less desirable than a single protracted absence, even when the time off work is identical. J. B. Fox and Scott (1943) suggest that there are indications that the number of days absent

Table 3.2 Some personnel indices used as criteria

Indices	Examples
Job attendance	• number of times late • average number of minutes late • total absences • certified absences • uncertified absences • frequency of absences • average duration of absences • percentage labour turnover • half-life of a cohort of recruits • percent dismissed • voluntary turnover
Career progression	• job level • number of promotions • number of times considered for • promotion • number of times 'passed over' • speed of promotion • salary level • salary increase • difference between actual salary increase and increase expected from tenure
Accidents	• accidents per year • accidents per 'mile' covered • accidents per unit of production
Training weeks	• needed to reach standard • marks at 'end' of training

is a more reliable criteria. Absences are used in about 6 per cent of validity studies. Perhaps the most dramatic form of non-attendance is labour turnover. If employees leave shortly after they have been engaged, the organisation has wasted the resources devoted to their recruitment, selection, training and providing a workstation. Also, termination of employment can be viewed as clear evidence of a mismatch between the person and the job. Although labour turnover is a clear dichotomous act (people either leave or stay), its interpretation is often far from clear and it is contaminated by other factors. Workers may be properly selected but their induction, training or supervision may be inadequate and cause them to leave. Generally, it is only reasonable to expect a selection process to predict labour turnover within the first few months of employment; after that period other influences may be much more important. It should also be noted that turnover is strongly influenced by possibilities of alternative employment (Behrend, 1953; Stark, 1959). Turnover is used in about 13 per cent of validity studies.

A set of personnel data which can also be used as criteria are indices of the individual's career progression. These criteria have the advantage that they are based on actual operational decisions which reflect the organisation's values and its view of the individual's competence. The most commonly used indices of career progression are job level, speed of promotion and salary progression. In most circumstances job level and speed of promotion are synonymous, except that job level is used in samples equated for length of services whereas speed of promotion can also be used in samples whose cases have different periods of tenure. A good example of the use of job level as a criteria is Anstey's (1977) study. Anstey used the rank achieved in the Civil Service after a period of 30 years to validate the selection procedure. Examples of the use of salary increase as a criteria are given by Hulin (1962), who compared the actual salary increase with the increase which would be expected for workers with the same length of service. Unfortunately, measures of career progression are fraught with difficulties. First, there is a conceptual difficulty. A selection system may be superb for selecting staff at, say, operative level but poor at selecting at supervisory level. Thus, if the selection system is used to predict promotion to the third level in an organisation it will produce poor results, but this does not mean that the system should not be used for operatives. There are other difficulties: promotion decisions may not be based on job competence, but instead may be based on social reputation or, as Wallace (1974) points out, the ability to get good ratings from the 'big shots'. Internal politics are rarely absent from the determinants of promotion decisions and in some organisations, promotions are little more than long service awards. Further, career progression may be heavily contaminated by external factors, such as labour market conditions and chance factors. In many situations a mediocre 'performer' in the right place at the right time stands a better chance of promotion than a good 'performer' who is in the wrong place at the wrong time. It can be argued that these chance factors become more important as job level increases and where promotion decisions are relatively infrequent. At lower levels there are usually more promotions and hence chance factors may be able to cancel each other out.

Accidents are sometimes used as criteria because they have a major impact on the person concerned and may involve the organisation in disruption and litigation. Nevertheless, accidents are often poor criteria. One disadvantage from a scientific viewpoint is the narrowness of range. Most people have no accidents per year, a minority have one, and only a tiny proportion have more than one. Effectively the range is from 0 to 1. A little extra discrimination can be improved by grading accidents according to their seriousness, but the essential problem remains. An additional problem arises from the instability of accident rates for individuals: the fact that a person has an accident this year does not mean that he or she will have an accident next year (Mintz and Blum, 1949; Ghiselli and Brown, 1955). Further difficulties in using accident statistics may arise from clerical errors in reporting accidents and from the fact that some workers are exposed to a greater risk of accidents than others. Perhaps one way of avoiding these difficulties is to change attention from actual accidents and instead observe the occurrence of unsafe practices (Whitlock, Clouse and Spencer, 1963). Accident statistics are used in about 1 per cent of validity studies.

Training information has many advantages as criteria. In many well established training courses all trainees have similar tasks, tools and time tables. Organisational contaminants – such as departmental politics and differential opportunities – have less impact upon a trainee because they are more distant and because the relatively short periods involved in training do not allow them to work to maximum effect. In many training schemes there is an 'objective' pass standard and the 'marks' are validated by an external body, which should reduce the possibility of the results being contaminated. Often, criteria of this kind are called 'knowledge tests'.

Thus training information, such as weeks needed to attain a 'pass' standard or marks at the end of courses, may provide good criterion information. Ghiselli (1966) was able to show that training data provide criteria that are reliable. The main disadvantages may be the artificial nature of some training environments and that the range of the information may be small. For example, most people in one company achieve efficient worker standard in either six or seven weeks and the criteria then becomes a two-point scale.

Judgemental Data

Person making the judgement

If production data or personnel data are unavailable, impractical or inappropriate, it may be necessary to utilise criteria which are drawn directly from judgements made by people. Usually these ratings are made by the individual's superiors, but they can also be made by peers, subordinates, the individual himself or herself and observers. Judgemental data (ratings) are used more frequently than any other type of criteria in about 45 per cent of validity studies (Landy and Rastegary, 1989).

Judgements made by superiors are almost an automatic choice because there is a widespread belief that a superior knows a subordinate's job and the degree to which he or she is competent. This approach is acceptable to most organisations. It is also relatively easy data to collect: it often boils down to a simple process of identifying the correct superior and mailing some kind of rating scale in a confidential envelope.

However, a deeper examination raises a number of questions. First, to what extent does the superior know about the job being performed? It may be years since he or she did the job him or herself. Second, to what extent can the competence of the subordinate be assessed? Analyses of managerial jobs (for example, Stewart, 1967; Mintzberg, 1973; McCall, Morrison and Hannen, 1978) show that managers spend most of their time in meetings with managers at their own level, and are able to devote only about 20 per cent of their time to their subordinates as a whole. Individual subordinates spend very little time with their bosses. Consequently, the basis on which superiors make their ratings is often very slim. A filtering process operates. Subordinates may actively manage the impressions they give to their boss by magnifying their successes and the difficulties they have overcome, while concealing their failures. All these factors may combine to make superiors' ratings very suspect criteria indeed. Other sources of judgements include ratings by peers, subordinates and self-assessments. These are discussed in greater detail in Chapter 12. Chapter 12 discusses these methods as potential predictors but they may nevertheless be used as criteria.

Under some rather special circumstances, criteria can be based upon judgements made by observers. This can be achieved only when the job is fairly simple, short cycle and where motivational influences are likely to be small. It can also be used in artificial situations where special tasks are constructed and observable performance can be assessed against known criteria. The biggest theoretical advantage of rating by expert observers is that it becomes feasible to train a small cadre of experts to overcome the deficiencies usually involved in judgements. Also it becomes feasible for one or two people to make all the relevant judgements, thus reducing the error due to raters' differing standards. Unfortunately, criteria from expert judgement can be obtained only in a narrow range of fairly artificial circumstances, and often generalising to the real world is suspect. Grant and Bray (1966) have shown that observer ratings are related to other criteria, and Bray and Campbell (1968) have used these criteria to evaluate a selection system for salesmen.

Traditional flaws

Most ratings, whether they are made by superiors, buddies, self or observers, suffer from a number of errors.

The *halo effect* refers to raters' lack of discrimination when describing the different aspects of the same employee. Thus, on a 7-point scale Phil receives ratings of 7, 7, 6 and 7 on intelligence, diligence, honesty and motivation. While this consistently good set of scores may be accurate, it may be a product of the halo effect. The most likely cause of the halo effect is the rater being over-impressed by a single characteristic. This impression 'spills' over to judgements of other characteristics and produces a 'halo' through which it is difficult to make accurate judgements of the other traits. The halo effect can work in the opposite direction, where an unfavourable characteristic reduces discrimination on other traits.

Leniency is the tendency to give ratings which are skewed in a favourable direction. An analysis of many appraisal forms will show a substantial proportion of employees in the 'very good' category, a very large proportion of employees in the 'good' category, a few employees in the 'average' and 'poor' categories and practically no one in the 'very poor' category. Explanations for the leniency effect are not hard to envisage. Few managers will admit that they tolerate subordinates who are below average because it may be taken to reflect on their own abilities as a manager. In addition, many organisations have a policy of showing subordinates the ratings their bosses have given, under these circumstances, superiors are reluctant to give average or poor ratings. First, there is a high probability that poor ratings will be contested and involve a lengthy appeals procedure; second, there may be a wish to avoid demoralising a poor worker.

The *error of central tendency* occurs because raters have a tendency to 'bunch' ratings together and not give extreme judgements. Consequently, most employees receive ratings that are within one point of the median rating, and the discrimination of the judgements is usually poor.

Contrast effects may compound the situation. Judgements do not take place in a vacuum, they take place in a certain order and context. Sequence and the context can distort the ratings. For example, a superior who has just correctly rated three subordinates as very superior will be rather less willing to give a fourth person the same rating.

The halo effect, leniency, central tendency and contrast effects may make ratings very suspect. In order to improve these judgements attention has been turned to more systematic methods of obtaining judgemental data for use as criteria (see Table 3.3).

Attempts at improvement

The most usual attempt to improve judgemental data is to develop some type of rating scale. The first stage is to define the number of scales. It is generally pointless to produce more than about nine different scales.

The simplest type of scale consists of a trait title plus some kind of continuum anchored at both ends. The rater simply puts an X in the appropriate position. For example:

Leadership   Good:___:___:___:_X_:___:___:Bad

This simple rating scale has two related weaknesses. First, the trait to be rated is ambiguously defined. To some people leadership involves

Table 3.3   Some ways of collecting judgemental data

Basic technique	● rating scales
Scales with anchors	● behaviourally-anchored rating scales
	● summated rating scales
Employee comparison methods	● employee ranking
	● paired comparisons

having an iron will, a god-like judgement and the ability to dominate others. To others, leadership means paying acute attention to the wishes and preferences of a group and maintaining a happy atmosphere. If these simple scales are used, there is usually no reliable way of knowing which meaning is being used. The second weakness of simple rating scales is the ambiguity of the scale positions. For example, what does a cross on the extreme left-hand side mean? Leadership on a cosmic scale or leadership that is just clearly discernable? Different raters will have different ideas and the divergence will contaminate the ratings as criteria. In an attempt to improve judgement data it is possible to be more specific when describing the trait and when defining the scale intervals. Examples are given in Figures 3.1 and 3.2.

There is an issue of how many scale points should be used. There is some evidence that people can reliably discriminate seven positions on most continua: in favourable situations we are able to discriminate among nine positions, and in unfavourable situations we are able to discriminate among only five positions. The number of scale positions chosen should generally lie within this range, with a preference for having more points at the upper end of the distribution. The rationale for this preference is quite straightforward: in most industrial situations raters are very reluctant to use the bottom two categories and, when this is taken into account, a nine point scale becomes (to all intents and purposes) a seven point scale.

Some industrial psychologists prefer to use rating scales with an even number of categories. This stratagem has the advantage of denying the rater the easy option of classifying people as average. He or she is forced to decide whether they are above or below average. However, the stratagem violates a simple fact of life: on most human characteristics, the largest single group of people are those who are close to the average.

Figure 3.2 demonstrates one final issue. The descriptions of the scale position (technically called 'anchors') are only given for alternate scale positions. This often produces a clearer and less cluttered layout and it caters for the eventuality where a rater finds it hard to decide which of two scale descriptions apply to a particular individual.

The refinement of rating scales has been carried furthest by P. L. Smith and Kendall (1963), who developed behaviourally-anchored rating scales (BARS). Smith and Kendall reasoned that much of the unreliability of ratings arise from the fact that neither traits nor standards of judgement are sufficiently defined. Consequently, much is

Figure 3.1   Improved rating scales

Improvement of trait description
CREDIT CONTROL

Knowledge of company guidelines and local area policy: setting and enforcing credit limits to assistant managers. Systematic checks on applications for credit.

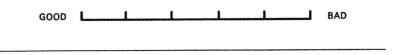

Improvement descriptions of scale intervals
CREDIT CONTROL

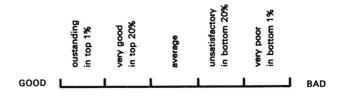

Improvement of both trait descriptions and scale intervals
CREDIT CONTROL

Knowledge of company guidelines and local area policy: setting and enforcing credit limits to assistant managers. Systematic checks on applications for credit.

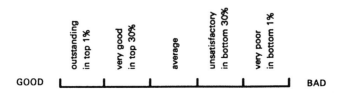

Figure 3.2   A practical example of a behaviourally-anchored rating scale

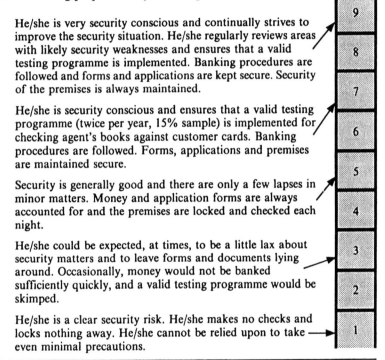

Security

Security is an important aspect of a branch manager's job. It includes taking normal care of premises and equipment, maintaining security of documents and maintaining proper security checks against fraud.

He/she is very security conscious and continually strives to improve the security situation. He/she regularly reviews areas with likely security weaknesses and ensures that a valid testing programme is implemented. Banking procedures are followed and forms and applications are kept secure. Security of the premises is always maintained.

He/she is security conscious and ensures that a valid testing programme (twice per year, 15% sample) is implemented for checking agent's books against customer cards. Banking procedures are followed. Forms, applications and premises are maintained secure.

Security is generally good and there are only a few lapses in minor matters. Money and application forms are always accounted for and the premises are locked and checked each night.

He/she could be expected, at times, to be a little lax about security matters and to leave forms and documents lying around. Occasionally, money would not be banked sufficiently quickly, and a valid testing programme would be skimped.

He/she is a clear security risk. He/she makes no checks and locks nothing away. He/she cannot be relied upon to take even minimal precautions.

---

left to the rater's imagination. If it is possible to construct rating scales which ask for specific judgements that are explicitly based upon behaviours which can be observed, then the agreement between raters should be much higher. Thus, an ideal scale for collecting judgements would consist of two parts: (1) a clear definition of the trait to be rated; (2) a scale with descriptions of specific behaviours which would be observed at different levels.

The construction of BARS usually proceeds in five steps. Step one involves the identification and definition of key aspects of job performance. Often this information can be directly obtained from the job description. Step two concerns the production of the behavioural anchors. A sample of superiors, experts or job holders is asked to give specific examples of behaviours shown by people who are good, average and poor on that aspect of performance. Usually, their examples are written out on file cards. The third step involves placing a scale value upon the anchors. The procedure is tantamount to the production of a Thurstone scale (see A. L. Edwards, 1957). A group of experts independently sort each anchor into one of, say, nine piles, according to whether it shows a high or low level of the trait involved. Fourth, those anchors which produce a wide range of judgements are discarded. Fifth, average scores of the remaining anchors are calculated and, on the basis of these averages, a selection is made so that the complete range from good to bad is sampled. Whilst it is possible to calculate the scale values of the anchors to several decimal points, in most practical situations it will be necessary to round them to the nearest integer.

The advocates of BARS point to two additional advantages: the process forces the organisation to consider carefully what it means by success and failure and, because the scales focus on actual relevant behaviours, it is relatively easy to gain acceptance for them. Early research (for example, J. B. Taylor, 1968) suggested that BARS were better than 'ordinary' scales and that their accuracy approached a level which was equal to administering an ordinary scale to 'four' raters and taking the average rating. However, subsequent reviews (for example, Schwab, Heneman and DeCottis, 1975, and Bernadin, Albares and Cranny, 1976) are less enthusiastic.

BARS are not the only attempt to reduce the errors involved in judgemental ratings. Summated ratings, forced choice questionnaires and methods of employee comparisons have also been used.

In some ways the method of summated ratings is similar to the BARS technique, except that the dimensions being rated are not made explicit, and the behavioural anchors from several dimensions are juxtaposed with each anchor being presented in a standard Likert-type format. Raters are asked to say how often the individual exhibits that piece of behaviour. The rater answers every item and a score is obtained by marking each answer on, usually, a 1–5 scale.

It is claimed that the method of summated ratings give criteria in which the halo effect is noticeably reduced. However, a considerable leniency effect may remain. Bass (1957) produced a scoring procedure designed to overcome this problem.

Another way of using a questionnaire to obtain judgemental data which can be used as a criterion is the method of forced choice technique. It is effective in overcoming the problem of leniency error. Leniency error arises when raters want to be nice to the people they are rating and therefore tend to give ratings which put other people in a sociably desirable light. The forced choice technique presents two statements which are equally socially desirable, but only one of which is a part of the criterion we want to measure. For example, both being happy and being efficient are socially desirable. A rater could be asked which of these traits is most typical of a worker. If the rater chooses efficiency then the worker has 1 added to his score, since efficiency is a part of the criterion. On the other hand, if the rater chooses happy, nothing is added. A scale is constructed of ten or more pairs of this kind and the criterion score is the total number of appropriate choices. Most forced choice questionnaires involve a variety of pairs and include pairs of favourable items and pairs of unfavourable items. Other formats are also possible. For example, it is possible to construct a tetrad involving a favourable pair and an unfavourable pair.

The disadvantages of forced choice ratings are relatively few. Sometimes raters dislike making decisions of this kind. They may feel that both items of a pair apply equally to an employee or, in the case of unfavourable pairs, that neither of the pair apply. In practice the construction of forced choice questionnaires is time consuming. The items must be devised, and then their social desirability must be established using a sample of 30 or more 'judges'. Uhbrock (1961) attempted to avoid some of this preparation by publishing the scale values of 2000 statements. Unfortunately, the sizes of his samples of judges was small and ideas of social desirability have probably changed in the years since Uhbrock published his paper.

Employee comparisons are probably one of the least frequently used methods of obtaining criteria from judgements. There are two main approaches: rank order and paired comparisons. The rank order method is simplicity itself: the superior simply ranks subordinates according to perception of the subordinates' merit. Despite its simplicity, the rank order method has two related disadvantages: It often forces a discrimination where there is little difference, and raters can find the task very difficult. To illustrate the problem of forced discrimination, suppose a supervisor in the pharmaceutical industry has four subordinates involved in running trials of an anti-arthritic drug. These subordinates can run 70, 60, 45 and 44 trials per month respectively, and they are rightly ranked 1, 2, 3 and 4 by their superiors.

However, this ranking implies that the difference between the first and second technicians is equal to that between the third and fourth technicians. The ranking also implies that there is a substantive difference between the third and fourth technicians where as, in fact, the difference is quite tiny.

The second method of employee comparison, the paired comparison technique, minimises some difficulties and is also uncomplicated. Every possible pair of employees is compared in turn and the best employee in each pair is identified. An advantage of the paired comparison technique is that, by using a number of psychometric procedures (see A. L. Edwards, 1957), measures can be obtained which are very discriminating and which have many of the properties of interval measures. Unfortunately, the paired comparison method has a major disadvantage: it can only be used with fairly small groups of people. If it is used with large groups it becomes unwieldy because the number of combinations increases exponentially with the number of subordinates involved. A supervisor with six subordinates will need to make 15 decisions and a supervisor with nine subordinates will need to make 36 decisions. In practice this disadvantage limits the use of the paired comparison method to situations where no one has more than about 12 subordinates.

Both methods of employee comparison have an additional, and usually fatal, limitation. They are quite effective for producing criterion information about subordinates who come within the span of control of one person; but whenever more than one superior is involved it is difficult, and often impossible, to equate the standards used by the different superiors. In effect this limits the sample size to about 12, and for most purposes a sample of 12 is too small.

Walk Through Testing or 'Hands on' Criteria

Since other criteria are often so faulty, some investigators set up special situations where as many influences as possible are controlled. In this way, simulated criteria are created. For example, it is almost impossible to obtain real criteria for a tank crew so simulated criteria were developed in which the subject was required to climb into a tank, operate the radio, operate the internal communication system, position the gun for firing and to reassemble a hand held weapon. The tasks were completed one at a time whilst being carefully observed and scored on a checklist. The scores are then used as a criterion. Sometimes, criteria of this kind are called 'Hands on' criteria. They are most frequently used when the 'real' operations may involve danger or irreversible consequences. The main disadvantage is that the simulations can be artificial.

The description of the main types of criteria has established one fact very clearly. *No criteria* are perfect. This simple fact must be borne continuously in mind because the imperfections in the criteria will tend to reduce the apparent effectiveness of our methods of selection. The greater the criterion's inadequacies, the greater the selection system's handicap in predicting effective performers.

THEORETICAL REQUIREMENTS OF CRITERIA

The problems surrounding the use of criteria have led to a detailed examination of characteristics which criteria should possess. Landy and Trumbo (1980) present an impressive list of 14 separate requirements which can be reduced to three main issues: reliability, validity and practicality.

Reliability of Criteria

To be of any use, a criteria must be reliable (see Chapter 6). Criteria should be consistent. If two sets of criterion data for the same individuals are collected at different periods of time, they should yield very similar results. The level of reliability will vary according to the criteria chosen. Ghiselli (1966) suggests that training data can be very reliable; on the other hand, many authors suggest that sales figures are often too unreliable to use.

Reliability of criteria can be boiled down into three main issues: the inherent unreliability of criteria; the time interval between sets of data, and the foibles of human judgement.

A clear example of the inherent unreliability of some types of criteria is given by a Dutch diamond broker which chose to evaluate its agents by using their sales figures as a criterion. Accordingly, they collected sales returns for the third week in September but, before making decisions on the basis of this information, they had the wisdom to check the reliability of weekly sales returns. They collected the same data for their agents in the second week of October, correlated the two sets of data and obtained a correlation of -0.2! This is not an isolated example of the inherent unreliability of criteria. Jenkins (1946) summarised the situation at that time:

Various predictive efforts in World War II have failed because the very performance that was to be predicted has proved inherently unstable. Number of hits scored by an aircraft gunner on a towed sleeve is a criterion possessing a delightful degree of objectivity. All studies of this criterion, however, find the individual scores so low in reliability as to be without value.

Often the reliability of criteria can be improved by basing them on a longer time interval. In theory, the appropriate time interval should be determined empirically. For example, the diamond brokers could have collected two sets of monthly sales figures, two sets of quarterly sales figures, two sets of half-yearly sales figures, and so on. They could then produce correlations for the different time periods and plot them on a graph to produce Figure 3.3. On the basis of this graph, it could be concluded that half-yearly sales figures would be the optimum choice since the additional reliability of the yearly and two-yearly figures would not justify the additional delay. Although 'reliabilities' tend to increase with very long time intervals, in practice the imperatives of a business environment prohibit studies of this kind: few organisations can afford the luxury of a four-year study (two years for the first data set and two years for the second) to determine whether to use half-yearly or two-year figures.

A slightly different issue concerns the time interval between obtaining the two sets of criterion ratings. Here the situation gives no surprise. The shorter the time interval, the higher the reliability. For example, Bass (1962) obtained a correlation of 0.6 when there were six-month intervals between collecting two sets of data. When the time interval was 42 months the correlation fell to 0.3. This kind of relationship bodes well where the whole process of selection, from job analysis to final evaluation, takes place within a very short period of time, but it also implies that longer-term studies have to contend with an additional source of error since the same long-term forces may intrude between, say, the selection of a metallurgist and an evaluation, two years later, of his ability to develop new kinds of abrasives. R. A. Henry and Hulin (1987, 1989) contend that slow changes in the nature of the job, and therefore the criteria, are one of the reasons why, over a period of time, validities tend to decrease. They tracked criteria which might be used for the selection of baseball players, such as the number of runs and pitcher performance. They showed that over a ten-year period, the correlation with the criterion performance in the first year steadily declined. They also noted that the decline in validities could be

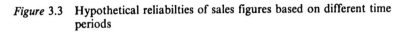

Figure 3.3 Hypothetical reliabilties of sales figures based on different time periods

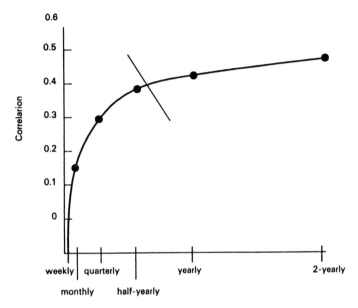

caused by changes in individuals or by changes in job demands. Ackerman (1989) contested the claim that validities always decrease with time, especially when the job includes non-repetitive work which cannot be 'automated'. It would appear that validities increase in about 16 per cent of cases.

The third issue concerning the reliability of criteria involves the 'foibles' of human judgement. Jenkins (1946) provides another delightful scenario. Instructors were required to fill out a detailed form giving critical comments on various phases of each flight completed by students. In actual fact certain instructors gave only a general grade, leaving detailed grading to a clerk who had not seen the flight. The clerk then dutifully supplied the detailed grades in a fashion which gave an overall distribution of conventional form. In another example, instructors saved all their forms to fill in at a weekend. Further doubts on the reliability of clerically-recorded data can be obtained from most examinations of medical records which almost invariably record body temperatures of 98.4°F, in spite of known monthly cycles and well established differences arising from the way that the temperature is taken. Thus the research on the reliability of criteria makes quite depressing reading. According to orthodox procedure, the output of a selection system is compared with criterion data and, if there is no relationship, the selection system is abandoned. It is clear that many systems have been unfairly rejected. In many situations, it may have been better to keep the system but change the criteria.

Validity of Criteria

Validity in the context of criteria can be taken to mean 'Do the criteria we use accurately reflect "true" performance at work?' Whilst in theory it is an easy question to pose, in practice it is very difficult to answer. We have no direct telephone line to a deity in the sky who can tell us for certain the true answer. In the absence of a communication from an all-knowing deity, we must proceed one step at a time by making logical deductions. The issues involved in the validity of criteria boil down to these main points: coverage; contamination; dynamism; and interrelationships among criteria.

Comprehensive coverage is important, as Ghiselli (1956) noted, because most jobs are complex and require the incumbent to achieve many objectives. For example, an operative in a nuclear reprocessing plant may be required to process fuel rods (1) quickly, (2) safely, (3) at minimal expense, whilst (4) maintaining good social relationships with both colleagues and superiors. Ghiselli also notes that each of these objectives can be achieved in different ways. As a trite example, one worker may achieve objectives by means of brute strength, another may use craft and guile, whilst another may achieve the same results by charming colleagues to do the work. Furthermore, each of these methods could be evaluated in several different ways: by examining personnel records, by examining output figures or by questioning a worker's superior. This example is a simplification, but it implies that there are 36 different criteria which could be used with the job of a nuclear fuel-processing operative. In theory we can only be totally conclusive if we use all 36. In practice it would perhaps be adequate to use a sample of six or seven criteria. This sample should be carefully drawn so that most salient features are represented. It is quite clear that, except in very unusual circumstances, a single criterion is not adequate. P. L. Smith (1976) gives a list of 11 authors who have made a plea for the use of multiple criteria. Probably the most famous exhortation to use multiple criteria is Dunnette's (1963b) call to junk *the* criterion. He says:

> Much selection and validation research has gone astray because of an overzealous worshipping of *the* criterion with an accompanying will-o-the-wisp searching for the best single measure of job success. The result has been an oversimplification of the complexities involved in test validation and the prediction of employee success. Investigators have been unwilling to consider the many facets of success and further investigation of the prediction of many success measures and instead persist in an unfruitful effort to predict *the* criterion. Thus, I say: junk *the* criterion.

Notwithstanding these exhortations, in practice most studies only use one criterion. Lent, Aurback and Levin (1971) found that 85 per cent of studies used only one criterion. According to Landy and Rastegary (1989) decades later, only about 10 per cent of validity studies use multiple criteria.

Contamination of criteria is also concerned with the content of criteria, but it focuses upon things which should *not* be present. Unfortunately, criteria are particularly susceptible to insidious forms of bias which may remain undetected, and which are often difficult to quantify and remove. The number of potential contaminators is almost endless, but two categories are particularly important: job contaminators and illusory successes.

Some criteria are contaminated by job influences since workers rarely run the same race. There may be differences of equipment, design of product or the length of product run. A clear example of contamination by job influences is when crude sales figures are used as criteria for salesmen: some salesmen sell popular lines and some salesmen have very favourable territories. In other situations, departmental power and prestige can be important contaminants. Thus departmental power and prestige can help even mediocre employees to corner a lion's share of the resources and to land the plum assignments, while more talented employees in other departments are left to be content with the crumbs. This phenomena can be seen in the civil services of many countries in the world: a first posting in the Treasury is often an almost automatic passport to a high-flying career.

Illusory success was highlighted by Wallace (1974) who noted that it is difficult for us to predict actual success itself but we are more successful in predicting who people *say* are successful. In some organisations at least, the road to the top is paved with mimicry. The implications can be startling; 'If we are, indeed, embarked upon a venture which will lead us to pick people who can get good ratings, especially from the big shots, what are the implications for progress in business and societal endeavour? How to succeed in business by satisfying the guardians of the status quo.'

A slightly different perspective arises out of the phenomenon of 'policy capturing', where criteria are used which reflect the point of view of the organisation's decision-makers. In other words, the criteria attempt to 'anticipate or predict how (and on what bases) operating managers will make their decisions' (Klimoski and Strickland, 1977). Policy capturing does not necessarily contaminate criteria. In some situations the explicit objective is, rightly or wrongly, to forecast future decisions.

The *dynamic nature of criteria* is often overlooked but it needs to be considered because the nature of criteria changes over a period of time. For example, in the early days of computing, economy of computer time and memory were important criteria for the success of programmers. However, the costs of computer memory and time have fallen dramatically. User friendliness and ease of interfacing with other systems are now more important aspects of a programmer's work. Clearly, in today's situation, it would be silly to continue evaluating the selection system on its ability to select programmers who economise upon computer memory. This is possibly an extreme example but, in other contexts, a gradual accumulation of obsolescence can affect criteria and this may produce an apparent lowering of the effectiveness of a selection system. Bass (1962), for example, investigated the effectiveness of three tests and 'peer' ratings over a 48-month period by seeing how well they predicted supervisors' opinions of salesmen. He found that all methods of selection became less effective as time progressed and that, after a three-year period, meritorious performance became less contingent upon ability in comparison to esteem and popularity.

The *predictability of criteria* was raised by Sackett, Zedeck and Fogli (1988) who compared four criteria for supermarket check-out operatives. Data were collected on the accuracy and speed of dealing with a standard trolley of groceries. Both types of data were collected under two conditions. In the condition of *maximum performance* operatives knew they were being tested and presumably worked as hard and as accurately as they could. In the condition of *average performance* they were unaware they were under scrutiny and presumably worked at their average rate. Sackett, Zedeck and Fogli (1988) collected the data for 635 new employees and 735 experienced employees. The median intercorrelation between the different criteria was low (0.11), indicating that the 'worth' of individuals would overwhelmingly depend on the criteria which was chosen. The data was also correlated with a supervisor's rating. It was found that with existing employees the highest correlation (0.36) was with maximum speed. With new employees, the highest correlation was with maximum accuracy (0.23). In general, the correlations were highest for existing employees and for data collected under maximum effort conditions. The major implications from this study are that the use of different criteria can produce significantly different validities and that some criteria are easier to predict than others.

Practicality of Criteria

In an attempt to meet objections there is a temptation to produce more complex and comprehensive criteria. Often there is a tendency to produce an exhaustive list of criteria which is too long, too time-consuming and too expensive for use. The practicality of criteria must be borne in mind. The main considerations are:

(a)   cost;
(b)   acceptability to the organisation;
(c)   time taken to collect data;
(d)   time at which data are available;
(e)   acceptability to collector;
(f)   ease of analysis;
(g)   volume of information available.

If these considerations are violated it is much more difficult to persuade organisations of the need to produce criteria against which the selection system can be evaluated.

In the haste to get a selection system 'off the ground' there is a compelling temptation to avoid the intricacies and difficulties of obtaining satisfactory criteria. It is alluring to proceed directly to the production of personnel specifications and the testing or interviewing of candidates. The lure should be resisted for, as Krug (1961) notes, '*a programme of personnel selection can be no better than the criteria which define it*'.

4 Personnel Specifications

An earlier chapter dealt with the first step of scientific personnel selection – namely, job analysis – which culminates in the first key document in the selection process: the job description. However, before systematic selection can proceed a second key document must be produced: the personnel specification.

Job analyses are, essentially, statements of the job to be done, either in terms of the tasks to be achieved or the *activities* a worker must perform. However, the objective of any selection system is to choose the candidate who possesses the most suitable *characteristics*. It is this step, from tasks and activities to characteristics, which is undertaken when a personnel specification is produced. It is a step which is as important as any other. It is, therefore, quite amazing to discover that there has been very little research into into the way that the inferences are made from statements of a job description to the statements of the personnel specification. There is little or no research on such obvious aspects as the cues that are used, the conventions adopted and the reliability and validity of the process. Because there is so little research, it is necessary to rely on experience and tradition, or upon intuitive methods derived from general psychological principles.

STRAIGHTFORWARD APPROACHES TO PERSONNEL SPECIFICATIONS

Experience and tradition lead towards a straightforward method of producing job descriptions based upon some type of plan: the most ubiquitous is the seven point plan developed by Alec Rodger. Often it is called 'Rodger's seven point interview plan' and this indicates a common confusion. This plan is not a scheme for conducting an interview. The plan provides a simple but scientifically defensible personnel specification. The main points of the seven point plan are shown in Figure 4.1. The plan is very practical.

*Figure 4.*1   Rodger's 'seven-point plan'

1	*Physical make-up*	includes health, physique, appearance, grooming, demeanour, strength, speech.
2	*Attainments*	include educational qualifications, training successfully completed, licences, professional associations, offices held in clubs and societies, success in competitions, occupational experience, career progress.
3	*General intelligence*	involves the ability to identify the key aspects of a problem, deduce the relationships between these aspects and use logic to deduce the next step. It is sometimes useful to distinguish between the intelligence an individual *can* use and how much he or she *normally* uses.
4	*Special aptitudes*	includes numerical reasoning, verbal reasoning, memory, mechanical reasoning, spatial reasoning, musical aptitude, artistic aptitude, manual dexterity.
5	*Interests*	outdoor, mechanical, scientific, persuasive, artistic, literary, social service, clerical, practical, intellectual.
6	*Disposition*	cheerful, relates well to people, stable, easily thrown off balance, assertive, can handle difficult situations, independent, experimenting, etc.
7	*Home circumstances*	include domestic commitments, mobility, family support, freedom to work certain hours.

Another well-known plan was devised by Munroe Frazer (1966) and consists of five points:

(a) impact on others;
(b) acquired knowledge;
(c) innate abilities;
(d) motivation;
(e) adjustment.

A personnel specification is usually produced by referring to the job description and systematically working through one of the plans, noting the characteristics required under each heading. Of course the characteristics identified will not be of equal importance. It may be useful to make a distinction between those characteristics which are essential and those which are desirable. An example of a personnel specification drawn up in this way is given in Figure 4.2.

Figure 4.2   Example of a personnel specification

Job Title:	*Upholsterer*	
Location:	*Glossopdale*	

1 *Physical characteristics*	Essential:	• Able to work in standing position
		• Able to bend at waist
		• Free movement of all limbs
		• Normal colour vision
	Desirable:	• Neat and clean appearance
2 *Attainments*	Essential:	• Time-served apprenticeship
		• Member of trade union
3 *Intelligence*	Desirable:	• Not in bottom third of population
4 *Special aptitudes*	Essential:	• Spatial ability and ability to work with patterned material – in top 20% of population
		• Manual dexterity
5 *Interests*	Desirable:	• Practical and manual interests, especially working with wood or fabric
		• interests requiring cleanliness, eye for detail and care over final presentation
6 *Disposition*	Desirable:	• Self-sufficient approach to life and willingness to work on own with only infrequent social contact
		• Willingness to work at a job which offers only a minimum level of variety (that is, not suitable for strong extrovert)
7 *Home circumstances*	Essential:	• Absence of commitments which could present difficulties to shift working
8 *Contra-indications*		• Medical history of rheumatic or muscular disease or back trouble
		• work history involving minor accidents

When drawing up a personnel specification bear three extra points in mind. First, it may not be necessary to include every point. If personality has no bearing on the ability to do the job then the section on 'disposition' can be omitted. Second, it is important to avoid over-specifying requirements. Use the categorisation 'essential' sparingly. Be aware that many physical disabilities do not impair performance. Third, ensure the specification is fair to everyone, and does not indirectly discriminate. Be particularly careful to ensure that specifications under the heading 'home circumstances' do not offend particular subgroups or violate equal opportunities legislation.

MORE COMPLEX METHODS OF PRODUCING PERSONNEL SPECIFICATIONS

Sometimes a more sophisticated approach is justified. There are two main possibilities: job component analysis or intuitive methods based upon theory of human characteristics. In addition, there are several less known methods, such as Fleishman's ability requirements approach (Fleishman and Hogan, 1978) and repertory grids (J. M. Smith and Stewart, 1977; J. M. Smith, Hartley and Stewart, 1978; Smith 1980).

Job Component Analysis

The PAQ has the advantage that the job elements it identifies can be specifically linked to human characteristics. Shaw and McCormick (1976) and E. J. McCormick, Cunningham and Thornton (1972) describe how each rating can be given a weight reflecting the relevance to a particular characteristic. The weighted ratings are then added up to produce an estimate of the level of the characteristic needed. The process is repeated for other characteristics. In fact there are two methods of proceeding: the cross product approach and the critical behaviour approach depending upon how weights are assigned. An excellent example of job component analysis is given by Sparrow, Patrick, Spurgeon and Barwell (1982). They analysed the job of a machine setter for an injection-moulding machine. An abbreviated profile is given in Figure 4.3.

Intuitive Method Based on Theory

If the job component approach, the repertory grid approach or perhaps the ability requirement approach (Fleishman and Hogan, 1978) are not

Figure 4.3　Abbreviated aptitude profile for the job of setter

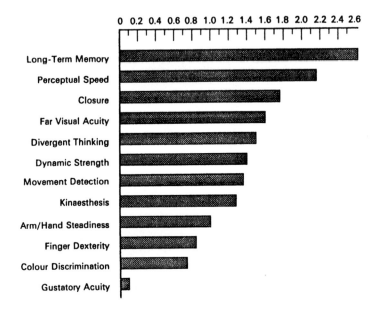

The mean weight of each aptitude for the job

Source: Sparrow *et al.* (1982), p.159.

appropriate for a particular situation, it becomes necessary to rely on a more 'intuitive' method. Clearly, however, the 'intuitions' should not be based upon guesswork, but should be guided by knowledge and experience and by theories and classifications of human characteristics. Many classifications exist, but the following classification has some merits. Its outlines are implicitly accepted by many psychologists (for example, Guion, 1965; Cronbach, 1970; Anastasi, 1982; see also Fleishman and Quaintance, 1984, Chapter 7). It divides human characteristics into four main areas: mental abilities, manual abilities, temperament, and motivation and interests.

Mental abilities

There is often an obvious need to select among applicants according to their mental ability, and consequently it is frequently included in personnel specifications. Often the term is used synonymously with 'intelligence', and many definitions exist. Perhaps the most specific, analytical and accepted definition is given by Spearman's (1927) three neogenetic laws:

The apprehension of reality is the extent to which an individual can identify, understand and absorb the different components of a problem

The eduction of relationships is the extent to which an individual can identify the way in which the various components of problems are related to each other

The eduction of correlates is the extent to which an individual can identify the logical consequence of the relationships and deduce the next step

In a nutshell, intelligence is the ability to identify the constituent parts of a problem to understand how they relate to each other and so to work out the next step. These basic mental operations underlie the tasks involved in many jobs, such as research scientist, area manager, teacher, investment analyst, nurse or personnel officer.

There is, however, a complicating factor. Does the type of question have any effect? For example, does it matter if problems involve numbers, words, shapes or levers and pulleys? It is a debate which has been largely settled. The main advocate of separate types of intelligence was L. L. Thurstone (1938), who administered 57 different tests to a large sample of university students and found that separate abilities existed depending upon the type of question he asked. He identified nine primary mental abilities. There have been criticisms of Thurstone's work. His initial study was restricted to university students, so the overwhelming majority would have been highly intelligent. This was tantamount to eliminating the influence of general intelligence and favouring less important aspects. In fact, Thurstone and L. L. Thurstone (1941) repeated their study with relatively unselected primary school children and admitted the existence of a general intellectual factor.

Probably the most accepted analysis of the structure of intelligence is Vernon's (1960, 1969) hierarchical structure which is shown in Figure 4.4. According to Vernon's model, the most pervasive aspect of intelligence is g but two domains, which largely overlap with g, can be distinguished: verbal-educational and practical. Subdomains which overlap with both g, $v{:}ed$ and $k{:}m$ can also be distinguished.

In practical terms, these underlying theories of the structure of intellect imply that in most personnel specifications it will be adequate

Figure 4.4   Schematic representation of Vernon's model of intelligence

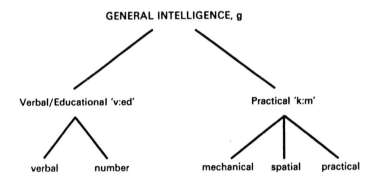

GENERAL INTELLIGENCE, g

Verbal/Educational 'v:ed'   Practical 'k:m'

verbal   number   mechanical   spatial   practical

Source: Vernon (1960, 1969).

to refer only to 'general intelligence'. Sometimes, however, it will be necessary to refer to major group factors such as $k:m$ or $v:ed$. Minor group factors, such as spatial, or verbal, will only need to be specified relatively infrequently. However, another argument points in the opposite direction and suggests that requirements should be as specific as possible in order not to rule out competent candidates. For example, if a garage specifies high general intelligence when it actually requires high mechanical ability, it will exclude people of average general ability who are particularly competent in mechanical matters.

One aspect of mental ability which was of considerable concern in the 1960s was creative thinking. The concern arose out of the belief that creativity was not the same thing as intelligence. Unfortunately, however, the evidence is not conclusive. Many different measures of creativity have been produced but they tend to correlate poorly with each other. This implies either that a single trait of 'creativity' does not exist or that our present techniques for measuring it are not adequate. Furthermore, some studies (for example, Getzels and Jackson, 1962) have shown that measures of creativity correlate as highly with measures of intelligence as they do among themselves. In the light of these problems, it seems prudent to include creativity in a personnel specification only when it is a clear precondition to successful performance.

Manual abilities

Manual, or psychomotor, abilities are 'physical' abilities which enable one to 'do' things and they involve muscular control and movement. Typical examples of psychomotor skills are: inserting an integrated circuit into a home computer, typing and standing to attention. Psychologists have attempted to classify psychomotor abilities. However, the outcome of these efforts has been rather different: a pervasive general factor has not emerged. Perhaps the most authoritative analysis of motor skills has been the work of Fleishman (1966) and Fleishman and Quaintance, 1984) who identified 11 factors in psychomotor skills and eight aspects of physical proficiency. The 11 factors in psychomotor skills were:

1. *Control precision*: fine control, rapid and precise actions
2. *Multilimb co-ordination*: the simultaneous co-ordination of several limbs, especially the hands and feet
3. *Response orientation*: involves directional actions made under speeded conditions in response to a stimulus (which is usually a visual stimulus)
4. *Reaction time*
5. *Speed of arm movement*
6. *Rate control*: involves making continuous adjustments to a moving target
7. *Manual dexterity*: involves the manipulation of fairly large objects
8. *Finger dexterity*: involves the manipulation of tiny objects
9. *Arm/hand steadiness*
10. *Wrist and finger speed*
11. *Aiming*: placing an object in an area under highly speeded conditions

Fleishman's eight factors of physical proficiency concern a separate but related area, and were derived from studies of performance of 60 different physical fitness tests. The eight factors are:

1. *Flexibility of trunk and back muscles*
2. Ability of muscles to make *rapid flexing movements* and recover from strain or fatigue
3. Ability to *exert force over a brief period of time*
4. Ability to *exert force repeatedly* over a period of time
5. *Strength of trunk muscles*

6. Ability to *co-ordinate movements when moving the body*
7. Ability to *maintain balance*
8. *Stamina* and *endurance*

Temperament

There are thousands of words which could be used in a personnel specification. To add to the difficulty, personality theorists often invent new, *ad hoc* terms which are ill-defined, overlap and generally serve to obscure the situation. There is a statistical approach which does not rely upon any specific theory of personality and which reduces a mass of data to a relatively small number of recurrent trends. The factor analytic approach has been applied to personality and five recurrent trends have emerged (Digman, 1990). They are: extroversion, disagreeableness, willpower, neuroticism and openness to experience.

Definitions of extroversion abound but it may be thought of as a general tendency of people to direct their energies outwards. It is the opposite of introversion, where people direct their energies inwards towards their own thoughts and feelings. Extroverts seem suited to jobs which involve dealing with people and making quick, practical decisions. Extroverts also seem suited to jobs offering a wide variety of tasks or settings. Introverts, on the other hand, seem suited to jobs where they work on their own or in the company of a few long-term colleagues, in a stable environment on one or two long-term projects. Extroversion can be subdivided in much the same way as intelligence. Cattell, Eber and Tasuoka (1970) suggest that extroversion is composed of warmheartedness, dominance, enthusiasm, adventurousness and group dependence. H. J. Eysenck (1970) suggests that extroversion is composed of sociability, impulsiveness, activity, liveliness and excitability.

Disagreeableness or, as Cattell calls it, 'tough poise', seems to be related in the activation level of the cerebral cortex. People who have tough poise can handle life's problems at an objective, logical level, whereas those low on this factor operate at a 'feeling' level. It seems to be composed of critical ability, practical realism, and a down-to-earth approach.

Willpower reflects the degree to which individuals can control their actions so that longer term considerations take priority over immediate reactions. It includes such things as dependability, super-ego strength and prudence. According to Cattell it consists primarily of two things: conscieniousness (the susceptibility to control by the expectations of others) and social poise (the control exerted by one's self perception).

Neuroticism refers to a 'brittleness' of temperament: the likelihood of 'snapping' under stress. Well-adjusted people can usually cope with distractions, do not ordinarily lack energy and they usually have a variety of interests. Cattell, Eber and Tatsuoka (1970) call the factor 'anxiety', which is composed of being easily affected by one's feelings, timidity, sensitivity, worrying, poor self-sentiment and tension.

The fifth major personality factor is concerned with independence, radicalism and self-sufficiency. Openness to experience reflects a willingness to consider new ideas, a flexibility of thought and a readiness to indulge in fantasy. It is also associated with cultural interests, creativity and intelligence.

Interests

In many situations interests will be included on the personnel specification. For example, a personnel specification for a manager might specify administrative, persuasive and computational interests. Similarly, a personnel specification for a forestry worker might specify outdoor and scientific interests.

Unfortunately there is no agreed list of interests: each author seems to adopt his or her own list! Figure 4.5 gives a general list. The choice of interest categories has been made on largely pragmatic grounds, except perhaps the categories used by Holland (1959), who structures his classification into a hexagon in clockwise order of intellectual, artistic, social, enterprising, conventional and realistic interests, on the basis of their closeness to each other.

Of particular importance to those drawing up personnel specifications for management jobs is Saville and Holdsworth's (1983) list of managerial interests. As Figure 4.5 shows, they view management interests in terms of both management functions and management skills.

Motivation

The inclusion of motives in a personnel specification is relatively infrequent. When it is included it is often in a general form, such as 'the applicant must be keen'. However, in many situations it is clear that motivation has a major influence on successful performance. Unfortunately, psychological theory offers very little help in identify-

Figure 4.5   Some interest and personal values categories

Interest categories

Outdoor	Literary
Mechanical	Musical
Computational	Social service
Scientific	Practical
Persuasive	Medical
Artistic	

Personal values

Theoretical	Social
Economic	Political
Aesthetic	Power

Managerial interests (from Saville-Holdsworth)

Functions	Skills
Production operations	Information collecting
Technical services	Information processing
Research and development	Problem-solving
Distribution	Decision-making
Purchasing	Modelling
Sales	Oral communication
Marketing support	Written communication
Personnel and training	Organising things
Data processing	Persuading
Finance	Developing people
Administration	Representing

---

ing the motivational traits which should be included in a personnel specification.

The locus of control should, perhaps, be considered first. Rotter (1966) suggested that people can have varying beliefs about the degree of control they have over their lives. People with an internal locus of control generally believe that their own characteristics and their own behaviour determines the rewards and punishments they receive. People with an external locus of control believe they are determined by factors outside themselves such as luck, fate or more powerful people. This approach has resulted in a great deal of research, reviewed by Phares (1976) and Lefcourt (1976).

One of the most comprehensive list of needs was drawn up by Murray (1938), whose long list included three needs which are particularly important: need for affiliation, power and achievement. A person who has a high need for affiliation enjoys working with others and will make an effort to win friendships and maintain associations. A person who has a high need for power attempts to control the environment and to influence or direct other people. He or she expresses opinions forcefully and enjoys leadership roles. A person with a high need for achievement tries to excel by maintaining high standards and achieving objectives by faster, cheaper, better methods. Achievement motivation is probably the most extensively reviewed human motive.

THEORETICAL ISSUES

The theoretical issues of personnel specifications are probably the most ill-defined and unresearched aspects of selection. Not only is there a dearth of research, but much of that which is available confuses the production of a personnel specification with the other stages of the selection process. The most obvious theoretical issues are reliability and validity.

Reliability of Personnel Specifications

Reliability is *not* an important issue when the required characteristics are derived by objective procedures. For example, in job component analysis, the attributes required for a job are obtained by applying a predetermined set of weights to the results of an inventory. In these circumstances coefficients of 0.99 or even 1.0 should be obtained, provided the analyst is competent and careful.

However, reliability *is* an important issue when methods such as the intuitive approach are used. In essence, reliability of personnel specifications obtained will have two major aspects: 'repeated measure' reliability and 'inter-rater' reliability. Repeated measure reliability arises when the same person is asked to read a job analysis and specify the characteristics which a worker will need in order to perform the job. After a short delay (of about one week) the process is repeated, and the two specifications should be very similar. Establishing 'repeated measure' reliability is conceptually straightforward. Unfortunately, no empirical comparison of this type could be located. We simply do not know how consistent people are when they make judgements about the characteristics which workers need to be able to perform jobs.

Inter-rater reliability arises when separate analysts read a job description and then specify a list of required characteristics. If the procedure is reliable, there is a strong relationship between the two lists. Fortunately, there has been some research which suggests that separate raters can achieve a satisfactory level of agreement. For example, Schmitt and Fine (1983) obtained multiple ratings on requirements of jobs for reasoning, mathematics and language, and obtained correlations of 0.86, 0.87 and 0.78 respectively. In a similar vein, Marquardt and McCormick (1972) obtained ratings by psychologists on 76 attributes. The median index of agreement was 0.90.

A classic study by Trattner, Fine and Kubis (1955) adds an extra ingredient by comparing the way that the specifications were derived. One group of analysts rated the requirements for ten different jobs on the basis of a written job description. Another group of analysts made the same ratings on the basis of observing incumbents. The results were encouraging; the coefficients between the ratings of mental and perceptual requirements were good and in the range of 0.87 to 0.96. Slightly surprisingly, the coefficients for physical aptitudes, such as hand–eye co-ordination and manual dexterity were lower and ranged from a puny 0.08 to a robust 0.87. Results of this kind are encouraging. It is probable, but not certain, that high inter-rater reliability implies high repeated measure reliability. In conclusion, the available evidence strongly suggests that the requirements contained in a personnel specification can be reliably deduced from the information contained in a job description.

Validity of Personnel Specifications

Reliability is important, but it is not enough. Methods must be valid. For present purposes validity can be taken to mean that personnel specifications are an accurate reflection of the human characteristics needed to perform a job. Unfortunately there is no simple way of assessing this. We do not have 'God-given' statements which can be used as a perfect standard. However, by using a 'boot-strapping' approach some progress can be made. One of the most straightforward is by Sparrow *et al.* (1982). Using a sample of only 14 tool setters, they first used the PAQ to analyse a job, then they obtained an attribute profile. From the attribute profile they chose a battery of psychological tests. The scores on these tests produced a high multiple correlation of 0.92 with the manager's assessment of the performance of the 14 tool setters.

Trattner, Fine and Kubis's (1955) study followed a similar rationale. They obtained the average test scores for workers in ten jobs. They also obtained estimates of the mean scores from analysts. Finally they compared the estimates with the actual scores. For tests of mental and perceptual characteristics they obtained acceptable correlations of 0.6 and 0.7. However, for tests of physical aptitudes the correlations were only 0.01 and 0.27.

Another investigation by Parry (1968) asked psychologists to estimate the validity of certain psychological tests and then compared these estimates with actual validities. The rationale was that if the psychologists believed a test measured a characteristic which was not required by a job, they would estimate a low validity. If they thought that the characteristic was relevant, and might therefore be included in a personnel specification, they would estimate a high validity. Furthermore, the accuracy of the psychologists' intuitions could be checked by comparing the predicted validities with the actual validities. Unfortunately, however, Parry found only a moderate relationship.

Probably the most extensive and sophisticated attempts to determine the validity of personnel specifications were made by Mecham and McCormick (1969), Mecham (1970) and Marquardt and McCormick (1974). These studies were based on about 8000 questionnaires from 141 jobs. It was therefore possible to deduce three separate indices for each job: the mean score, the potential cut-off scores and the validity coefficients. Each of these indices could, in turn, be correlated with the data on the personnel specification. The correlation between the personnel specification and the mean test scores was good: about 0.73. The correlation for the potential cut-off score was also good: about 0.71. However, the correlation between the personnel specification and validity was mediocre: about 0.39. It must be remembered that these figures give a global view. When correlations for individual subscores were examined it emerged that relationships involving mental abilities, such as general intelligence, verbal intelligence, numerical intelligence and clerical perception, were high. However, the relationships for *some* physical abilities, such as finger dexterity and manual dexterity, were lower.

5 Dealing with Candidates

The chapters on job descriptions, criteria and personnel specifications dealt with the preparation before a vacancy arises. The more thorough this preparation the easier it is to deal with events when an employee hands in a resignation or extra employees need to be recruited. Little 'theory' is involved; practical administrative experience is the greatest requirement.

ATTRACTING A FIELD OF CANDIDATES

A later chapter demonstrates the importance of attracting suitable candidates but, for the present purposes, a common-sense rationale is sufficient: the greater the number of applicants, the greater the probability that one of them will give a precise fit with the personnel specification. However, two particular points should be noted. First, there is an emphasis upon *suitably qualified* candidates. A large number of applications from non-runners is a handicap rather than advantage. Second, the generalisation 'the more applicants the better' is only true up to a certain point. It takes time and effort to process applications. A very large number of applications can overwhelm the capacity of the recruiters and the care and consideration given to each application is degraded. In the light of the costs involved in dealing with large numbers of applicants and the deterioration which it may entail in the decision process, it is sometimes said that in ideal situations there should only be one applicant: the one who is eventually hired. In practice, it would be dangerous to adopt this approach. As a rule of thumb, the recruitment process should aim to produce a field of about ten well-qualified applicants, and in addition there will probably be a collection of applications from less suitable people. Success in attracting a good field of qualified applicants will largely depend upon the recruitment media.

RECRUITMENT MEDIA

Internal advertising is usually the cheapest and quickest way of advertising a vacancy. It involves an announcement of the vacancy at a meeting, a memo on notice boards or an insert into the company newsletter. Internal transfers of this type have the following advantages:

(a) the process can be completed quickly;
(b) more will be known about the applicant;
(c) there will be fewer formalities and legal implications;
(d) training requirements are reduced because the employee will already know much about the organisation;
(e) advertising costs are reduced;
(f) general morale can be improved if it is felt that the company looksafter its present employees and gives them 'first refusal' of any openings which arise.

However, internal recruitment also has disadvantages. The most important are the long-term consequences for the organisation. A policy of internal recruitment denies the company access to new ideas and approaches. Without even being aware of the situation, the organisation can become smug, complacent and out of touch. Another disadvantage arises from the tricky diplomatic situations which arise when an internal application is refused: a high proportion of rebuffed employees may resign within a short period. One of the disadvantages of internal recruitment is that it often does not solve the problem: it merely transfers it elsewhere.

Internal advertising can work in another way. Existing employees may pass on the information to someone who is looking for a job. Often this is a suitable approach because:

(a) applicants can find out a lot about the job from existing employees and they are therefore likely to make a better decision;
(b) home circumstances of such applicants are likely to be appropriate (for example, they are is likely to be locals);
(c) such applicants, if appointed, will try hard not to let down the person who recommended them.

In addition, the employee who makes the recommendation has a vested interest in making sure that the person recommended comes up to scratch. Generally they act as a source of guidance and advice which may make both induction and training easier tasks. To have a recommendation of this kind accepted by management may motivate existing employees. The main disadvantages of seeking recommendations from existing employees is the diplomatic situation which can arise if a recommendation is refused. Furthermore, in some situations, especially in small organisations and units, it may not be in the organisation's interests to be dependent upon a small cohesive group of friends. Strauss and Sayles (1980) maintain that two-thirds of newly-hired employees learn about their job through informal recruitment of this kind. A disadvantage of both direct and indirect internal recruitment is that it tends to perpetuate the status quo, and the status quo may be unfair to newly arrived minority groups.

The decisions about whether to recruit internally needs to be taken in the light of circumstances. The most usual pattern is to rely exclusively upon internal recruitment at senior management levels. Ironically, perhaps, this is the level at which it is most important to ensure an inflow of new ideas and expertise into the organisations.

Vacancies boards are perhaps the second easiest recruitment media. Often a smart, up-to-date notice board outside the entrance of the organisation is a good way of advertising a vacancy. They tend to attract local recruits as they travel to work. Traditionally vacancies boards have been used as a recruitment media for skilled and semi-skilled jobs, but there is no intrinsic reason why they cannot be used for secretarial, professional and managerial jobs. Vacancies boards have two main disadvantages. First, if the organisation has a chronic labour turnover problem, the situation is clear for all to see. Second, the trivial task of keeping the board up to date, especially removing past vacancies, often defeats even the best managed organisation.

Future vacancies files contain information from two main sources: the documents of unsuccessful applicants for other vacancies and speculative applications of people who have contacted the company on the chance that a suitable vacancy may exist. Future vacancies files can be cheap and very effective. People are often delighted to think that a company has not simply discarded their past applications. However, future vacancies files need to be managed carefully. An effective system of classification and cross-indexing is necessary and there must be regular procedures to weed out files which are too old or where several job offers have been refused.

Government employment agencies can be found in most towns and their services are free. They can offer nationwide services, and in many situations government agencies undertake the preliminary sifting of applicants. Unfortunately these agencies have two problems. First, the service may have a poor image and some employers may believe that good applicants will use other methods. Consequently, some employers only use the government system as the medium of last resort. The second problem arises from the link between the state service and the payment of unemployment benefits.

Private recruitment agencies charge fees and tend to specialise in particular occupations, such as clerical, technical or managerial groups. The exact methods of operation can vary from merely acting as a clearing house for applications to managing the whole recruitment process. The fee will depend, in part, upon the services used. Many agencies maintain a register of suitable, qualified personnel and offer a preliminary interviewing service. The advantage of using private agencies is that they have an up-market image and a company can avail itself of expertise as and when it is needed rather than having to bear the cost of employing specialists on a full-time basis. They have a further advantage in that some applicants prefer to make their initial approach to an intermediary rather than to a specific company. The main disadvantage of private agencies are the fees and the fear that agencies will take a short-term view and will recommend unsuitable applicants in order to claim their fee. In practice, these disadvantages do not necessarily occur. Private agencies can be a cost-effective method of recruitment.

Headhunters are a particular type of private recruitment agency. They are almost exclusively used for top jobs. The rationale of headhunting is that the ideal candidate is probably not looking for another employer and is too busy to read job advertisements. Therefore, if the post is important, a company should act proactively, and seek out the best person. Headhunters perform this service, usually by using an extensive network of contacts, monitoring trade media or by identifying the employees of competitors and suppliers. Once they have identified a 'prospect' headhunters research the prospect's performance and career. If the results are positive, contact will be made and the vacancy discussed in general terms at a neutral venue. The company's name is only revealed to the prospect and the prospect's name is only revealed to the company when all checks have been made and where preliminary negotiations have been successful. Discretion is one of the main advantages of the process. The main disadvantage is the cost. There are also ethical considerations, not least of which is the propriety of the present employer 'hoarding' talent which could be better used elsewhere. Headhunting executives in order to obtain specific technical and commercial knowledge from competitors involves serious legal dangers.

Unions and professional organisations can often be an excellent source of recruits, especially when there is a strong tradition of employing only union members. In some professional bodies, including the BPS and the APA, the system is highly organised and the methods include appointments memoranda and offering facilities at conferences and conventions. Unions and professional organisations can be useful recruitment media even when systems of this kind have not been highly developed. An informal telephone call to the branch secretary can often produce a useful field of candidates.

Probably the majority of jobs are advertised in a newspaper, and a number of decisions have to be made. First, it is important to decide upon the category of newspaper to be used: should it be national, regional or local? Second, specific newspapers must be chosen. To a large extent newspapers specialise in certain types of job adverts. They may even specialise further by carrying specific types of job advertisements on certain days, for example, Monday, Civil Service; Tuesday, creative and media; Wednesday, academic and teaching; Thursday, sales; Friday, production. Even when a publication (or combination of publications) have been chosen, a further choice of the type of advertisement is necessary.

Lineage advertisements are the cheapest type and are used for small advertisements where you pay for the number of lines used. The advertiser has no control over the appearance of the advertisement. The finished product may look cramped, hard to read, and will appear along with scores of similar advertisements.

Semi-display advertisements allow the use of differing typefaces, give headings and more space. The advertiser still has little control over the final appearance but the result is easier to read and is more distinctive. The main disadvantage is its increased cost. Some guidelines for producing lineage and semi-display advertisements are given in Figure 5.1.

Classified display advertisements are the most expensive and are usually spread over several columns. The advertiser has almost total control over the final appearance, and pictures, diagrams and logos can be included. Fordham (1975) draws attention to the need for creative talents in copy-writing and visualisation in order to obtain maximum benefit. He suggests that a display advert should achieve four objectives.

(a) attract reader's attention (it must catch the reader's eye and clearly identify the audience to which it is directed);

(b) arouse interest in the company and the job;

(c) explain the remuneration in terms of salary, benefits and prospects;

(d) incite the reader to action (that is, make an application).

The same considerations apply to job advertisements in the technical press except that the readership is usually much more specific and, since trade journals appear less frequently, timing is a crucial element in success.

Figure 5.1   Guidelines for producing newspaper advertisements

1   Get a copy of the paper you intend to use.

2   Be careful over *timing*. Avoid Bank Holidays, Budget Days, days when there is a lot of news. Fridays are said to be good days to advertise a job.

3   The first few words are crucial; start with the title of the job to be filled, or the type of work. If possible, start your advertisement with a word that begins with A, B or C (it will then get to the top of the column).

4   The first line or headline must catch the reader's eye and arouse interest. So start with the most interesting information and work down to less interesting information.

5   Use short words and short sentences. One sentence should contain one thought. Use plenty of paragraphs.

6   Generally, it is best to avoid box numbers. They lower the response, and should only be used in special circumstances.

7   Salary or salary range should be quoted whenever possible. References to 'attractive salary' are meaningless and a waste of space. Benefits should be included. Prospects for promotion can also be included.

8   Inclusion of telephone numbers increase response rate, but be sure to brief the people who may answer the telephone.

9   In some cases give information about the company, its size, location and product.

10 Tell people how to respond: for example, call at the office, write or telephone. Is an application form available?

Liaison with educational institutions may be an important way of recruiting young employees, and this can operate at three levels. At its simplest, an employer simply writes with details of vacancies. At a more organised level, personnel officers will establish a relationship with the school's career teacher. At its most systematic level, the college or university will offer facilities for advertising and interviewing.

The electronic media are a relatively untapped method of recruitment. Local radio and television are potentially powerful media but the cost is high and only a very short, general, advertisement can be transmitted. Consequently, the use of these media can produce too many ill-suited applications. Electronic and moving 'billboards' suffer the same disadvantages, in perhaps a more acute form. The advent of teletext and the use of cable TV offer a way around this limitation and allow the presentation of a simplified job description so that potential applicants can make an informed decision.

Whatever recruitment media are chosen to attract a field of candidates, it should be remembered that an important secondary function of the advertising will be to enhance the image which the public has of the organisation: job advertisements will be noticed by a substantial proportion of suppliers, competitors and customers and will play a part in forming their image of your organisation. Similarly, a job advertisement will receive a great deal of attention and speculation from present employees. It can fill them with pride and it can also fill them with shame.

The media chosen to attract applicants have three implications for equality of opportunity. First, media should be chosen so that all suitable applicants, regardless of sex, race or creed, have a roughly equal chance of seeing the advertisements. Second, under the vast majority of circumstances the text of any advertisement should not state or imply that any one sex or racial group is more suitable or will be given favourable treatment. Third, while it is unlikely to evoke legal action, it is bad practice to produce advertisements and recruitment literature which presents the sexes and racial groups in stereotyped roles.

Before the advert appears it is vital to make two administrative checks: is any additional information promised in the advertisement available? Have arrangements been made to handle the replies (for example, have the office staff and telephonist been briefed)?

METHODS OF APPLICATION

The job advertisements should clearly state how the applicant should apply. The most common methods are: (1) personal visit 'on spec' to the personnel department; (2) by telephone; and (3) written response. The usual result of a telephone or written contact is to send the potential applicant an application pack which will consist of four items.

1 A short letter thanking applicants for their interest, stating the closing date, and drawing their attention to the enclosures.
2 An application form.
3 A description of the job.
4. A reply envelope.

APPLICATION FORMS

In most cases, a good application form is an essential part of selection and serves five functions. First, the most important function of an application form is to select a short list of applicants who will be invited to an interview. Second, a good application form should be an aid to the interview itself. It should be easy to read, provide a framework for the interview and provide convenient spaces for the interviewer to make short notes. The third function is to build up a future vacancies file: applicants may not be suitable for the present job but they may be suitable for one that arises in the near future. Fourth, an application form can help analyse the labour market and identify the recruitment media which brings the best kind of response. Using this information, recruitment advertising can be targeted with accuracy and wastage can be reduced. The fifth function is often overlooked but is of great importance. The application form fulfils a public relations function. The form will be distributed to perhaps 100 people. Even if they decide not to apply, they will give the form close attention. A well-produced form projects an image of an efficient, fair and well-run organisation.

Most firms will need three separate application forms in order to cater for different categories of staff. They are: (1) A form for school leavers; (2) A form for professionally-qualified staff and management; and (3) A form for other employees. In some situations a bespoke form will be needed. Figures 5.2 and 5.3 give guidelines on the construction of application forms and their contents. For more precise guidance it will be necessary to refer to standard texts such as B. J. Edwards (1975) and Tavernier (1973).

Figure 5.2 Checklist for constructing an application form

---

1 It should be marked CONFIDENTIAL and *treated* as such. Completed application forms should not be circulated.

2 In general, arrange items in a chronological sequence.

3 The layout should give enough room for the answers.

4 Use clear and concise words: that is, short words and short sentences.

5 Standardise form sizes: use A4 good quality paper.

6 Avoid underlinings: use different sizes of type instead.

7 Instruct applicant to complete the form in BLACK ink so that it will photocopy.

8 It *must* contain the name and address to which it should be returned and the closing date for the return of the completed form.

9 It should contain a warning not to send testimonials or the originals of other documents (these can be requested at a later stage).

CURRICULA VITAE

At senior managerial, professional level and jobs where written communication is important, it is generally better to ask applicants to send copies of their curriculum vitae (CV) since the way that an applicant writes a CV may be a valid indicator of how good he or she will be at the job. However, the use of CVs may give rise to two problems. First, information from different applicants is likely to be given in a different order and formats. Inevitably, this makes the initial sifting procedure more tedious. At its worst it can mean that some good applicants omit important information. In order to avoid this difficulty, requests for a CV should specify essential information. The

Figure 5.3 Checklist for contents of application forms

Application forms should start with the type of job sought and the date of any previous applications. They should also cover some of the following items:

1 *Personal details*

   (a) name, address and telephone number
   (b) date and place of birth
   (c) sex, marital status, dependents
   (d) height, weight, state of health

2 *Family background*

   (a) relations employed in company
   (b) occupations of other members of family

   This section needs handling with care. Young people in particular may be sensitive about the status of their parents' jobs. However, this information is often useful.

3 *Educational background*

   In general, do not ask for details of education before the age of 11. Possible items are:

   (a) schools attended (name and type, with dates)
   (b) examinations taken, and grades obtained
   (c) school offices, scholarships, or prizes
   (d) college or university; nature of courses; grades obtained; dates; offices held; extra-curricular activities

4 *Vocational training*

   (a) type of training (for example, apprenticeship/articles, place of training)
   (b) professional qualifications; date of qualification; present grade of membership
   (c) fluency in languages: written, oral

5 *Employment history*

   Complete chronological record of all jobs with:

   (a) name and address of employer
   (b) dates, nature, scale of duties and to whom responsible
   (c) reasons for leaving
   (d) starting and finishing salaries

Allow plenty of space for details of last employment and ask when they would be free to start work.

6 *Leisure interests*

(a) hobbies
(b) membership of societies and offices held

The exact range, depth and intensity of these interests can be ascertained at interview.

7 *Self-assessment*

Towards the end of the form ask the applicant about

(a) personal likes, dislikes and special job interests
(b) future aims and ambitions

---

second problem arises because an executive may not have produced the CV personally, but may have used the services of professional agencies.

PRODUCING A SHORTLIST

Very occasionally it is possible to make a decision solely on the basis of the information given in a written application. More often written applications are used as a first sieve. The most common sieving procedure is to sort each application into one of three piles:

Possibles: applicants who seem to have a good chance of succeeding at the job
Doubtfuls: applicants who are at the margin of suitability
Rejected: applicants who are clearly unsuitable

The objective is to end up with about six applicants in the 'possibles' pile. If there are fewer, reconsider the candidates in the doubtful pile to see if any can be reclassified, perhaps using slightly less stringent criteria. If the first sieve results in more than six 'possibles', it is they who are subject to further scrutiny.

After a decent interval of about a week applicants who are doubtful and rejected are informed of the decision.

THEORETICAL ISSUES IN ATTRACTING A FIELD OF APPLICANTS

Selection as a Social Process

Herriot (1989) argues very convincingly for viewing selection as a social process which consists of a series of episodes. At the end of each episode, both the organisation and the candidate make a decision whether to continue to the next. The elaborate choreography between the applicant and employer starts when the applicant becomes aware of the vacancy via an advertisement or, say, a brochure. On the basis of the information available, he or she estimates the match between their expectations and their knowledge of the organisation. If the gap is wide, no further action is taken. If the gap is low, the candidate fills out a form. The organisation then compares the application form and its expectations of candidates. If the gap is wide the relationship is terminated. If the gap is narrow the applicant is usually invited to an interview; and so the procedure continues until the organisation or the candidate terminates the relationship, or a job offer is made and accepted.

The advantages of explicitly stating this process are two-fold. First, it reminds selectors that the applicants have power, too. Second, it prompts research into the information which applicants use to determine whether an organisation meets his or her expectations. Schuler (in press) suggests that the results might be organised under four headings: information, participation, transparency and feedback. Organisations transmit *information* both intentionally and unintentionally. Evidence suggests that, at least initially, candidates are most concerned about receiving functional information. However, greater weight seems to be placed on information obtained from personal sources such as interviewers or colleagues; many studies have shown that candidates are very sensitive to the style of the interviewers. In general, interviewers who maintain a high level of eye contact, who comment about feelings and who disclose information about themselves create the most favourable impression. Some results (see Thornton, in press) also suggest that applicants are more likely to attend further interviews and accept job offers. When 'warm' interviewer behaviour was not displayed applicants were more willing to pursue further contacts with the organisation only when the interviewer presented a high level of information. Generally, applicants feel that tests give them little information about the job.

Not surprisingly, candidates prefer methods which are *participative* and where they feel they can exert some *control*. Consequently there may be a tendency for applicants to prefer non directive methods of selection, or methods which have been designed not by specialists, but by people like themselves.

Transparency is the degree to which the candidate can easily perceive the revelance of the procedures they complete and how the information can be used. This issue is particularly important when tests are used, and there is research suggesting that tests and assessment centres are more acceptable if the applicants are given details about their construction, use and interpretation.

Finally, candidates seem to prefer methods which provide them with *feedback* on how well they are doing. There is some evidence to suggest that this is true even if the feedback they receive is negative.

Effects of Using Different Channels of Attracting Candidates

There are some data which suggest that employees recruited by some sources are better than those recruited by other sources. Usually it is maintained that informal sources, such as recommendations, are better than formal sources (such as advertising). De Witte (1989), for example, reviews five studies in which labour turnover of those recruited by advertising was 51 per cent. The labour turnover for spontaneous applicants was 37 per cent and the labour turnover for applicants recommended by existing employees was 30 per cent. As the same type of result has been obtained in several investigations various hypotheses have been put forward to account for it.

The first of these hypothesis was the 'better waters' hypothesis. It was suggested that the different recruitment methods fished in different waters and that some waters contained a better quality of fish than others. Presumably, according to this hypothesis, the best people do not reply to newspaper advertisements or make themselves known to recruitment agencies: they speak up for themselves, or their friends and relatives speak up for them.

The second hypothesis was the 'better info' hypothesis. It was argued that people who were suggested by other employees or relatives were better and more realistically informed about the job than those who applied through newspapers and agencies. Thus they were in a better position to assess their own suitability and perhaps the least suitable did not bother to apply at all. Consequently the average 'quality' of informally-referred applicant tends to be higher. Better information might also influence labour turnover. Better informed candidates are likely to have a more realistic view of the job and consequently would be less likely to leave when faced with the job itself. It is arguable that candidates from informal sources have discussed the job with the person who recommends them and that the job has been accurately described, warts and all. Candidates replying to newspapers, on the other hand, were probably obtaining their information from glossy brochures produced by the company's public relations department. When actual experience failed to match the high expectations, a substantial proportion would find employment elsewhere. The 'better info' hypothesis fitted in beautifully with the Zeitgeist of the time: work in progress in the USA was showing that labour turnover among candidates who were given realistic job previews of the job (RJPs) was lower. More recent research has cast some doubt upon the effectiveness of RJPs. Some reviewers have concluded that RJPs (see Chapter 10) have little impact on turnover whilst other researchers suggest that an RJP only works when it is based on first-hand experience rather than a film or demonstration.

The third hypothesis to explain the apparent finding that informal sources of recruits produced a better quality of employee is the 'cynics' hypothesis. This contends that the result is little more than a self-fulfilling prophecy. Some studies used ratings by the supervisor as their measure of employee quality. Unfortunately, supervisory ratings can be notoriously subjective. Supervisors usually know how an employee has applied and many supervisors firmly believe in the importance of local knowledge and personal contact. Perhaps subconsciously they allowed their feelings and knowledge to affect the ratings they gave.

However, all this speculation proved unnecessary because the scientific validity of the finding that informal sources produced better candidates fell into doubt. Some of the early studies failed to control for the effects of seniority and tenure, and had lumped together jobs of different kinds. Older employees tend to stay with an employer for longer. There is also a tendency for informal methods to be used with senior positions. Consequently, when all types of jobs are mixed together in an investigation an illusion is created. Recent work which has carefully controlled age and job level has failed to replicate the findings of ten years ago. It does seem to be a case of one step forward and one step back, but this should not daunt us in further work on the effectiveness of different recruitment media. It remains an area where a lot is opined but little is known.

Satisfaction with and Effectiveness of Different Media

A survey by the British Institute of Management and the Institute of Personnel Management (1980) investigated the way a sample of 335 companies recruited managers. No fewer than 77 per cent recruited managers internally and the most common media for external recruitment were the local and national press; but, as Figure 5.4 shows, the pattern varies according to both the management function and level. Figure 5.4 also shows the company's perception of different recruitment methods.

Pollock and Lake (1983) give the results of a survey of 50 employers' and 50 recruitment consultants' views of the requirements of CVs. The majority preferred a clear working document with no photograph. Most preferred to have details of the last job first and information about the duties, responsibilities and achievements under each job rather than a table of appointments followed by a description. Details of educational background, salaries and benefits (including whether a car had been provided in the last job), nationality and a clear statement of career aims were considered to be especially important information.

The applicant's view of recruitment media is an important issue but there has been even less research in this aspect. The results of one survey by the Consumers' Association (1983) are given in Table 5.1.

Table 5.1   Applicants' use of, and success with, recruitment media

Recruitment media	*% use*	*% success*
National press	47	11
Local press	56	22
Trade press	30	15
Agencies	22	11
Specialist agencies	27	28
Job Centres	56	11
Professional and executive register	39	7
Speculative applications	42	23
Personal contacts	50	51

Source: Consumers' Association (1983).

Figure 5.4 Use of, and satisfaction with, recruitment media

Category of worker	Senior Management	Middle management	Junior management	Engineering	Sales Marketing	Personnel	Computer	Accounts	Technical	Satisfaction (1–5 rating) with method	Strong advantages	Strong disadvantages
	% of companies using media for:											
National press	65	45	20	48	66	35	29	40	39	3.5	N	F
Local press	28	56	71	59	44	49	55	53	50	3.7	C,Q	F
Trade journals	38	45	36	49	40	48	51	45	57	3.2	S	F
Private agencies	11	21	28	18	16	13	27	26	18	2.7		C,P
Selection consultants	35	15	6	14	18	14	11	18	12	2.8	S	C,P
Headhunters	15	3	1	4	5	6	0	6	5	2.5	S	C,N,P
Government agencies	12	25	28	27	17	19	19	19	26	2.2		P
Professional registers	6	8	6	9	7	4	6	10	10	1.9	S	E,P
Personal recommendations	26	24	21	27	27	20	21	16	25	–		
Direct application	10	18	20	19	15	13	16	11	20	–		
Internal recruitment	–	77	–	–	–	–	–	–	–	4.1		

Notes: C = Costs; F = Confidentiality; N = Number of Applications Generated; P = Public Relations; S = Suitability of Applicants

SOME UNANSWERED QUESTIONS

Clearly research in this area is in its infancy. The data which exist are sparse, at a descriptive level, and focus largely on the perception of custom and practice. We know very little about which advertisements and recruitment media are successful in terms of attracting applicants who will make good employees. We know little about the processes which lead potential applicants, especially those applicants who are contented in their present job, to attend to the recruitment media. We know little about the processes by which employers use the information in CVs and application forms to select a short list of candidates. We know little about the way that recruitment methods affect a company's public relations. These uncertainties mean that attracting a candidate and handling the response is, at present, more an art than a science.

Part II
Psychometrics

6 Requirements of Measures: Practicability, Sensitivity and Reliability

Once the short-listed candidates have been identified, the next stage is to subject them to a procedure to measure the personal qualities listed in the personnel specification. There are many different measures from which to choose. Eventually a decision between the different methods will need to be made. The most logical way is to set out, in advance, the requirements which good selection methods should meet. In practice, there are four main requirements. In order of pre-eminence they are practicability, sensitivity, reliability and validity. This chapter deals with the first three; the next chapter deals with validity.

PRACTICABILITY OF MEASURES

Except in the most unusual situations, practicability is the most important requirement. Even if a measure has all other virtues, if it is impractical its use will not be maintained.

Acceptability to those Involved

The employment of any selection method depends upon whether people perceive it to be useful. This perception does not have to be unanimous but there must be a consensus at the appropriate level and place within the organisation. Probably most important are the perceptions of *senior management* since, in the last analysis, they decide the deployment of the organisation's resources. The perceptions of *selection specialists* are also important. Their experience and technical knowledge adds weight to their views. The technical aspects and practicality are probably the most important considerations to selection specialists, although tradition will play a significant part.

A selection method must also obtain the approval of the *candidates*. At the very least, the results will be distorted if candidates disapprove

93

and fail to take proceedings seriously. Cronbach (1970) gives a delightful example of the importance of the candidates' perceptions: an Italian bus company discovered that applicants believed that the more elaborate testing facilities in the capital gave them a fairer chance. Finally, the method of selection may attract the attention of *political and pressure groups*. Again Cronbach provides an example: 'The British military selection programme had to satisfy a Labour cabinet insistent that poor boys have a fair chance to become officers.' More recently, some companies have abandoned certain selection methods in favour of less efficient ones because they are unwilling to attract the attention of minority groups and become involved in protracted litigation which would prove costly even if they sustained their case.

Operational Aspects

At a practical level, operational aspects of measures are also important considerations. The main operational aspects are: cost-benefit, time considerations, manpower and facilities. The basic point is that a selection system must produce more benefits than its cost. The difficulty lies in establishing whether this is true. With care it is fairly easy to establish the costs of a selection system, but establishing the benefits is much more difficult and can in itself be an expensive activity (see Chapter 13). The main costs are set out in Figure 6.1. In a large organisation with a clearly defined selection department, the costs will be easy to identify since most accounting systems will treat the department as a cost centre.

The second operational aspect concerns timing. Flexibility and lead time are particularly important. Generally, a selection system which can be quickly adapted to changing circumstances is more practical than a system which requires rigid adherence to predetermined procedures. Similarly, methods which can be completed within a short time span of two or three weeks are usually more practical than multi-stage procedures which drag on for several months. The different selection methods vary in the demands they make upon able and qualified people. Unfortunately the situation is complicated by the fact that the need for qualified personnel is clearer for some methods than others.

The final aspect concerning the practicality of a measure concerns the facilities required. Graphology and reference checks require minimal facilities. Tests require booklets and answer sheets: they also

Figure 6.1   Main costs in a selection system

---

1   Labour costs of personnel involved in selection and associated clerical work

- salary
- pension contributions
- holiday entitlements
- employment taxes

2   Set-up costs

- costs of training staff in selection methods
- costs of engaging consultants
- costs of maintaining records
- costs of obtaining criterion measures

3   Equipment and accommodation costs

- rent or apportionment of accommodation costs
- heating, lighting, cleaning
- rates and taxes
- cost of materials, for example, tests
- stationery, postage, telephone

4   Costs paid to applicants

- travelling expenses
- accommodation expenses

5   Advertisement costs

---

require small pieces of equipment. Some work sample tests, such as a test of ability as an airline pilot, can require expensive simulators.

On its own, practicality of a selection method is not enough: selection at random with a pin is very practical, but few organisations knowingly use methods of this kind! Practicality must be supplemented by other aspects.

CRITERION-BASED SCORING SYSTEMS

One approach to scoring people is to determine the level of skill that is needed for a given purpose and then devise a test to see whether or not they have reached that level. Often measures of this kind can be regarded as measures of mastery. Possibly the clearest example is the driving test. Experts have established that, in order to be a safe driver, an individual must be able to drive in traffic, know the Highway Code, perform a 'hill start', turn at appropriate junctions, complete an 'emergency stop', and so on. A test is then constructed in which these operations are required, and failure in any one operation means a failure in the whole test. An individual's performance is not related to the performance of anyone else. In principle, all entrants could pass or all entrants could fail. The use of criterion based tests is probably becoming more prevalent. For example, the BPS accreditation for competence in testing stipulates a list of competences which individuals must have before they are deemed fit to use psychological tests. Many educational qualifications (such as GCSE) now specify a series of criteria which students must meet in order to be awarded a certain grade. This contrasts with some previous systems whereby the top so many per cent were given grade A, the next so many per cent were given grade B, and so forth.

Criterion-based measures tend to be characterised by the following features:

- the items of the measures are highly specific;
- the measures are closely linked to some kind of education or training;
- the result is usually a pass/fail basis although performance may be organised into a series of levels;
- candidates are usually allowed several attempts, often interspersed with further tuition, until they achieve the criterion level.

The main disadvantages of criterion-based tests are:

(a) the criteria may be difficult to establish objectively: for example some psychologists might contend that some of the competences required by the BPS are not necessary for effective test use
(b) criterion-related tests are often too specific; requirements may change over time and the test become too easy (the test results may be so specific that they are useless in making decisions for a related job);
(c) in situations where repeated attempts are allowed the ultimate success rate is high and is of little use to organisations who wish to select 'the best' rather than those who are merely 'competent'.

Criterion-related tests also give rise to special issues concerning reliability and validity (see Berk, 1984).

NORM-BASED SCORING SYSTEMS

Sensitivity and Discriminability

Other things being equal, the more a measure discriminates among applicants, the more useful the measure will be. Some selection methods are less discriminating than others. For example, one of the authors was involved in a selection situation which used several different measures on the same group of people. To ensure comparability between the methods, the participants were placed in one of five categories, 5 being the most favourable. The results can be seen in Table 6.1. The most discriminating predictor was the test and the least discriminating was the interview. Indeed, the spread (standard deviation, or sd) of the interview was only about half the spread of the tests.

Table 6.1 Sensitivity of five measures in selection

Type of measure	Mean	Standard deviation
Tests	3.1	0.98
Group discussion	2.5	0.84
In-Basket	2.8	0.75
Manager's reference	3.2	0.64
Interviews	3.0	0.54

n = approximately 155 depending on measure.

Scoring Systems

The scoring system used to report the results is closely related to the degree to which a measure can discriminate. Crude measures can only adopt a crude scoring system and complex scoring systems should be used only with measures with good discrimination. The initial score given by a measure is the *raw score* and at its simplest it consists of the crude number of right answers. However, raw scores have very little use and can be quite misleading, as the cautionary tale of John

Michael demonstrates. On arriving home one day he informed his mother that he had 'got 10 for arithmetic today'. Mummy, being delighted that her offspring was at last showing some gumption, decided to encourage the simpleton by buying him a new bicycle. John Michael had faithfully reported his raw score of 10. What he had not reported was that the test was out of 200 and that the average mark of his classmates was 120! Adequate scoring systems aim to prevent misunderstandings of this kind. In essence, there are three main types of scoring systems: intuitive, positional and systems based upon the normal curve.

Intuitive systems

The simplest system is based upon pure intuition, where someone experienced in selection has stored in their memory experience of past situations. Current information can be matched with a past situation and an evaluation made.

Positional scoring systems

Except in the crude sense that, on most measures, the higher the score the higher the potential, the raw score is not very useful. To make sense of a score, it is necessary to compare the score with those obtained by similar people. In other words, it needs to be compared with a set of *norms*: a table which shows how a representative sample of people would have fared on the measure. Great care should be taken in choosing appropriate norms. Usually it is better to use 'local' norms, but work by Hunter, Schmidt and Hunter (1979) suggests that norms should not be based on small samples of less than, say, 400 people. As the name implies, positional systems refer to the position of individuals in respect to those in the normative sample and there are four main systems.

The simplest positional scoring system simply allots an above average or below average category. Although it is simple and quick, this method wastes so much information and is so crude that it should be used only when all else fails.

Ranking is only slightly more complex and gives better discriminations. By convention, the best candidate is given a rank of 1 and so on until the worst candidate receives the highest number. However, rankings are best avoided: they can magnify small differences and they can shrink large differences. Furthermore, a rank in itself does not indicate a level of merit or competence; the top rank can mean that an individual is merely the best of a bad bunch; the bottom rank could mean that an individual is only slightly worse than a field of superb candidates. Ranking systems are also notoriously difficult to analyse.

Percentile scores are the most refined type of positional score. Percentile scores attempt to place a person in a representative queue of 99 other people who have been arranged in order of their score. Thus someone with a percentile of 52 would be fifty-second in the queue. Percentile systems are easily understood by lay people and they allow fine discriminations. Their main disadvantage is that they do not accurately portray the difference between two scores. For example, there will only be a small absolute difference between two people at the 55th and 60th percentile, while there will usually be a substantial difference between two people at the 90th and 95th percentile. It should be noted that a percentile score says nothing about the percentage of questions answered correctly. The decile system is similar to the percentile system but gives a cruder classification. It tries to place people in a representative queue of 10. The decile system is rarely used but it has the advantage of avoiding over-interpretation of scores, and it does not require such large standardisation samples to obtain a set of norms.

A five-category grading system is slightly more sophisticated than a ranking system. It is easily understood and is sufficiently refined for many personnel decisions. The most ubiquitous version of this system is as follows:

A = Top 10% of candidates
B = Next 20% of candidates
C = Middle 40% of candidates
D = Next 20% of candidates
E = Bottom 10% of candidate

This scheme has the advantage of placing the maximum discrimination at the extremes of the spectrum and it prevents over-interpretation of scores.

Scoring systems based on the normal curve

If a large sample of people is taken and one of their characteristics (such as height) is measured, the results can be cast into a frequency diagram, as shown in Figure 6.2. When the midpoints of each class

Figure 6.2   Normal curve showing height of a sample of 36 women

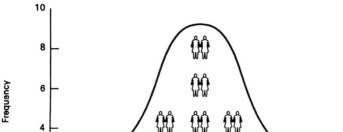

Figure 6.3   Two examples of a normal curve showing how mean and standard deviation may vary

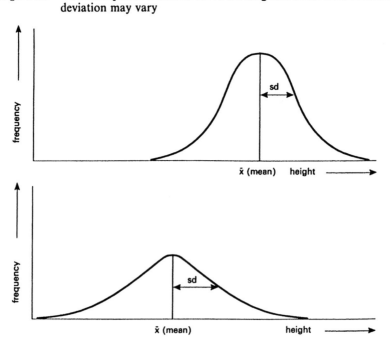

interval of the frequency diagram are joined, it is highly likely that a normal curve is produced in which most people are near the centre and there are fewer and fewer people at the extremes. The normal curve has two main characteristics: the mean and the standard deviation. The mean shows the average score and the standard deviation is a measure of the spread (see Figure 6.3). It is possible to construct several scoring systems based upon the normal curve. There are five main ones.

Z scores are the simplest type of score based upon a normal curve, and they simply state how many standard deviations a person is above or below the mean. Someone whose Z score is exactly average would have a score of 0: someone whose Z score is −2 would be two standard deviations below average. It is easy to obtain a Z score from a raw score: simply subtract the average from the raw score and then divide the result by the standard deviation. For example, the AH4 intelligence test has a mean of 75 and a standard deviation of 15. Someone with a raw score of 90 would have a Z score of 1: that is, (90−75)/15. Someone with a raw score of 45 would have a Z score of −2: (45−75)/15. In most practical situations, Z scores are not used because they involve decimal points and plus or minus signs which are notoriously liable to be omitted when copying out results. Furthermore, Z scores appear to be crowded because most people lie in the −2.5 to +2.5 range. Although simple, Z scores are rarely used, they are important because they form the basis for the other types of standard scores, such as quotients, T scores, stens and stannines. To obtain a standard score, the Z score is usually multiplied by a constant to expand the range. Then a further constant is added to remove any minus sign.

The *quotient system* is probably the best known standard score. It is frequently used with intelligence tests and it is usually based on a mean of 100 and a standard deviation of 15. Thus someone with a Z score of +1.5 would obtain an IQ of 122.5 100+(1½×15). Just to add some confusion, it should be noted that some tests use quotients based upon a mean of 100 and a standard deviation of 20. Unfortunately quotients offer too fine a discrimination for most measures and they invite over-interpretation of trivial differences.

T scores were named after Thorndike; they adopt a mean of 50 and a standard deviation of 10. Although T scores are convenient and practically the whole population will have a score between 1 and 99, they are rarely used because they still invite over-interpretation.

Sten scores (standard scores to ten) are used by some of the most popular psychological tests. The system adopts the mean of 5.5 and a standard deviation of 2. Ninety-nine per cent of the population have scores between one and ten. Stens have the disadvantage of involving half points and analysts need to allow two digits in their computations to cater for those who score the maximum.

Stannines (standard scores to nine) are similar to stens except a mean of 5.0 is adopted. Consequently, decimal points are needed less often and the huge majority of people have scores between one and nine.

It is possible to convert between percentiles, quotients, Z scores, T scores, stens and stannines, but to avoid confusion it is better, within an organisation, to adopt only one system.

RELIABILITY

The Standard Error

Even if a measure is both practical and sensitive, it will be inadequate if it is not also reliable. Reliability is often defined as the extent to which scores on a measure are free from random error. Reliability is usually, but not always, synonymous with consistency. The best way of establishing the reliability of a measure is to use it repeatedly on the same object. For example, 100 specimens of one person's handwriting could be obtained and each specimen independently rated on a trait such as extroversion. The 100 ratings of this one person could be collated and a histogram produced. Like most distributions, the histogram would have a mean and a standard deviation. The mean could be taken to be the 'true' position and the standard deviation could be taken as an index of how much random factors influence measurement. Usually, this is called the *standard error* of a measure. In approximately two out of three situations the random factors will be less than one standard error, and consequently in two out of three situations we can be sure that the true score lies within one standard error of the scores we observe. Thus the standard error of measurement is particularly important in interpreting a score, as it tells us the confidence we can have in our observations. Providing the scoring system is constant, measures with smaller standard errors are best. In essence, this analysis follows the classical analysis explained in more detail by J. P. Campbell (1976, pp. 189ff.) which views a score as two separate components: the true score and random error. Lumsden (1976) provides a witty, provocative and disturbing critique of this view.

Correlation Coefficients and Reliability

Estimating reliability by measuring the same thing a large number of times is usually possible in the physical sciences. In industrial psychology, this method is usually impractical. Few volunteers are prepared to submit to 100 interviews or be content to complete a questionnaire *ad nauseam*. A different method of establishing reliability is needed. Instead of obtaining 100 scores from one individual, it is usually easier to obtain, say, two scores on 100 people. The two scores can then be correlated with each other and the correlation can be used as an index of reliability since, if a measure is reliable, it should produce two very similar scores for each person and therefore a high correlation. Furthermore, given a few statistical assumptions, it is possible to calculate a standard error from a reliability coefficient using the formula:

$$\text{standard error} = \text{standard deviation} \times \sqrt{1 - \text{reliability coefficient}}$$

Often it is more convenient to express reliability in terms of a correlation because the computing procedure for a correlation automatically reduces scores to a common scale. Under most circumstances the correlation coefficients can be interpreted as shown in Table 6.2. Reliability coefficients obtained in this way directly give the percentage of variance which is systematic. Thus a reliability coefficient of 0.9 means that 90 per cent of variance is sytematic and 10 per cent is error. Under most circumstances, selectors are reluctant to use measures with reliabilities of less than 0.7.

Methods of obtaining reliability coefficients

To obtain a correlation coefficient, it is necessary to have two scores for each candidate. The different ways of obtaining these pairs of scores give rise to the four main methods of estimating reliability.

Parallel form reliability is used when there are two equivalent versions of a measure. Sometimes this type of reliability is termed the coefficient of equivalence. Parallel form reliability has a number of disadvantages. First, and obviously, it is necessary to produce a parallel form of the measure. This increases costs and can involve extra delay. Consequently parallel form reliability is only used when different versions of the measure exist for other reasons. A second difficulty is the problem of ensuring that both versions are equally

Table 6.2   Interpretation of reliability coefficients

	Verbal label						
	Excellent	*Good*	*Acceptable*	*Poor*		*Abysmal*	
Reliability coefficients	0.9	0.8	0.7	0.6	0.5	0.4	0.3
% random	10	20	30	40	50	60	70
% systematic variance	90	80	70	60	50	40	30
Signal/noise ratio	9.0	4.0	2.3	1.5	1.0	0.6	0.4

satisfactory. If one of the versions is less satisfactory than the other, the correlation between them will reflect the reliability of the least satisfactory version. The consecutive administration of the two measures produces a third set of difficulties. For example, in responding to the first version a candidate may be more alert, give greater thought to the answers and be less sure about the purposes of the procedure. In responding to the second version, the candidate may have become bored or so sophisticated that she can perceive the purpose of the procedure and adjust her responses in order to fool the selector. These influences arise from procedures to estimate reliability and not from the measure itself. They will tend to produce an underestimate of reliability. A fourth problem with parallel form reliability is the influence of temporary and irrelevant states in the candidates. For example, if both versions of a measure are administered on a day when a candidate is feeling on top of the world, then the score on both versions may be a little higher. Another candidate may be operating in the face of what feels like a terminal hangover and both of these scores are depressed. Because these temporary influences operate on both versions they tend to inflate the observed level of parallel form reliability.

Internal consistency is a type of reliability which has similarities with parallel form reliability. At its simplest it consists of a split-half reliability. In essence the two scores used to compute the correlation are obtained by dividing the items of a measure into two halves. In principle this can be done with most measures, but it is easiest with tests. For example, one-half of a test might be the odd-numbered items and the other half might be the even-numbered items. A score is then obtained for each half and the two scores correlated. This initial correlation is an appreciable underestimate of the true reliability. It is known that short scales are less reliable than longer ones, and the initial split-half correlation is based on scales that are only half the length of the actual scales. The initial estimates must therefore be corrected for length using the Spearman-Brown formula (see formula 4.2 in Appendix IV). Split-half correlations have one particular disadvantage. The way that the items are divided among the two halves is arbitrary. With very short measures which are not uni-dimensional this can reduce the level of the reliability estimate. For example, suppose there is a short test of arithmetic ability covering the operations of add and multiply. It is quite likely that the test designer used a spiral omnibus format in which the first and third (and so on) questions are additions and the second and fourth (and so on) questions are multiplications. The unwary might then attempt an odd-even split-half reliability which would correlate additions against multiplications. It is probable that the resulting coefficient would be smaller than one obtained from two halves, both of which contained additions and multiplications.

An alternative to the split-half method is the item-whole correlation, which also applies mainly, but not exclusively, to psychometric tests. Here the score on each item is correlated with the total score. There are as many correlations as there are items and, since it is mathematically wrong to take a simple average of a set of correlations, the median item-whole correlation is usually chosen. The item–whole correlation may be spuriously high because there is self-contamination (that is, the score of an item is included in the total score against which it is correlated). A correct analysis would make appropriate subtractions from the total score before it is correlated. Probably the best indices of a measure's internal consistency are coefficient alpha and Kuder–Richardson's formula 20. These indices, in effect, compute the mean values of all possible split-half reliabilities. The Kuder–Richardson (1937) formula is generally used where the items are scored in terms of pass and fail, and Cronbach's (1951) alpha is used when items are marked on a continuum.

Test–retest reliability, in spite of its name, is relevant to other selection measures. To establish test–retest reliability, the same measure is readministered to a sample after a short interval. Often this type of reliability is termed *stability* (see Cureton, 1971). Test–retest reliability does not entail the problems arising from changes from one version to another, but additional issues arise. Some candidates will learn from their first experience and their scores will show subsequent improvement. Differential changes will tend to depress the level of the reliability coefficient obtained. The time interval used in a test–retest study may be of crucial importance. A very short interval (such as one or two days) increases learning effects. On the other hand, a long interval of a year could encompass genuine changes. The genuine changes are wrongly included as error and thus the reliability estimate is depressed. Most test–retest studies involve an interval of between one and three months.

Inter-rater reliability is a different issue which is encountered when a measure involves some subjective evaluation by a judge, such as evaluating an interview or performance in a discussion group. In these situations a check should be made on the consistency of the raters. Usually, an unambiguous scoring system is devised and raters are trained in the use of the system. Next, two markers independently classify a small, but representative, sample of results. Differences between the two markers should be discussed and reconciled. The markers then independently score a full sample and the two sets of independent marks are then correlated. An inter-rater reliability of less than 0.9 is not normally acceptable. Some authors, such as Cattell (1957) and Guion (1965), refer to inter-rater reliability as 'conspect reliability'.

Setting 'Cutting Scores'

Some organisations set thresholds in selection. For example, one international firm of management consultants has a policy of not hiring candidates whose IQ is less than 130. However, it is known that the test is not perfectly reliable. The test–retest reliability is 0.84, so someone who scores slightly less than 130 could have a true score which would take him or her over the limit. The question is, at what point is it so unlikely that the true score is over 130 that rejection of a candidate is fully justified? The firm considers the risks and decides that the line should be drawn at the point where the chances of someone's true score being less than 130 are less than 1 in 3 (or 33 per cent). The level of risk chosen of accepting a poor candidate is usually called the alpha (α) level.

The first stage in the calculation is to determine the standard error (se) of the test using the formula:

$$\text{se} = \text{sd of scale} \times \sqrt{1 - \text{reliabilty}}$$

With a reliability of 0.84 and a standard deviation of 15, the standard error is 6: that is,

$$15 \times \sqrt{1 - 0.84} = 15 \times \sqrt{0.16} = 15 \times 0.4 = 6$$

The second stage is to multiply the standard error by the Z, score, which cuts the acceptable probability in the normal curve. The table of areas and ordinates of a normal curve (Appendix I) shows that, according to the laws of chance, a Z score of -0.43 will 'cut off' the bottom 33 per cent of cases. Consequently, the standard error of 6 is multiplied by 0.43 to give a margin of error of 2.58. So the margin of error which must be allowed is 2.58 (6 × 0.43). The consultancy company therefore draws the line at 127 in the knowledge that anyone scoring below 127 has a less than one in three chance of truly meeting their standards.

It should be noted that, in applications of this kind, the probability levels are usually much lower than the 0.05 and the 0.01 significance levels commonly used in statistical inference testing. Inference testing is traditionally concerned with avoiding type I errors (in our terms, accepting the hypothesis that the candidate will turn out to be a good employee when in fact he or she will not) and this may involve a high level of type II error (in our terms this means rejecting the hypothesis that they will turn out to be effective when in fact he or she will be effective). In selection there is much greater emphasis in balancing the types of error so alpha levels of 0.33 (Z = 0.43) or 0.25 (Z = 0.65) are commonly used. A more detailed discussion of type I and type II error is given in the next chapter.

Confidence Limits about Scores

Similar calculations can be made to establish the confidence intervals around a score. For example, the 95 per cent of instances closest to the mean stretch from the 2.5 percentile to the 97.5 percentile. The z scores for these percentiles are -1.96 and $+1.96$. The 95 per cent confidence limits are the standard error multiplied by the Z score, i.e. $1.96 \times 6 = 11.76$. Appendix II give the confidence intervals associated with various reliabilities on most of the major scaling systems. Note that when establishing cutting points one-tailed Z scores are used, and when establishing confidence limits two-tailed Z scores are used.

Standard Error when Two Scores are Added Together

Sometimes selection decisions are based on the scores from two measures. For example, one engineering firm bases its decisions on a test of numerical reasoning and a test of spatial reasoning. The two sets of scores are first converted into reasonably comparable scoring systems (out of 10). The interview score and test score are then added. The question arises, what is the standard error of this composite? The answer can be obtained from the formula:

$$se_{comp} = \sqrt{se_1^2 + se_2^2 + 2r_{12}se_1se_2}$$

It can be seen that to calculate the standard errors of a composite, the standard error of both scales (se_1, se_2) and the correlation between the scales (r_{12}) are needed.

In the case of the engineering firm, the standard error of the test of numerical reasoning is 2 and the standard error of the spatial test is 3. The correlation between the tests is 0.7. It follows from the formula that the standard error of the composite is 4.6: that is,

$$\sqrt{4 + 9 + (2 \times 0.7 \times 2 \times 3)} = \sqrt{4 + 9 + 8.4} = \sqrt{21.4} = 4.6$$

Another firm in Glossop selects its engineers using a test of numerical reasoning and a test of verbal reasoning. By a strange coincidence, they also have respective standard errors of 2 and 3 but the correlation between the tests is only 0.2. The standard error of this composite is 3.9: that is,

$$\sqrt{4 + 9 + (2 \times 0.2 \times 2 \times 3)} = \sqrt{15.4} = 3.9$$

The only material difference is the lower correlation between the tests, and this has resulted in a more reliable composite with a lower standard error (3.9 as opposed to 4.6). This example demonstrates the basic principle that *more reliable composites are obtained when there is little correlation between the measures that are combined.* However, this should only be done when both tests are valid. Amalgamating a valid test with a different but invalid test is likely to increase the reliability but reduce the validity, of the composite!

In the Glossop examples the situation is fairly straightforward. The two tests were weighted equally and so each result had a weight of one.

However, in some circumstances one score is given a higher weight because, perhaps, it is more valid. Formulae for these situations are given by Guilford and Fruchter (1978, pp. 387ff).

Establishing the Difference between Two Scores

Sometimes, especially in vocational guidance and placement decisions, two scores are obtained and it is necessary to establish whether there is any real difference between them. For example, a firm in Poynton recruits a young graduate, Julie, for one of three posts, an accountant, an information officer or a general administrator. Julie has no preference other than that she should go to the job for which she is most suited. To resolve the issue, the firm asks Julie to complete two tests: a test of verbal reasoning and a test of numerical reasoning. It reasons that if Julie is best at numerical problems she should become an accountant, if she is best at verbal problems she should become an information officer, and if her abilities are evenly balanced, she should go into general administration. Her sten scores on the tests were numerical 7.6 and verbal 8.5. There is clearly a detectable difference but is the difference significant? The difference could be due to chance. The two tests have respective reliabilities of 0.8 and 0.9. As they are sten scores the standard deviation is 2. The correlation between the tests is 0.4. The standard error of the difference between the two scores can be calculated by first obtaining the standard error of each test using the formula

$$se = sd_{scale}\sqrt{1-\text{reliability}}$$

and then substituting these standard errors into the formula:

$$se_{diff} = \sqrt{se_1^2 + se_2^2 - (2 \times r_{12} \times se_1 \times se_2)}$$

The standard error of the difference between Julie's two scores is 0.87: that is,

$$\sqrt{0.894^2 + 0.63^2 - (2 \times 0.4 \times 0.89 \times 0.63)}$$

$$= \sqrt{0.80 + 0.40 - (0.8 \times 0.56)}$$

$$= \sqrt{1.2 - 0.45}$$

$$= \sqrt{0.75}$$

$$= 0.87$$

The actual difference of 0.9 is therefore about one Z score. Statistical tables show that this could happen by chance 16 per cent of the time. This is well short of the traditional 5 per cent and 1 per cent levels of significance, but traditional methods have undervalued the importance of type II errors. Julie decides that it is just as important to avoid underestimating her talents by excluding her from a suitable job as to avoid putting her into a job where she did not have enough talent. Consequently, Julie and the company decide she should take up a job in the information office.

Down the road in Hazel Grove, John and his company are facing similar decisions. The tests are different but their reliabilities are identical, 0.8 and 0.9 respectively, standard deviations are also 2. Even more surprisingly, his scores (7.6 and 8.5) are identical to Julie's. The only difference is that the Hazel Grove tests hardly correlate with each other: a measly 0.16. Calculations show that the standard error of the difference between his two scores is about 1.00. The difference between his scores is 0.9 standard errors. This would occur by chance in 91 per cent of occasions. Comparisons with Julie's results show that *decreasing the correlations between measures increases the standard error of the difference*. This is directly opposite to the effect on the effect on the standard error of the *sum* of two scores. Consequently, it is vital to be sure whether the standard error relates to the *sum* or the *difference* between two scores.

Length and Reliability

Where a measure is obtained by adding up subscores, the number of subscores has a strong influence on reliability. The classic situation is where a test score is obtained by adding the number of correct answers to a series of questions. The same principle applies to combining the scores given by several interviewers or by combining the references from several sources.

In general, the more subscores aggregated, the more reliable the measure (see Gulliksen, 1950). Guilford and Fruchter (1978, p. 432) give a formula for calculating the number of subscores needed in order to obtain a total score of a given reliability. The logic is quite simple. A score consists of two parts: the first part is a true reflection of a person's ability; the second part consists of random errors, such as misunderstanding the word of a question or a momentary surge in concentration, and it distorts the true score. For each subscore the distortions will be relatively large, but when subscores are aggregated the random errors tend to cancel out. The more subscores aggregated, the greater the probability that the cancelling out will be exact. However, there are two important qualifications. The additional scores must be as good as the scores to which they are added: adding rubbish will reduce reliability. Second, there comes a point of diminishing or even negative returns: candidates become bored or even annoyed by a long-winded procedure.

Attenuation of Range and Reliability

The use of correlation coefficients to estimate reliability is complicated by the way in which the sample is obtained. The sample must reflect the population on which the selection method is to be used. In particular, the sample must cover the whole range of the population because, if the range is attenuated, it will produce a lower coefficient of reliability and make the proportion of error variance seem much larger. A fuller discussion on the effects of restriction of range is given in the next chapter on validity.

ITEM RESPONSE THEORY AND LATENT TRAIT THEORY

Traditional psychometrics are usually concerned with the results from whole questionnaires but the hegemony of this global approach is being challenged by latent trait theory and item response theory, which focus on the replies to individual questions.

The basics of latent trait theory are quite simple. Every *set* of questions will measure some quality or trait in the individual. This trait is a function of that particular collection of questions. It is an abstract and statistical quality which may not, but usually does, relate to some psychological or physical characteristic. People may be placed on a continuum according to how much of the trait they display; furthermore, the questions may also be placed along the same continuum according to how much of the trait they require. Probably the simplest example is to imagine a test similar to the digit span subtest on the Wechsler Adult Intelligence Scale (WAIS). Subjects are asked to repeat random sequences of digits and there can be any number of digits between one and twelve. To increase reliability, two sequences are given at each level so there are questions A, a, B, b, C, c, . . . L, l. The lowest score would be zero and the maximum 24. An individual's score would be the number of sequences repeated correctly. The trait that is measured is short-term memory and, using the total score on the test, individuals could be placed on a continuum according to the size of their short-term memory.

This simple test could be given to 16 000 people and their responses to each item could be recorded. Initial analysis would probably reveal that no one scored less than 3 or more than 18 and, by a very convenient statistical fluke, there were exactly 100 people with each score from 3 to 18! It would then be possible to analyse each question by seeing how success or failure on that question relates to the total score on the tests. Usually, this is done by counting the number of people with each total score who pass the test. Then a cumulative distribution is calculated and represented in an ogive which usually produces the shape of a lopsided letter S. Figure 6.5 shows how the results might be for an item (item F): almost everyone with a total score of 10 gives an incorrect answer; about half with a score of 13 are correct; and almost everyone with a total score over 14 gives the correct answer to item F.

The procedure is repeated for items A to j (see Figure 6.4). With all these items, the shape and slope of the ogive is the same – only the position (the average score of people giving correct answers) differs – so there is only one important parameter to be taken into account: the level of difficulty of the item.

Using the data for this parameter, it would be possible to construct a much more efficient test. The test would start by giving item F, which is in the middle of the continuum for the latent trait 'short-term memory'. If the answer was correct, item H could be given. If this is answered incorrectly, item G could be given and an incorrect answer here would give the person's position on the latent trait. (To be thorough, we might also want to check the conclusion by giving items f, g and h. Knowing someone's score on item F would give a clear idea of their score on the latent trait within the range 9–14.) This procedure has noteworthy advantages over conventional testing. First, the procedure is much more efficient as the person's position has been determined with many fewer items – only 6 compared with the 24 in the whole test. Second,

Figure 6.4   Basic item analysis for a hypothetical test of short-term memory

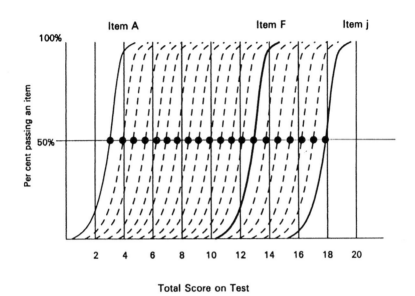

different people will be given different combinations of items but their position will be given on the same latent trait. Third, a person's position could be compared with the position of someone who has been tested on an entirely different test *provided* the other test measured the same latent trait. The one parameter method of item analysis was developed by Rasch (1966) and expounded by Anderson (1983). It was claimed to be robust and not unduly disturbed by other factors.

However, 'Rasch anlaysis' was criticised because it left out some key considerations. In our example so far, the shape of the ogive has been identical for all items. In practice this is rarely so. The item analysis of items K to I showed a different pattern. The sequence for the subject to attempt to remember in item K was 1, 2, 2, 5, 5, 6, 6, 8, 8, 9. Although, this is a 10 digit sequence, repetition means that the average difficulty level is only 6. Despite the fact that the parameter 'difficulty' is the same for items F and K, the ogives (figure 6.5) show that the responses to the items are quite different. In some ways item K is a little easier

Figure 6.5 Item analysis for a hypothetical item in a test of short-term memory

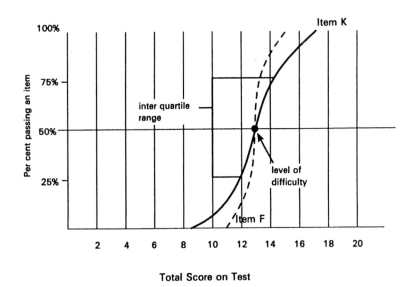

Total Score on Test

(the numbers form an ascending series) and in other ways it is a little harder (it is necessary to remember which numbers are repeated). Consequently, the level of difficulty is less clear cut and the S shaped ogive is more stretched: knowing someone's reply to item K would not give such a clear guide to their score on the latent trait (within the range 9–15).

The slope of an ogive can be expressed in several ways. The most convenient is probably the interquartile range: if all the people who pass an item are placed in order of total score, the interquartile range is the difference between the score of the twenty-fifth person and the seventy-fifth. Usually, however, the slope of an ogive is expressed as a standard deviation – the greater the standard deviation the longer the slope. Under most, but not all, circumstances items producing ogives with a steep slope are preferred, but it depends on the individual. If we were trying to determine whether someone's short-term memory was 6 or 8, then item F would be better. However, if we were trying to determine whether someone's short-term memory was 3 or 5, item K would be a better choice. Thus a two-parameter model (difficulty and slope) is a more powerful method.

Many psychometricians, such as Lord (1980), advocate a three-parameter model. The third parameter is usually the likelihood of guessing the correct answer: for example, by answering at random. In a multiple choice question with two options, the probability of guessing the right answer is a lot higher than for a question with five plausible options.

The level of guessing is related to ability: those who have not got a clue guess more often! The procedure is generally an iterative one. The total score, first calculated on a crude basis of one mark for each correct answer, is used to determine the level of difficulty and slope. Some items are then eliminated or modified on the basis of this information. A more accurate total score for each person can then be calculated and the new figure used to estimate the level of guessing. The guessing may then be subtracted from the new total score to give a still more accurate estimate of ability. These more accurate estimates of ability can be used in item analysis and so on. Iterations of this kind are continued until they stabilise: that is, until there is no noticeable difference between the results from two successive cycles.

If the sample of subjects is sufficiently large, the characteristics of each item can be determined quite accurately and will not need to be determined again if applied to another sample. In other words, item parameters are invariant of the sample from which they are obtained: item F would give a reading of 13 whether the initial sample was a group of primary school students or a group of PhD students. Thus, once a bank of items has been established, item response theory provides some very powerful tools. It will be possible to make requests such as, 'I would like to be 95 per cent sure of Pamela's short-term memory to within plus or minus one point.' Then, under the guidance of a computer (which would be essential for the many complex calculations), the items which give most information about Pamela's short-term memory would be administered. The items giving most information will depend on previous answers. For example, if Pamela has already given two correct answers to items with 7 digits, it is almost a total waste of effort to administer an item with 3 digits. Under the guidance of a computer, items will be administered until a given level of reliability is reached. If only a low level of reliability is specified, perhaps only 3 items will be given. If a high level of reliability is specified, perhaps 10 to 13 items will be given.

7 Requirements of Measures: Validity and Meta-Analysis

DEFINITIONS OF VALIDITY

Even if a measure is practical, sensitive and reliable, it is a poor measure unless it is also valid. For example, the circumference of the head might be suggested as a measure of a candidate's intelligence. This measure would be practical since it would only take a few seconds to obtain. It would be discriminating because the circumference of heads varies by up to 75 mm. It would be reliable because, with reasonable care, a second reading would give more or less the same answer. Yet head circumference is unlikely to be used because it is not valid as an index of intelligence: it has only a very slight relationship with intelligence itself.

Whilst everyone agrees that validity is a 'good thing', there is much less agreement upon its definition. However the most acceptable definition is that *validity is the correctness of inferences that may be made from it*. Thus, in a strict sense, measures do not have validities. It is the *inferences made from them* which have validities. A measure can be used for different purposes and it can therefore have different validities. An 'extroversion' test may be valid for selecting bank clerks but invalid for selecting investment analysts. The relativity of validity contrasts with the specificity of reliabilities; given a specific sample and method, reliability will remain static. Indeed, Cureton, Cook, Fischer, Laser, Rockwell and Simmons (1973) seem to imply that, provided the length of a test is held static, the reliability will remain the same.

A more technical definition of validity is the systematic variance which is related to a criterion. The technical definition needs more explanation. In the previous discussion on reliability, scores were divided into two parts: the random (error) variance which produces the unreliability of a score, and the systematic variance which produces the true score. This systematic variance can be further subdivided into those parts which are unrelated to a particular

117

inference (for example, test familiarity, bias, seniority or length of service) and the part which is related to a particular criterion (for example, ability or personality). Validity is concerned with the size of the latter portion.

TYPES OF VALIDITY

Many different ways of assessing validity have evolved, but there is no universally agreed method of classifying methods of establishing validity. APA (1954) initially distinguished four types of validity: content validity, concurrent validity, predictive validity and construct validity (Cronbach and Meehl, 1955). This view was subsequently revised (APA, 1966) and in 1974 a three-fold classification was made into content, criterion-related and construct validity.

CONTENT VALIDITY

Content validity is often divided into two types: *face validity* and content validity proper. This distinction is essential because face validity is not, in the true sense of the earlier definitions, a type of validity at all. Face validity is concerned with people's perceptions of a test's validity: not with validity itself. This does not mean that face validity is unimportant. Indeed, in many situations it has greater practical importance because it can determine whether an organisation decides to adopt a measure and it determines the level of rapport with candidates. The importance of face validity seems to increase with the age and seniority of the applicants. Fortunately, face validity can often be improved by using examples and wording that are appropriate to the group concerned.

Content validity boils down to a matter of sampling: does the measure adequately cover the operations which are relevant to success in a job? For example, if a job required general mathematical ability and an interviewer asked only questions concerning additions and division, the interview would not have content validity because subtraction and multiplication would have been overlooked.

An advantage of content validity is that it is usually easier to establish than other kinds of validity. The first stage is to define the domain to be measured by examining job descriptions and consulting experts. On the basis of these enquiries a specification is built up. Sometimes it may be necessary to employ judges to categorise behaviours. Content validation of this kind is particularly pertinent to job samples since it is necessary to demonstrate that the sample is in fact representative of the job itself. Unfortunately, content validity involves a number of practical and conceptual issues. In practice it is often difficult to define the domain of tasks to be sampled and experts may not be available. The conceptual difficulties are much greater. Guion (1977, 1978), Tenopyr (1977) and others have pointed out that content validity is evaluated by showing how well the content of the measure samples the class of situations about which conclusions are to be drawn. In other words, content validity is about the construction of measures. But this lies outside the earlier definition that validity is concerned with the *inferences made from scores*. Messick (1974) makes the point explicit: 'Content coverage is an important consideration in test construction and interpretation, to be sure, but in itself it does not provide validity. Call it "content relevance", if you would, or "content representativeness", but don't call it "content validity".'

CRITERION-RELATED VALIDITY

In selection, criterion-related validity is usually the most important type of validity, and it is concerned with predicting an applicant's behaviour in certain situations. 'Prediction' in this definition must be taken in a broad statistical sense rather than in the sense of a sequence of time. Three main types of criterion-related validity can be distinguished: predictive validity, concurrent validity and synthetic validity.

Predictive Validity

Predictive validity is, from a scientific standpoint, the most desirable type of validity. It refers to the extent to which a measure can predict the scores of applicants on some future assessment. For example, a company installing an optical fibre communication system might give applicants a test of finger dexterity. It does not use the scores to select applicants. Instead, it hires all applicants. After a period of three months, when the applicants have settled down in their jobs, the company collects information on how many circuits each applicant instals in a specified time. It establishes the predictive validity of the dexterity test by comparing the test scores with the production data, by plotting a scattergram with the test score along the bottom and the criterion score on the vertical axis as shown in Figure 7.1. The scattergram can then be inspected to see if there is a relationship

Figure 7.1   Example of a scattergram between a predictor (in this case a test) and a criterion

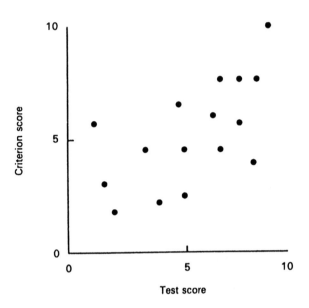

between the measure and the criterion. Visual inspection can be arbitrary. It is usually better to rely upon a correlation coefficient as a statistical index of the relationship between a measure and a criterion.

Although predictive validity has great theoretical appeal, in practice it is rarely used outside the armed forces and a few government organisations. The reasons are easy to determine. First, in its pure form, predictive validity requires an organisation to hire all applicants, even those who seem patently unsuitable. Few organisations are prepared to sacrifice such large resources on the altar of scientific purity.

Restriction of range

Consequently, data are often only available on a narrower band of candidates. This is called *restriction of range*. Restriction of range nearly always lowers a correlation coefficient and makes it seems smaller than it truly is.

A hypothetical example demonstrates the effect of restriction of range. A company gives 20 applicants with names A–T a work sample test and ranks the candidates on their scores as shown in column (ii) of Table 7.1! There is an all knowing deity in the sky which knows what the future performance of all 20 applicants will be. The deity ranks the applicants on their true ability (column iii). The correlation between columns (ii) and (iii) represents the true validity of the work sample test. The intermediate workings of the correlation are given in column (vi) and the final correlation of 0.80 is impressive. It indicates the test is valid and that the organisation should pay great heed to the test scores when it decides who to hire.

In practice, however, let us assume that the firm is reluctant to hire the applicants who do badly on the work sample test and only offers employment to the top ten candidates. After a time the production data for the successful candidates is collected, without error, automatically by computer and the successful candidates are ranked on their actual performance. The ranks are according to performance and are given in column (iv). Notice that the order of the successful candidates' performance is identical to the ranks given by the deity, except that some have been pushed up a little to fill the gaps left by two candidates who were wrongly excluded by the firm (that is, candidates O and L). The correlation between the work sample and performance for the restricted range is only 0.32 (intermediate computations are in column (vii), and if it did not know better the organisation might conclude that it should only take heed of the test scores when they are extreme high or low scores.

Fortunately, in some circumstances it is possible to allow the worst candidates to be screened out and then to make a statistical correction to the results. There are two formulae. The first is used when the restriction occurs at an even earlier stage and where only some applicants are subjected to a measure (for example, only those who pass the interview are given tests). Thus when the restriction of range is in the predictor measure, formula 4.3 in Appendix IV is used.

Restriction of range can also occur in the criterion data. Even the most affluent and tolerant organisation will fire or transfer the worst applicants who make a botch of everything they touch and who are a danger to themselves and colleagues. Furthermore, there is usually 'voluntary turnover' from poor performers who sense their failures and who decide to quit while they are ahead. Thus, even in the best planned predictive study criterion scores tend to be higher than those for a

Table 7.1 Demonstration of the effects of restriction of range and attenuation of criteria

Applicant	Work sample rank (ii)	True performance rank (20) (iii)	True performance rank (10) (iv)	Supervisor's rank (10) (v)	D^2 (ii–iii)² (vi)	D^2 (ii–iv)² (vii)	D^2 (ii–v)² (viii)
A	1	4	4	5	9	9	16
B	2	5	5	4	9	9	4
C	3	1	1	1	4	4	4
D	4	7	7	7	9	9	9
E	5	2	2	8	9	9	9
F	6	10	8	2	16	4	16
G	7	14	10	10	49	9	9
H	8	12	9	9	16	1	1
I	9	6	6	6	9	9	9
J	10	3	3	3	49	49	49
K	11	13			4		
L	12	9			9		
M	13	15			4		
N	14	11			9		
O	15	8	NOT HIRED	NOT HIRED	49		
P	16	16			0		
Q	17	18			1		
R	18	20			4		
S	19	17			4		
T	20	19			1		

$\sum D^2$	264	112	126
$6 \times \sum D^2$	1584	672	756
$N(N^2 - 1)$	7980	990	990
$6\sum D^2/N(N^2 - 1)$	0.20	0.68	0.76
rho $= 1 - \dfrac{6\sum D^2}{N(N^2 - 1)}$	0.80	0.32	0.24

perfect sample would be. To correct the restriction of range of this kind use formula 4.4 in Appendix IV.

In addition to the necessity to hire all applicants, predictive validity has another practical disadvantage: it inevitably involves a time delay. This time delay can be very substantial. For example, to train a policeman fully takes more than two years. If it takes a year to amass a sufficient sample of recruits then, allowing time for organisation and analysis of the study, predictive validity will take almost four years. In a commercial environment the organisation could become bankrupt while it awaited the results.

Attenuation of criteria

Unfortunately, yet another phenomenon may reduce apparent validity. Earlier, in the chapter on criteria, it was pointed out that inaccuracies in the criteria (attenuation of criteria) make *the measure* seem less accurate. This is demonstrated by the remaining columns in Table 7.1. Let us suppose that the supervisor cannot operate the computer which collects the true performance, and instead uses his or her own judgement to rank the ten selected applicants on their performance (most validity studies use supervisory assessments as the criteria). The supervisor's ranking is given in column (v). Notice that the supervisor's ranking is not very different from the computer's. His or her subjectivity has only resulted in the inversion of the order of two pairs A and B, and E and F. The correlation between the computer and the supervisor is 0.55. Yet, look at the influence this has had upon the apparent validity. It has shrunk further to a measly 0.24. The company could easily conclude that the work sample has no use as a selection device whereas, in fact, the true validity is 0.8.

This is a clear example of how restriction of range and criterion contamination usually reduce a true validity coefficient. In a real situation, however, a much larger sample would be needed and, a product moment correlation would probably be used. The simpler rank order correlation was used here so the reader could easily verify the calculations. It is clear, however, that what appear to be very different validities are, in fact, entirely consistent when restriction of range and attenuation of criteria are taken into account.

Concurrent Validity

Concurrent validity avoids these practical problems, but is less scientifically pure. In essence, concurrent validity involves obtaining the measures and the criterion information at the same time. Usually, this means that a sample of existing employees is obtained and subjected to the selection measure. At about the same time, criterion information is collected. The criteria and the scores are then correlated in the normal way. The results of a study of concurrent validity are available within weeks or months, and there is the further advantage that the method is relatively cheap. Unfortunately, concurrent validity also suffers disadvantages. Almost all concurrent studies suffer severe restriction of range: the worst employees may have been promoted to other work, so this restriction of range will spuriously reduce the level of validity. A second problem arises from motivational factors: volunteer employees in a concurrent study may not be as motivated to produce their best performance whereas most applicants in a selection situation will try very hard. Motivational factors in concurrent validation will probably understate the actual validity. Cronbach (1970, p.137) quotes an analysis of 70 studies in which concurrent validities were slightly smaller than predictive validities.

A special type of concurrent validity is the *nominated groups technique*, where two groups are assembled which are strongly believed to differ on a particular characteristic. The measure in question is applied to the groups. If the measure is valid, it should differentiate between the groups. For example, if a group of bank managers and a group of confidence tricksters were assembled and specimens of their handwriting given to a graphologist for evaluation, the bank managers should, presumably, achieve higher scores for honesty from the graphologist.

Synthetic Validity

Synthetic validity is sometimes called job component validity, and was pioneered by Lawshe (1952) as a method applicable to small firms. The first stage of obtaining synthetic validity is to analyse the jobs within an organisation in terms of the degree to which they require a certain characteristic. Next, the measure is applied to everyone in the organisation and the average score for each job is calculated. Finally, the average scores are correlated with the requirements. For example, a small company may be interested in evaluating a test of mental arithmetic. First it ranks each job on the level of mental arithmetic demanded (such as accountant, estimator, general manager, supervisor . . . janitor, tea lady). Second, everyone in the firm completes the mental arithmetic test and the average score for each job is obtained.

Jobs are ranked according to the average score of the occupants. Third, the two sets of ranking are correlated. Although synthetic validity was designed for use in small companies, it can be used in larger investigations. Probably the best example of this use is McCormick's (1959) study. Mossholder and Arvey (1984) provided a review of the current status of synthetic validity approaches.

CONSTRUCT VALIDITY

In essence, construct validity attempts to answer the questions, 'What is the psychological meaning of the scores and how do the scores relate to other measures?' Cronbach and Meehl (1955) say that 'construct validation is involved whenever a test is to be interpreted as a measure of some attribute or quality which is not operationally defined'. The problem for the investigator is, 'What constructs account for variance in test performance?'

Although Cronbach and Meehl's comments specifically mention tests, the same considerations apply to other measures. Their definition contains two related elements. First, construct validation *is not* particularly concerned with predicting behaviour which is operationally defined (for example, 'conducts an average of 40 blood group analyses per day'). Second, construct validation *is* concerned with the attribution of more general traits, which are usually derived from psychological theory: for example, 'is able to persist with highly boring, technical operations'. We can never open up the brain to observe persistence in the face of boredom: we can only infer these psychological constructs from behaviour. In this particular example it is easy to specify the behaviour which would indicate persistence and boredom. In many situations the inferences are more complex: for example, what pieces of behaviour typify leadership or insight? Bechtoldt (1959), however, was not happy with the idea of construct validity. He felt that there is little essential difference between predictive validity and construct validity as they are both involved in the process of building scientific theories; in the case of construct validity the chain of inferences may be longer but the chain ultimately ends in some kind of observable behaviour.

In practical terms, construct validity is established in three main ways. First, there is *correlation with a single alternative measure* which is believed to be an accurate reflection of the construct involved. For example, suppose that a graphologist claims that the space between words in handwritten script is a reflection of intelligence. The construct validity of space between words could be established by correlating the size of spaces with scores on an established test of intelligence. To establish the full construct validity of a measure, many individual studies of this kind would be required. For example, we may need additional correlations with academic performance, and a rating by a superior. Unfortunately, the results of these studies may be contradictory, especially if the studies use small samples and alternative measures which are themselves questionable.

Exploratory factor analysis is a powerful tool in establishing the construct validity of a measure and is a way of simultaneously investigating several relationships. The use of factor analysis in this context is complex and best explained by an example. Suppose it was necessary to explore the construct validity of interview ratings: we wanted to know what psychological constructs are being measured. One way to do this would be to collect a series of scores on, for example, three tests of intelligence, two ratings of intelligence, a rating, and biographical information. Every combination of these scores could be correlated and a correlation matrix produced.

In essence, factor analysis is a statistical technique for identifying the underlying trends in a matrix of correlations. A computer scans the matrix and when it locates a trend (a factor) it extracts its influence from the matrix. The computer then scans the remaining matrix for another trend, and so on until all the information is extracted. In extracting factors in this way, the computer combines those scores which are measuring the same constructs and produces a more general composite which should overcome the drawbacks of its constituents. In this example there would be an intelligence factor, and probably factors concerning sociability and verbal fluency. It is then possible to correlate the interview scores with the factors to determine the factorial composition of interviews (that is, loadings). The loadings could then be inspected to determine the factorial composition of the measure. By squaring the loadings and multiplying by 100 it is possible to calculate the percentage variance due to a factor. Table 7.2 shows how the loadings might emerge.

The results from this hypothetical example suggest that the main component of interview scores is verbal fluency, which determines about 36 per cent of the differences between individuals. Among other things it suggests that intelligence plays a minor role and that 38 per cent of the differences between individuals are due to influences which are not included in the analysis.

Table 7.2   Hypothetical factor loadings for interview scores

Factor	Loading of interview score	% of variance
Intelligence	0.1	1
Sociability	0.4	16
Verbal fluency	0.6	36
Job experience	0.3	9
	Variance accounted for	62
	Variance not accounted for	38
	Total variance	100

Thus factor analysis can be a powerful tool in establishing the composition of a measure. However, two very strong notes of caution are necessary. First, the sample sizes must be large: as a rule of thumb there should be four times as many people as there are scores for each person. Second, great care should be taken in determining which scores should be included in the factors which emerge. In the example, the inclusion of several intelligence tests guaranteed the emergence of intelligence as the first and largest factor. However, the actual loadings with factors should not be directly affected. In the hypothetical example intelligence emerged as the first and most important trend, but nevertheless it did not correlate heavily with the interview scores. This two-stage approach, involving first the extraction of the factors and then a correlation of the measure in question against the factors, is scientifically pure but cumbersome. In practice, the interview scores would probably be included in the analysis itself and the correlations between the interview scores and the factors would be produced in terms of loadings.

Factor analysis can help to determine the construct validity in another way; it can help to assess the dimensionality of a measure. This arises when a total score is obtained by adding a series of subscores. For example, the total score on an arithmetic test is usually obtained by adding the scores from individual questions. In these cases the factorial composition of a measure can be explored by correlating the result of every question with the result on every other question. The correlation matrix can then be factor analysed. The results of the analysis will show how many different qualities are being assessed by a measure.

The nature of the different dimensions can be deduced from the pattern of the loadings. For example, a factor analysis of the questions in the arithmetic test might produce five factors. The first factor might have significant loadings on practically all questions and could be interpreted as a general numerical factor. Factor 2 might load mainly on questions involving addition problems and might be interpreted as an 'addition' factor, and so on. In this situation the results are fairly simple but generally factor composition is more complex.

The exploratory approach to factor analysis, described above, relies on statistical criteria to explore and establish the factors underlying a set of data. An alternative approach to exploring the factor structure of a measure may be used when one holds firm, a priori hypotheses about the underlying factors. This approach involves specifying the underlying factors that are expected and using statistical procedures to confirm or refute the existence of the factor structure. *Confirmatory factor analysis* techniques have been developed more recently than the well-established exploratory procedures and are derived from the work of Joreskog (1969). Several computer programs have been developed which allow researchers to utilise the mathematical procedures developed in the confirmatory factor analysis literature (see Joreskog and Sorbom, 1988; Bentler, 1989).

Convergent-discriminant validity is usually associated with D. T. Campbell and Fiske's (1959) paper. Convergent-discriminant validity is founded on the axiom that a measure *should* correlate with measures gauging the same construct, and *should not* correlate with different constructs. Thus, if ten measures are collected, and three of these measures (test score, arithmetic questions at interview and reference from superior on candidate's arithmetic ability) concern arithmetical ability, then the intercorrelations should show a certain pattern. With valid measures, the three measures of arithmetic ability should show high intercorrelations among themselves but not with other variables such as temperament or biographical details. If the measures are invalid they show low correlations among themselves and high correlations with irrelevant measures. An excellent example of convergent-discriminant validity is given by Thompson (1970).

EVALUATING VALIDITY COEFFICIENTS

Whichever method is used to estimate validity, it is necessary to decide whether the validity is sufficient. Usually this decision boils down to evaluating whether a correlation coefficient is big enough. The issues raised in the other sections of this chapter show that this is a complex decision which needs to take account of many factors. However, the following benchmarks may be used as a rule of thumb guide:

Over 0.5	excellent
0.40–0.49	good
0.30–0.39	acceptable
less than 0.3	poor

It must be emphasised that these are only general guidelines and that many factors must be taken into account.

Rundquist (1969) noted that validity coefficients rarely exceeded 0.5 and suggested the existence of a *prediction ceiling*. In 1974 Wallace provided statistical models to suggest that observed validities in the region of 0.5 are as much as can reasonable be expected. This ceiling may not necessarily reflect the true validities of the measures as much as the inadequate criteria and the samples that are used in our studies. The point is neatly demonstrated by Sparks (1970). He generated data whose characteristics were known precisely, and he demonstrated that observed validity coefficients of 0.17 to 0.22 became significant correlations in the range 0.4 and 0.45 when a number of scores were combined and when some inadequacies in the criterion were taken into account.

Unfortunately the situation is still more complex. It is often found that if a validity study is repeated with a different sample, the second validity coefficient is lower than the initial estimate. This phenomenon is known as *shrinkage* and it can arise in two ways. First, there are changes which occur over time, in terms of social structure, education or physical fitness, which alter the relationship between a measure and a criterion. In theory there is no reason why these changes should not increase validity, but in practice they nearly always decrease validity coefficients. A classic example of the shrinkage phenomenon is given by Kirchner and Dunnette (1957). Second, shrinkage is particularly large when measures are combined using the statistical technique of multiple regression. For example, multiple regression analysis might show that, for a sample of 100 engineers working on the installation of a Gandalf Switch, the combination 0.4 − an interview rating (IR), plus 0.8 − score on a mechanical reasoning (MR) test, plus 0.2 − rating of a reference (R) produces a validity coefficient of 0.64 which is almost certainly an over-estimate. The multiple regression technique tends to include some of the chance variation in the scores and the validity is inflated.

When the formula $(0.4\,(IR) + 0.8\,(MR) + 0.2\,(R))$ is tried out on a second sample, there is a different set of chance variations which do not match the formula and are rightly excluded. The obtained validity falls to 0.37 and it generates the impression that the validity has diminished. To overcome this difficulty a process of *cross-validation* may be adopted. Generally, a sample of 100 would be split into two parts – about 68 candidates for the main sample and 32 as the *holdout* sample. The initial validation would be conducted on the main sample, but the results would then be checked out by applying the formula to the holdout and recomputing the validity. However, this strategy may be misguided. The precision of a correlation coefficient depends, in part, on the size of the sample and the bigger the sample, the more accurate the correlation. By using a holdout technique we reduce the size of the sample, often replacing one accurate estimate with two inaccurate correlations (from the small holdout sample) which will be used as the standard for the better correlation. Unless large samples are available, it is probably better to avoid the holdout design and estimate the 'shrinkage' by statistical means. The formula is given in Appendix IV (4.5).

Taking all these factors into account there seems to be an upper limit of about 0.65 for validity coefficients, and these levels are usually only achieved by selection procedures which combine many different methods and which extend over a period of several days. Using these extended methods, Bray and Grant (1966) and Anstey (1977) obtained very high validities of 0.66 or higher, and A. Jones (1981) obtained reliabilities of 0.65 to 0.86.

People as Moderator Variables

In an effort to raise the level of validity coefficients beyond the ceiling which seems to exist at about 0.65, many people have turned their attention to identifying moderator variables. The logic behind moderator variables starts with the idea that some people are more predictable than others, and then it seeks to eliminate the least predictable people. Finally it applies measures only to those predictable people who remain. For example, a bank might have difficulty in accurately selecting investment analysts using an interest test. On subsequent analysis it discovers that the interest scores of applicants who are neurotic are almost useless: sometimes a high interest score produces a good performance, sometimes a high interest score produces a poor performance. On the other hand, the interest scores of stable individuals are good predictors of future performance. Thus the bank would be able to improve its selection of investment analysts by first giving a test of neuroticism to select those applicants whose scores can be predicted, and then giving an interest test to provide the basis for the actual selection.

Using this kind of rationale, Ghiselli (1960) was able to use a measure for the selection of taxicab drivers whose initial validity was 0.22 but, by concentrating on the third of applicants whose success was most 'predictable', he obtained a validity coefficient of 0.64. In the same paper Ghiselli describes in detail how, by constructing a predictability index and using it to screen out individuals whose scores were not predictable, he raised two validity coefficients from 0.22 to 0.86 and from 0.15 to 0.78. Similarly results were obtained by Frederiksen and Melville (1954). They used the accountant scale on the Strong Interest Blank as a measure of compulsiveness, and in 11 out of 15 cases they found it easier to predict the subsequent success of people who were not compulsive. The findings were less clear cut when the study was replicated using a separate sample (Frederiksen and Gilbert, 1960). Clearly the use of moderators could raise the levels of validity coefficients in selection contexts. However, a word of warning is necessary. Abrahams and Alf (1972a and 1972b) contend that much of the improvement brought about by use of moderators is illusory and is merely the consequence of pratfalls and artefact. Dunnette (1972) and others are less convinced by Abrahams and Alf's reasoning.

Moderator effects are also important in another context in personnel selection: when we are interested in whether a selection procedure will work in a variety of different situations (that is, will validity generalise or is validity moderated by situational factors?). For example, a selection procedure may work well in a large engineering company but will it work in a small computer consultancy? The role of situational moderator variables and validity generalisation is taken up more fully later in this chapter.

The Bandwidth–Fidelity Dilemma

Cronbach and Glesser (1965) draw attention to a dilemma which faces many selectors: should their selection system concentrate upon accuracy or spread? Suppose personnel managers in the aerospace industry wish to select mechanical engineers to instal and test rotor blades of jet engines. They know from past experience that successful engineers need to be conscientious, have good numerical ability, spatial reasoning and mechanical comprehension. Further, for reasons beyond the personnel managers' control, the selection process is restricted to a 45-minute interview. What should be done? Should they spend the entire time obtaining a very precise measure of one aspect of the candidate, such as conscientiousness, or should they share the time of the interview, obtaining less accurate estimates on all four requirements? This essentially is the bandwidth–fidelity dilemma. Cronbach and Glesser (1965, p. 99) wrote:

> This dilemma may be described in the language of the communications engineer as a choice between 'wideband' and 'narrowband' tests. In using a particular channel, such as a telegraph wire, one may either crowd many messages into a period of time, or give a single message slowly and repetitively. The former, more varied, message has greater 'bandwidth'. The wideband signal transmits more information, but the clarity or dependability of the information received is less than for the narrowband signal except under ideal communication conditions. Random errors can seriously confuse the wideband signal; this is spoken of as a lack of fidelity. The tester's situation is analogous. If he concentrates on facts relevant to a single decision, he gets a much more dependable answer than if he spreads his effort. But, by concentrating, he leaves all his other questions to be answered on the basis of chance alone.

Cronbach (1970) came to the conclusion that:

> While no general rule can be given . . . it is clear that the greatest amount of time should be given to the most suitable questions. When several questions are of about equal importance, it is more profitable to use a brief test giving a rough answer to each one than to use a precise test answering only one or two questions.

THE RELATIONSHIP BETWEEN RELIABILITY AND VALIDITY

One of the oldest canards of psychometrics is that reliability sets a ceiling upon validity. Indeed, in statistical terms, validity cannot exceed the square of the reliability. Thus, if a measure has a reliability of 0.9, validity cannot exceed 0.81. Using strict statistical definitions this generalisation is true. In some circumstances, however, the observed reliability is unduly low. In these situations it is perfectly possible for validity to exceed reliability. It occurs most often when measuring characteristics which change very quickly. For example, a measure of hunger may have a high validity but a low test–retest reliability because, in the interval between the test and the retest some people may have eaten a snack. A less extreme example concerns a projective test where applicants are presented with an ambiguous photograph and asked to tell a story about it. Assessing the true reliability of this test is very difficult because it has a kind of self-destruct quality and subsequent administrations are never quite the same since the first administration has already structured the mental field. Tomkins (1961) compared the situation to hearing a joke: it is just not the same a second time, but this is no reason to question the validity of the first laughter. Further, in ambiguous situations applicants may deduce that the selector wishes to hear a different answer the second time around (Winter and Stewart, 1977). Many measures stress imagination, creativity and variability in their instructions: for example,

This is a test of creative imagination . . . obviously there are no right or wrong answers, so you may feel free to make up any kind of story about the picture that you choose. The more vivid and chromatic the better . . . Remember this is a test of creative imagination . . . be as imaginative as you are able to be.

Winter and Stewart found that when such implicit expectations to be different were removed from the instructions, the reliability of the scores rose to a level where validity no longer seemed to exceed reliability.

VALIDITY GENERALISATION

The generalisation of validity coefficients has great practical significance and involves the question, 'If a measure is valid in the selection for one job, would it also be a valid method of selection for jobs in the same category, or even for all jobs?' If the answer to this question is yes, then a great deal of effort can be saved, since only the general validity of the measure must be established. If the answer is no, separate validities must be established for each job or even each situation.

Unfortunately the traditional answer to the question is the pessimistic one: general validity cannot be assumed. Consequently, textbooks of a decade ago recommended that validity should be established for each specific application. The logic seemed quite compelling. Authors such as Ghiselli (1966), who collected and catalogued validity studies, repeatedly found considerable variability from situation to situation, so validity was thought to be specific, not general. So powerful was this logic that the view is enshrined in authoritative documents such as the Equal Employment Opportunity Commission's *Uniform Guidelines for Employee Selection Procedures* (1978).

A more recent and sophisticated view suggests that, on the contrary, there is considerable generalisation of validity coefficients across jobs and situations. The more recent view states that validity coefficients usually contain several statistical artefacts which must be controlled before comparisons are made. The first two of the artefacts have been noted earlier in this chapter: the *restriction of range* and *reliability* of the criteria. Some validity coefficients are based upon studies of the population as a whole, while other studies are based upon highly selected samples. A restriction of range is likely to reduce the size of a validity coefficient and consequently this statistical artefact will produce different correlations even when the 'true' validity is constant. Similarly, some studies have used criteria such as training records, and other studies have used criteria such as trainer's ratings. Again, these differences alone will produce different correlations even when the true validity is constant. The third statistical artefact is probably more potent, and has been considered at length by Schmidt, Hunter and Urry (1976) and concerns the *sizes of samples* used in validation studies. They note that typical validity studies use small samples between 60 and 70, and frequently the sample size is as low as 30. This assertion is supported by other workers, such as Lent, Aurback and Levin (1971) and M. H. Jones (1950). More recently Monahan and Muchinsky (1983), in reviewing three decades of personnel selection research, found that the mean sample size of validity studies increased from 76 to 100 to 119 in the 1950s, 1960s and 1970s respectively.

Even allowing for the gradual improvement, Schmidt, Hunter and Urry (1976) suggest that sample sizes are too small to be sure of detecting a measure's validity. They show that when a measure's true validity is 0.5 and the criterion reliability is 0.6, and where the range has been reduced by 40 per cent, a sample of 172 subjects are needed to have a 90 per cent chance of detecting the measure's validity. Schmidt, Hunter and Urry (1976) go on to give tables showing the sizes of samples required under various conditions. To support their arguments they quote a study by Brogden. In a well-executed large sample series of studies, it was found that when army occupations were classified rationally into job families, tests showed essentially identical validities and regression weights for all jobs within a given family. Further, new jobs also fitted this pattern. Finally, these validities have held constant since the end of the Second World War. Brogden concluded that when methodological artefacts are controlled and large samples are used the obtained validities are, in fact, quite stable and similar across time and situations for similar jobs.

Pressing the argument home one stage further, Schmidt, Hunter and Pearlman (1981) reported two empirical studies. They first examined validity figures for five categories of clerical jobs and indicated that with the possible exception of one of the ten tests, tests valid for one job family are valid for all job families. Their second study was not limited by the fact that the jobs were drawn from the same type of occupation. The 35 jobs included: dental assistants, radar repairers, military police, clerks, welders and personnel specialists. Again the results indicated general validity. Schmidt, Hunter and Pearlman (1981) concluded, 'Contrary to widespread belief in personnel psychology, these results indicate that task differences between job families within an occupational area have little or no effect on test validities and validities and differences in test validity among entirely different jobs are small.' The empirical foundations of these two studies are extraordinary. Study 1 is based on a total sample size of 368 877 and study 2 is based on 211 022 individuals. The total sample base is almost 400 000.

The implications of these findings are quite profound. At a banal level they suggest that over the last 30 years some industrial psychologists have wasted a great deal of effort in pursuing small-scale validity studies. Yet in most situations practical constraints, such as cost or the limited number of people actually in an occupation, prohibit large-scale studies. It would follow that only the largest organisations or government departments are able to conduct satisfactory validity studies. Fortunately, the results also imply that, once established, the validity coefficients can then be generalised to other situations.

META-ANALYSIS AND VALIDITY GENERALISATION

Studies such as those by Schmidt, Hunter and Schmidt (1990) were able to obtain such large samples because they used the technique of meta-analysis. In essence meta-analysis provides a method for cumulating the results of many separate studies and deriving a quantitive estimate of the effect size (for example, the correlation between predictor and a criterion).

Meta-analysis procedures were derived, more or less independently, by two different research teams. The earliest published work was by Glass (1976). At almost the same time, Schmidt and Hunter (1977) published theirs. The most useful books for personnel selection specialists are Hunter, Schmidt and Jackson (1982) and Hunter and Schmidt (1990), although other sources are worth consulting (see Glass, McGaw and Smith, 1981; Cooper, 1984; R. Rosenthal, 1984). The meta-analysis procedures developed by Hunter and Schmidt are distinctively different from others (Glass, McGaw and Smith, 1981; R. Rosenthal, 1984) and have the most direct relevance to personnel selection research; theirs is the only approach developed specifically for occupational psychology.

What is Meta-Analysis and Why is it Useful?

Within occupational psychology there are many research issues of common interest to investigators. Within personnel selection for example, many investigators and practitioners are interested in the criterion-related validity of different selection methods (such as interviews, psychometric tests and assessment centres). As earlier parts of this chapter explain, criterion-related validity may be estimated by a correlation between the predictor and criterion. Large numbers of validity studies have been conducted on many personnel selection methods. Although a group of studies may look at the same selection method (say, interviews), they differ in some ways: sample size, criterion measure, job type and organisation involved, and so on. Almost certainly, and perhaps not surprisingly, they will also produce rather different results. For, example the results given in Table 7.3 from eight small samples would not be unusual. When inspecting a set of results like this the main question that arises is, 'Do these data suggest that general mental ability tests show criterion-related validity or not?' This is precisely the kind of question that meta-analysis was designed

Table 7.3 Correlations between general mental ability test score and work performance in eight different studies

Study	r	n	Size of organization in which study was done
1	0.31*	69	Large
2	0.05	43	Small
3	0.37*	75	Large
4	0.22	53	Small
5	0.31	26	Small
6	0.10	22	Small
7	0.61*	34	Small
8	0.38*	70	Large

Note: *p < 0.05

to address. Before we can look closely at how meta-analysis can help with these kinds of results it is useful to see how the results might have been interpreted without the benefit of meta-analysis.

Consider first why it is that the correlations are not the same. Most people realise that when different samples are used to calculate a statistic (the mean, the standard deviation, or a correlation) each sample will produce different results. Even two samples of 500 would probably not produce identical results, though they would both be better estimates than samples of 50. The *average* from the two samples of 500 would be an even better estimate of the true population correlation (referred to as rho from now on), but is the population correlation (rho) greater than zero or not?

This is similar to the problem involved when we ask whether a selection method shows criterion-related validity. Stating it in this way emphasises the important extra step of specifying the population(s) for which the method will show validity.

The underlying correlation between general mental ability and work performance could be the same for each sample even though, due to sampling error, the values obtained for each sample are different. On the other hand, of course, the observed values for the correlation coefficients could be different because the underlying correlation is different from study to study. For example, it *could* be that the correlation between general mental ability and work performance is strong when the job involved is complex, but much weaker for simple, routine work. The crucial problem is one of recognising whether variation in observed results is due to statistical artefacts (such as sampling error) or a real difference. Until the development of quantitive meta-analysis procedures it was impossible to distinguish between the two sources of variation: sampling error or true variation. Indeed the situation was often exacerbated by investigators failing to recognise the existence of artifactual variation. Examination of the observed results in Table 7.3 (which include artefactual and true variation) may produce misleading conclusions, since artefactual variation may be interpreted as real.

Effect sizes and statistical significance

At face value Table 7.3 seems to suggest that the relationship is stronger in large organisations compared with small ones, since four out of the eight correlations are statistically significant and three of these are drawn from large organisations. As the analysis conducted later will show, this conclusion would be wrong. This illustrates a second and related problem in interpreting the results in Table 7.3. The statistical significance of an effect (correlation) is a function of two things: the size of the effect and the size of the sample (see R. Rosenthal, 1984, for an extremely lucid exposition of these points).

Previously, it was explained that the scatter in results is highest when small samples are used. Consequently, a bigger effect is needed in order to show through the random effects. Thus, even if the size of the effect is not different a larger sample size may produce statistical significance and a smaller sample may not. This point is illustrated in studies one and five in Table 7.3. To put the point as clearly as possibly, counting significant findings alone may lead to erroneous conclusions; looking at effect sizes *and* sample sizes focuses attention in the right place and will provide a more accurate basis for interpretation. As the formulae and example presented later will show, this is precisely where attention is focused in meta-analysis. An alternative way of estimating statistical significance involves calculating an interval around the observed value. The confidence interval provides an indication of the range within which the true value for the statistic estimated (from the sample) is likely to fall. The general form of the equation to estimate a confidence interval is:

Population = Sample ± error
value   value   variation

The error of estimation is based on the standard error for the statistic being estimated and the level of statistical significance chosen. For correlations a good estimate of the standard error (se_r) is given by:

$$se_r = \frac{(1 - r^2)}{\sqrt{n - 1}}$$

Thus, the confidence interval = z (chosen to give the appropriate probability of a type I error: that is, α level) multiplied by se_r.

If the correlation is 0.31, and the sample size 50, the standard error of the correlation is:

$$\frac{1 - 0.31^2}{\sqrt{50 - 1}} = \frac{1 - 0.06}{\sqrt{49}} = \frac{0.90}{7} = 0.129$$

If the alpha level is 0.05 (two-tail) the appropriate Z is 1.96. So the confidence interval for the correlation is:

$$\pm 1.96 \times 0.129 = \pm 0.25$$

And we can be 95 percent sure that the true correlation is 0.31 ± 0.25, so the true correlation will be anywhere between 0.06 and 0.56.

Notice that if the range of values covered by the confidence interval does not include zero, this is the same as saying that statistical significance has been attained: that is, we are, say, 95 per cent sure that r is not zero. Therefore the null hypothesis is rejected.

Statistical significance and power

Most readers will be familiar with type I error which occurs when the null hypothesis is true (for example, there is no relationship between predictor and criterion, $r = 0$) but we make an error and reject the null hypothesis. In simple language, we conclude that there is a correlation when there is none. Setting a level of statistical significance (such as the 95 per cent level; $\alpha 0 = .05$) protects against type I error. If we classify a correlation as significant at the 95 per cent level there is only a 5 per cent chance that a type I error has been committed.

Readers may be much less familiar with another kind of statistical error, type II error, which occurs when the null hypothesis *is* false (that is, there is a relationship between predictor and criterion; $r \neq 0$) but we make an error and *accept* the *null* hypothesis. In simple language we conclude that there is no correlation where there is one: we fail to see an effect that is actually there. The probability of detecting an effect, if present, is known as the power of a statistical procedure. Even experienced researchers fail to appreciate the important link between power and research outcomes. Figure 7.2 provides a summary of the role of power in explaining research outcomes.

As Figure 7.2 illustrates, when effect sizes are modest (correlations of about 0.3 are common selection research) and sample sizes are small (less than 150) the power to detect the effect may be quite small. In other words, even if many individual studies in a collection of small sample studies do not show statistically significant effects, it does not

Figure 7.2   Statistical power and type ii error

- $\beta =$ probability of Type II error

  Power $= 1 - \beta$; i.e., power is the probability of correctly rejecting the null hypothesis

- As the probability of Type I error (α) *increases*
  power *increases*

- As sample size (n) *increases* power *increases*

- The larger the effect in the population the greater the power: i.e., stronger effects are easier to detect

  These four parameters (α, β, n and effect size) are related so that when three are known the fourth can be determined. When three of the four values are known the fourth may be determined from power tables (see, for example, Cohen, 1988)

- For example, if:

  $n = 50, \alpha = 0.05$; effect size $(r) = 0.3$

  then:

  Power $= 0.57$

  In this example the odds are only a little better than even (50/50) that the results from a sample will attain statistical significance, even though the underlying population correlation is 0.30! Out of every hundred studies (with $n = 50$) forty-three will appear to show no relationship if the only criterion used is that of statistical significance!

---

mean that there is no underlying effect: merely that the procedures used (in this case the small sample in each study) may lack the power to detect the effect. (Clear discussions of statistical power may be found in Cohen, 1988, and Hunter and Schmidt, 1990.) The potentially misleading effects of low power may be removed by collecting data from samples that are large enough. Meta-analysis provides a set of statistical procedures which enable investigators to combine the results from several separate studies, thus effectively pooling and combining the samples from each individual study. Meta-analysis procedures also enable investigators to estimate the amount of variation in observed results that is caused by statistical artefacts. The main statistical artefacts that will cause misleading variation in study results are sampling error, restriction of range and unreliability of measurement. The effects of these artifacts have already been explained earlier in this chapter. The main steps involved in meta-analyses are: (1) combine the results of all of the studies to give an estimate of the average effect size; (2) calculate the observed variation in effect sizes across studies; (3) estimate and remove the effects due to sampling error; (4) produce a 'corrected' estimate of the correct interval surrounding the effect size estimate.

Figure 7.3 provides the formulae needed to conduct a rudimentary (bare-bones) meta-analysis. In what is now termed a 'bare-bones' meta-analysis, the effects due to sampling error are estimated and removed but no attempt is made to correct for other artefacts (such as restriction of range or unreliability). Consideration of the material discussed earlier in this chapter makes it clear that the different artifacts will have different effects: sampling error will reduce confidence in the result and hence removal of sampling error will shrink the *variation* around the estimated mean correlation but will *not* alter the magnitude of the estimated correlation. Unreliability and range restriction affect the *magnitude* of the coefficient.

Formulae for conducting corrections for both restriction of range and unreliability are given in Hunter and Schmidt (1990). A worked example of a 'bare-bones' meta-analysis, using the results from Table 7.3, is given in Figure 7.4.

Interpreting meta-analyses

A large number of meta-analysis studies have now been conducted (see Hunter and Hirsh, 1987). In some of the earliest meta-analysis in the personnel selection field, one rather striking finding began to emerge

Figure 7.3   Meta-analysis formulae

---

1   Calculate sample size weighted, mean correlation across studies:

$$\bar{r} = \frac{\sum[n_i r_i]}{\sum n_i}$$

where r_i =observed value for r in the ith study
n_i =sample size used in ith study

2   Calculate observed variation in effect-size across studies.

$$\sigma_r^2 = \frac{\sum[n_i(r_i - \bar{r})^2]}{\sum n_i}$$

3   Estimate the variation due to sampling error:

$$\sigma_e^2 = \frac{[(1 - \bar{r}^2)^2 K]}{\sum n_i}$$

where K =number of studies

4   Variation after removal of sampling error,

$$\sigma_{rem}^2 = \sigma_r^2 - \sigma_e^2$$

5   Credibility interval for r, after removal of sampling error

$$\bar{r} \pm \sigma_{rem}^2 \; (Z, \text{ at appropriate level})$$

See Whitener (1990) for an explanation of the distinction between credibility intervals and confidence intervals in meta-analysis.

(see Schmidt, Hunter and Pearlman, 1981). These studies showed that artefactual variation, caused by sampling error, was often responsible for *all* of the observed variation in the correlations (validity coefficients) studied. This produced the surprising (at the time) conclusion that the validity of some selection procedures did not vary from one situation (for example, organisation or job type) to the next. In other words, the validity of the selection method was 'generalisable' from one setting to another. Some researchers have attempted to show that validities are generalisable across all jobs within very broad

Figure 7.4 A worked example of a bare-bones meta-analysis

r_i	n_i	$n_i r_i$	$r_i - \bar{r}$	$(r_i - \bar{r})^2$	$n_i(r_i - \bar{r})^2$
0.31	69	21.39	0.00	0.0000	0.0000
0.05	43	2.15	-0.26	0.0676	2.9068
0.37	75	27.75	0.06	0.0036	0.2700
0.22	53	11.66	-0.09	0.0081	0.4293
0.31	26	8.06	0.00	0.0000	0.0000
0.10	22	2.20	-0.21	0.0441	0.9702
0.61	34	20.74	0.30	0.0900	3.0600
0.38	70	26.60	0.07	0.0049	0.3430

$$\sum n_i = 392 \qquad \sum n_i r_i = 120.55 \qquad \sum n_i(r_i - \bar{r})^2 = 7.9793$$

$$\bar{r} = \frac{120.55}{392} = 0.3075 \qquad \text{1 weighted mean correlation}$$

$$\sigma_r^2 = \frac{7.9793}{392} = 0.0204 \qquad \text{2 observed variation in effect size}$$

$$\sigma_e^2 = \frac{(0.9054)^2 8}{392} = 0.0167 \qquad \text{3 variation due to sampling error}$$

$$\sigma_{rem}^2 = 0.0204 - 0.0167 = 0.0037 \qquad \text{4 variation after removal of sampling error}$$

5. At 95% two-tail level $Z = 1.96$. $\therefore 0.31 \pm \sqrt{0.0037}\,(1.96)$
$$= 0.31 \pm 0.12$$

To estimate the 90% probability that the lower boundary of rho is greater than zero use $Z = 1.28$ (i.e. $\alpha = 0.10$, one tail). This is often referred to as the lower boundary of the credibility interval.

NB: This example is for illustration only. The total n and the number of studies are not large enough for meaningful conclusions.

families (Pearlman, 1980a; Pearlman, Schmidt and Hunter, 1980). Many researchers in the personnel selection field are sceptical about some of the more extreme arguments for validity generalisation, but there are also several widely accepted conclusions. The most important conclusion, in many ways, is that sampling error is responsible for most, if not all, of the variation in validity coefficients for cognitive ability tests. Over-simplified a little, this finding (see Schmidt, Hunter and Pearlman, 1981) shows that, regardless of the situation (type of job or type of organisation) cognitive ability tests will predict work performance reasonably well; variations observed from one study to another are mostly due to sampling error. Cognitive ability tests are probably the only selection method for which reasonably extensive validity generalisation is widely accepted.

For many other selection methods, although meta-analysis studies have shown that some of the observed variation may be caused by sampling error, there is often evidence that substantial variation remains even after sampling variation has been removed. When this happens it suggests that other factors may *moderate* the validity coefficient so that there are true differences from one setting, or set of circumstances, to another. Robertson and Downs (1989), for example, found that the validity of trainability work-sample tests was lower for longer follow-up periods. Weisner and Cronshaw (1988) found that interview validity was moderated by interview structure, with structured interviews producing better validity. The procedures involved in searching for and identifying moderators are explained in detail in Hunter and Schmidt (1990).

Meta-analysis and the criterion-related validity of selection methods

A large number of meta-analysis studies have now examined the validities of most of the main personnel selection procedures. Some of the studies have focused on specific methods (see Gaugler, Rosenthal, Thornton and Bentson, 1987, on assessment centres); whilst others (such as Schmitt, Gooding, Noe and Kirsch, 1984) have covered several selection methods. The findings of these studies are raised at relevant points in other chapters of this book when the particular selection methods concerned are being discussed.

A definitive critical appraisal of the contribution of meta-analysis to personnel selection is impossible, partly because the field is still developing and partly because it is beyond the scope of this book. It should be stressed that meta-analysis procedures have been widely debated within the scientific literature (see Schmidt, Hunter, Pearlman and Hirsh, 1985; and Sackett, Schmitt, Tenopyr, Kehoe and Zedeck, 1985) and are not without criticism either of a general kind (see Guzzo, Jackson and Katzell, 1986) or specific attacks on certain elements (for example R. Rosenthal's (1984) critique of the use of corrections for unreliability). There is no doubt, however, that the procedures of meta-analysis have made a major contribution to the scientific study of personnel selection.

8 Bias in Selection

DISCRIMINATION AND TYPES OF BIAS

Discrimination is the essence of good selection: an employer tries to discriminate between applicants who will be good workers and those who will be poor workers. Such discrimination is right and proper; it increases organisational efficiency, it conserves society's resources and it saves many individuals the stress and strain of struggling to cope with jobs beyond their capabilities. However, this discrimination is justified only when it is based upon the ability to do the job concerned. In practically all circumstances the decision should not be influenced by the sex, colour, creed or politics of the applicant. If these factors are allowed to influence decisions it can mean that less satisfactory candidates are hired with inevitable organisational, individual and social consequences, and this is usually termed 'bias'.

Bias can be divided into two kinds: direct and indirect. *Direct bias* is the most repugnant: it involves a conscious decision to exclude or impede applicants, usually on the grounds of race or sex. Direct bias is unethical and usually illegal, and yet it is often hard to eradicate. Probably the best defence is for an organisation to have a widely known and clearly stated equal opportunities policy. Then the company should be prepared to take, and be seen to take, disciplinary action if, after proper investigation, an employee is shown to have violated the policy. Formally, two conditions apply when direct bias has occurred: the treatment is less favourable for the minority group; and the reason for this less favourable treatment is the membership of the minority group.

Indirect bias is probably less repugnant but it can be equally potent in producing unfairness and injustice. Indirect bias is usually unintentional, and arises when all groups are treated similarly but the effect is unfavourable to one particular group.

Sources of Indirect Bias

Personnel specifications are the first possible source of bias because it is possible to include requirements which exclude large proportions of minority groups. However, such requirements are permissible only if

146

they are necessary to the performance of the job. Pearn (undated) provides the following examples:

> An interesting case arose in the USA in the selection of police officers in which the height requirement effectively eliminated most female applicants. A job analysis was undertaken to determine the justifiability of the requirement. The study revealed that police officers had to be tall enough to fire the revolver across the roof of a police car . . . As a result the minimum height requirement was lowered, and the proportion of women able to comply became greater. Because women are, on average, shorter than men, a smaller proportion could comply, even with the reduced requirement. However, the new height requirement was clearly and demonstrably job related and is within the law despite a degree of disproportionate impact against women.

Thus the touchstone of an unbiased requirement in a personnel specification is the requirement of the job itself. Any requirement which is discriminatory must be job related. Indirect bias may arise in *job advertising*. For example, a company may have genuine equal opportunity policy but, by oversight, it may only advertise its vacancies in newspapers, magazines and media which are read exclusively by the majority population. A third source of bias is the *procedure used to select among the applicants* who present themselves. So much attention has been given to this source of bias that it deserves a section of its own.

Types of Evidence of Biased Selection Procedures

In spite of the fact that most people wish to abandon selection procedures which are biased, there is far less agreement upon what constitutes evidence of bias. Six main types of evidence may be offered:

(a) comments by unsuccessful candidates;
(b) Proportions engaged;
(c) expert opinions;
(d) experimental evidence;
(e) internal consistency;
(f) comparisons with subsequent performance.

Comments by unsuccessful candidates

A great many, possibly the majority, of rejected candidates feel that they have been treated unfairly. Undoubtedly some of these candidates have received a poor deal. Equally, undoubtedly, many of the other accusations are unjustified and arise from two major reasons. First, rejected candidates may rationalise their experience in order to maintain their self-pride. A second reason is that candidates often assume everyone else's interviews are perfect. Rejected candidates may support claims of bias by pointing to inadequacies in the selection procedure such as interviewers who are inattentive. Whilst these allegations may be true, they do not amount to bias. Very few interviews are perfect, and the interviews of successful candidates may be equally bizarre. Thus the accusations of rejected candidates provide very poor evidence of bias. Generally, action can only be taken where the occurrence of a specific and relevant irregularity is corroborated by independent evidence.

Proportions engaged

Sometimes the proportions of majority and minority groups among successful applicants is put forward as evidence of bias. For example, if a company advertises for steelworkers and ultimately makes offers of employment to 90 men and only 10 women, this could be seen as bias since about 40 per cent of the work force are women and the low proportion of engagements is the result of bias on the company's behalf. This type of reasoning led to the 'four-fifths rule' which is contained in the *Uniform Guidelines* (USA Government, 1978) on employee selection procedures. It says: 'A selection rate for any race, sex or ethnic group which is less than four-fifths (or 80 per cent) of the rate for the group with the highest rate will generally be regarded by the Federal enforcement agencies as evidence of adverse impact.' However, in the case of the steelworkers, the accusation of bias against women is almost certainly false because very few women chose to apply. Indeed, if only five per cent of the applicants were women, an engagement rate of 10 per cent needs to be seen in an entirely different light. These complications are recognised by the *Uniform Guidelines* which state: 'Greater differences in selection rate may not constitute adverse impact where the differences are based on small numbers and are not statistically significant, or where special recruiting or other programs cause the pool of the minority or female candidates to be atypical of the normal pool of applicants from that group.'

In order to meet this kind of situation a fair policy is sometimes defined as a system in which 'the proportion of minority applicants who apply is similar to the proportion of minority applicants who are accepted'. In other words, if 10 per cent of the applicants were women, 10 per cent of those offered jobs should be women. This line of reasoning is more compelling, and any company where the ratio of applicants to employment offers for minority groups is out of balance should look carefully at its selection procedures. Nevertheless, on its own this type of information does not provide conclusive evidence of bias because it involves the assumption that the level of ability in minority applicants and the level in the other applicants is exactly equal.

In the real world, local conditions may make this assumption untrue. For example, a light engineering firm in one of the valleys of South Wales expanded its production capacity and advertised for five production controllers. The firm happily accepted that men and women were equally suitable for the job. However, in spite of the fact that over 60 per cent of the applicants were women, all five of the successful applicants were men. Contrary to the first impressions, in the context of that particular company at that particular time, the hiring decisions are almost certainly unbiased. Two companies in the locality had recently closed. One was a large knitwear factory which employed many women, but on jobs with little relevance to engineering trades. The other closure was a car component factory employing five male production controllers. Local conditions produced a large pool of women applicants with little experience of the job and a small pool of male applicants with a great deal of experience.

However, what is sauce for the goose is also sauce for the gander. If there are special circumstances where it is fair to employ a higher proportion of majority group applicants, there must be circumstances where it is fair to employ a higher proportion of minority group applicants.

Expert opinion

Another approach to establishing bias in a selection system is to ask experts to scrutinise the methods used. For example, if an equal opportunities commission suspected a certain test is biased against a minority group, it could ask an expert psychologist, or even the test author, to look at the questions and pronounce upon their bias.

Past experience has shown that this is a very unsatisfactory type of evidence because experts rarely agree with each other and because their views may not be substantiated by scientific investigation. Little research in this area has involved measures used in selection. Efforts have largely concentrated upon the Wechsler Intelligence Scale for Children (WISC). Experts, including members of the American judiciary, maintained that several questions were biased against the negro minority (see McLoughlin and Koh, 1982). These views were supported by the test author's comments in a CBS programme. Wechsler himself accepted the cultural bias hypothesis in relation to one question about children picking a fight (see Miele, 1979). However, subsequent analyses showed that there are no significant differences between the black and white groups in any of the seven disputed WISC items and, indeed, 2 per cent more black children gave right answers to the 'fight' question, the bias of which was publicly conceded by Wechsler.

A slightly different tack was taken by Sandoval and Miille (1980) who asked 100 volunteers to judge the bias of 30 test questions. Previous analysis had shown that half of these items were more difficult for Mexican Americans. The volunteers consisted of 38 blacks, 22 Mexican Americans and 40 Anglo-Americans. the results indicated that the volunteers were not able to determine accurately which items were more difficult for minority students and that there was no significant difference in accuracy between judges of the different ethnic background. Similar results have been reported by Jensen (1980) and Cole (1981), who claimed that judges were not able to determine accurately the cultural bias of items on a standardised test. Jensen's study is particularly interesting. His judges either had a PhDs in psychology or were advanced graduate students working for PhDs in psychology and the judges were black, yet they too were unable to identify items which contained bias.

Experimental evidence

Several investigators (for example, Haefner, 1977; McIntyre, Moberg and Posner, 1980) have tried to investigate the potential bias of selection methods using experimental techniques which control as many influences as precisely as possible. In a typical investigation, standard descriptions of candidates are produced. Sometimes they are given a black identity, sometimes a male identity and sometimes a female identity. They are then mailed to a potential employer and differences in the responses are noted. As the descriptions are standard except for the racial and sex identity, any differences which emerge are evidence of bias. In practice, the methodology is often more complicated in order to ensure that the descriptions are equivalent and also to ensure that employers do not detect the purpose of the applications. Often student volunteers are used as judges instead of actual employers. More recently, specially prepared videotapes of interviews have been used rather than relying upon written résumés. This type of methodology has two main disadvantages: first, the artificial nature of the studies might produce results which are inaccurate and, second, it is not entirely clear whether interviews or application blanks are being examined for evidence of bias.

Internal consistency

Where a selection procedure has a number of component parts which can be scored independently, the relationship between the different parts can be used to detect bias. The situation is seen most clearly in tests but the principles apply to other measures. If test items are ranked in order of difficulty, biased items obtain different rankings from samples of majority and minority groups.

Comparisons with subsequent performance

Probably the best definition of a fair selection system is that 'candidates who are equally likely to be successful in performing the job are equally likely to receive a job offer irrespective of their sex, colour, age or creed'. This implies direct comparisons of candidates' scores on a selection measure and their competence at the job.

The simplest method of making this comparison is to use quadrant analysis, which is outlined in Chapter 13. For example, suppose a company has vacancies for widget-makers and it interviews 10 men and 10 women. Each interviewee is given a mark out of 10 on the basis of interview performance, and everyone who is interviewed is engaged. Then, three months later, after everyone has finished training and has settled down into the widget-making routine, the company collects data over a period of several weeks and works out the average number of widgets made per hour by each of the recruits. The company can compare interview performance with widget making ability by drawing a scattergram (see Figure 8.1).

Bias is most clearly shown in the top left and bottom right quadrants. The top left quarter contains the false negatives: the applicants who did badly at the interview but who turned out to be good employees. The bottom right contains the false positives: those

Figure 8.1   Bias in selection using quadrant analysis

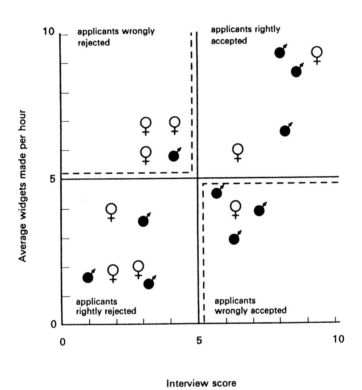

who interviewed well but turned out to be poor employees. If selection is biased against women, there will be proportionally more women false negatives and proportionately more men false positives; in other words, selection will underestimate the performance of the women and over-estimate the performance of men. The diagram shows how the results might appear for a very biased set of interviews. One man who was able to do the job would have been wrongly rejected, whereas three women would also have been wrongly rejected. This imbalance in the ratio of false negatives is direct evidence of sex bias. The fact that *some* women are wrongly rejected is neither here nor there; it is the higher proportion that matters. In practice the situation is more complex. Larger samples are needed and few employers would be prepared to employ everyone who applied: they would only hire those who were successful at the interview! Consequently, attention is usually confined to the false positives (the applicants who are wrongly accepted).

Regression analysis is more accurate and sophisticated than quadrant analysis. Instead of dividing the scattergram into quadrants, a trend line can be fitted to the data. The fairness of the regression line can then be inspected by looking at the distances from the regression line to the individuals on the scattergram. If the measure is fair, the distances above the regression line will be cancelled out by the distances below the regression line for both the majority and minority groups.

It should be noted that, to be fair, a measure does not need to be equally accurate for both groups: it is the balance of the inaccuracies which matters (Bartlett and O'Leary, 1969, case IV). The regression approach probably has the widest support. Ledvinka, Markos and Ladd (1982) comment:

> The regression model is the one that seems to be implicit in the federal selection guidelines . . . it has also found some acceptance by the federal courts in title VII cases . . . In fact, most validation research now includes analysis of regression lines for minorities and non-minorities. . . . that essentially tests for fairness as defined by the regression model.

In spite of the hegemony of the regression approach, three additional points must be noted. First, the short, non-statistical exposition contained in this chapter inevitably results in a great deal of over-simplification. More authorative expositions are given by Cleary and Hilton, 1968; Bartlett and O'Leary, 1969; Humphreys, 1973; and Jensen, 1974). Second, if fairness is defined in terms of equal prediction of ultimate job performance, then the way that the worker's competence is judged can be important. In an objective situation where all that matters is the number of objects a worker produces, there are few complications. But, as the earlier chapter on criteria implies, there are few jobs where this is the case and most validity studies depend upon the judgement of a superior. It is certainly possible for these criterion judgements to be biased either in favour of or in detriment to a minority group. For example, Boem (1972) and Bray and Moses (1972) suggest that findings of bias are associated with the use of subjective criteria and that validity differences seldom occur when objective criteria, are used. However, this possibility is less likely in the light of Schmidt, Berner and Hunter's (1973) investigation, which concluded that when irrelevant factors are controlled, subjective criteria are no more likely to generate instances of single group validity than are more objective criterion measures. Third, when the regression model does find that a selection measure is biased against a minority group, what are the likely consequences? A company should try to use an alternative measure which is known to be fair. In practice it is hard to know in advance whether the new measure will be fairer than the old measure, and the best an organisation can do is to choose a selection system against which bias has not been proved. But the lack of proof may be due to two possibilities: the device may be genuinely more fair, or it may be that the new device is biased but the bias more difficult to prove. For example, most psychological tests produce a score which can be directly related to performance, and its bias can be subjected to statistical analysis. Interviews on the other hand, rarely yield a quantitative score and they may or may not be more biased. It is difficult to subject the vague bias of an interview to statistical analysis.

If a measure is fair to the majority group but unfair to minorities, another possibility emerges. The organisation could retain the measure for use with the majority group and devise an equally valid but different method for use with the minority group. While this stratagem may be scientifically acceptable, in practice its use is doubtful. The obvious differences in treatment of the majority and minority groups would seem to be unfair and would undoubtedly attract a great deal of criticism even though the different procedures were introduced with the best intentions. Finally, it should be noted that there are other models which assess bias according to the relationship between scores and performance (see Thorndike, 1971; Cole, 1973; Ledivinka, Markos and Ladd, 1982).

Of these rivals to the regression model, Thorndike's constant ratio model has received the greatest attention. Thorndike holds that in a fair selection procedure, the pass marks on a test should be set so that the proportions of applications passing the test should be the same as the proportions of the groups who will satisfy the criteria for good workers. Suppose, for example, a company finds that 30 per cent of its successful workers are from a minority group but, when a single pass mark is used for all groups, only 20 per cent of the successful candidates are from that minority group. In these situations, Thorndike would advocate lowering the pass mark for the minority group until 30 per cent of those who are successful are from a minority group. This procedure attempts to eliminate unfairness in a situation where the two groups differ much more at the selection stage than in actual performance on the job and it is particularly relevant when the validity of the selection device is low. Thorndike's method is in essence a sophisticated quota system, but like all quota systems it shares the disadvantages that the average performance of those selected is reduced. Hunter and Schmidt (1976) comment:

> If lowered performance is met by increased rates of expulsion and firing, then the institution is relatively unaffected but (1) the quotas are undone and (2) there is considerable anguish for those selected who didn't make it. On the other hand, if the institution tries to adjust to the candidates selected by quotas there may be great cost and inefficiency.

LEGAL ASPECTS OF BIAS IN SELECTION

The principles described earlier in this chapter reflect the basic legal position that both direct and indirect discrimination is illegal. However, these principles need to be applied within the strict legal framework in force where the selection takes place. As this legal framework varies from country to country and is amended from time to time, all that can be done in a text of this kind is to emphasise the need to check legal requiements and keep abreast of any changes. In the UK, for example, the two main legal 'instruments' are the Equal Opportunities Act and the Race Relations Act.

In other countries there may be laws covering age discrimination, and in multi racial societies such as Malaysia, there may be enforceable quotas concerning the employment of groups such as Malays, Chinese and Indians.

CHECKING THE POTENTIAL BIAS OF SELECTION DEVICES

A previous section has argued that the only scientifically defensible way of establishing bias or its absence is a careful study relating predictions to subsequent performance. Consequently the first step is to ask protagonists of any selection measure if there have been any specific studies of this kind in relation to their specific measure. Often, for quite understandable reasons (for instance, there are insufficient numbers of a minority group to provide an acceptable sample size), a specific study of this kind will not be available. Under these circumstances, claims of fairness should be supported by studies quoted in the literature whose findings could be expected to generalise to the specific measure in question. Beware of the use of studies where the situation, sample or measure are not similar to the situation to hand and which may lead the generalisation of results to be faulty.

In the absence of supporting research, a number of other questions may give an indication of the fairness of a measure.

1. Were steps taken to ensure that the measure accurately reflects the requirements of the job? (This has, in the past, been the basis of a successful legal defence.)
2. Was there adequate minority group representation in the samples that were used to develop and standardise the measure?
3. Does the measure violate the 4/5ths rule for no apparent reason?

It should be noted that the fact a particular group obtains, on average, a higher or lower score is not good evidence that a measure is biased. It is almost certainly useless to scrutinise a measure to 'see' if it or the questions it uses are biased.

AFFIRMATIVE ACTION PLANS (AAPS)

If (because of selection or some other reason) bias exists, affirmative action can be taken. For example, a company might lower the acceptance score for minority groups; it could impose a quota system; or it could provide compensatory training. In extreme circumstances, it could dismiss majority group employees and replace them with member of the minority group. Affirmative action can take three basic forms: first, it can be ordered by a court of law or regulatory body, usually in the light of a legal plaint. Second, it can be the result of contract compliance or executive order whereby a large customer, usually the government, insists that people who supply them with goods implement a fair employment policy. Third, it can be voluntary. Affirmative action programmes (AAPs) can be very controversial and their legality may be challenged. Probably the most notorious case is the Bakke case, where an unsuccessful white applicant for medical school sued a college because, under an AAP, it had offered a place to a black applicant with a lower score. Almost all the experiences in this area are from the USA.

Kleiman and Faley (1988) reviewed six legal challenges to AAPs. In general, courts will support an AAP if, first of all, the purpose is clearly remedial. If there is an imbalance in employee composition, an AAP can be used to contact the balance. It is also possible to use an AAP to maintain a balance. One AAP concerned procedures for layoffs: teachers with the most seniority were laid off *unless* the percentage of minority personnel laid off was greater than the percentage of minorities employed. This rule was instigated to protect gains made by previous AAPs in selection and it resulted in more non minorities being laid off while minority teachers with less security were retained. In one interesting case, the Supreme Court rejected an AAP based on the 'role model theory'. It intended to employ more black teachers who could act as role models for black children (*Wygant* v. *Jackson Board of Education*).

Second, the plan must not unnecessarily trammel the interests of majority groups, In the *Firefighters* v. *City of Cleveland* case, it was argued that the AAP unjustly hurt members of the majority group who bore no direct blame for past discrimination, but the argument was rejected. However, courts have held that no person should be automatically excluded from consideration, and the degree of burden on innocent third parties should not be too high. Consequently AAPs involving the drastic consequences of dismissal are more questionable.

Third, less burdensome methods of affirmative action should be preferred. Before implementing an AAP, organisations should enquire whether alternative and less restrictive methods would achieve the same ends.

Finally, the elements of the plan should be reasonable. Generally, plans are reasonable if they are flexible (for example, quotas would be waived if no qualified blacks are available), temporary and designed to meet specific goals.

Kleiman and Faley (1988) suggest that research is needed on the impact of AAPs on employees (both those who are favoured and those who are denied favour) and the utility of AAPs to organisations.

WIDER ASPECTS OF AFFIRMATIVE ACTION

The first wider issue concerns the influence of company policy. Rosen and Merich (1979) asked 78 administrators in local government to evaluate resumes of male and female applicants and to suggest appropriate starting salaries. Two organisational policies were simulated: a strong commitment to fair employment and mere lip service to equal opportunities. The results indicated that the strength of the policy made little difference to general preferences, but a strong policy resulted in a *reduction* of the starting salaries thought appropriate for females.

The second wider issue concerns the cost of affirmative action. Usually the costs to an organisation and its customers are difficult to quantify. However, Arnold, Rauschenberger, Soubel and Guion (1982) attempted to calculate the cost of a policy of ensuring that 20 per cent of employment offers for steelworkers were made to women. Using the techniques outlined in the chapter on utility, they were able to estimate that the cost of the policy was approximately $2.8 million during one fiscal year. The calculations serve to remind us that affirmative action policies have their costs. Unfortunately the calculations do not provide an answer to the controversy surrounding affirmative action because the benefits remain unquantified. This chapter has aimed to set the theoretical basis concerning the bias of measures. The actual bias of specific measures will be given when each of the measures is considered.

Part III
Selection Methods

9 Psychological Tests

Psychological tests are carefully chosen, systematic and standardised procedures for evoking a sample of responses from a candidate, which can be used to assess one or more of their psychological characteristics by comparing the results with those of a representative sample of an appropriate population. This definition implies a wider range of procedures than the common stereotype of pencil-and-paper questionnaires, although it remains true that the vast majority of tests are in fact pencil-and-paper tests. The definition involves six main components.

First, tests are *systematic* and are constructed according to some logical framework which guides the questions which are included and the order in which they are presented. For example, most tests attempt to cover all relevant aspects of a characteristic and generally tests start with easy items and progress to more difficult ones. Tests may be contrasted with references where the referees may report any information they wish in any order they prefer.

Second, tests are *standardised*, so that all candidates receive fair and equal treatment. As a slight oversimplication, standardisation can be taken to mean that all candidates are:

(a) faced with identical tasks;
(b) given identical instructions;
(c) required to perform in very similar settings;
(d) have their responses evaluated in an identical way.

This standardisation in tests may be compared with interviews where many aspects are allowed to vary willy-nilly and candidates may be treated quite differently.

Third, questions are only a small *sample* of the questions it would be possible to ask. The adequacy of this sample will play a major part in determining the adequacy of the test. A typical test will ask between 100 and 300 questions compared with the much smaller number asked at an interview.

Fourth, tests aim to evoke *responses* which can be scored: candidates must do something. This contrasts to selection devices such as biographical data, references, palmistry and astrology in which the candidate is passive.

Fifth, assessments are made in terms of *general human characteristics*, which are psychological constructs such as intelligence, extroversion or outdoor interests. This aspect differentiates psychological tests from work samples which are tests which focus upon specific jobs. This distinction is very useful and works adequately in most cases, but the distinction between psychological tests and work samples is not clear cut: for instance, there could be considerable overlap between a psychological test of mechanical reasoning and a work sample test for a motor mechanic job.

Sixth, the candidates' scores can be compared and interpreted in the light of the *scores of a representative and relevant sample*. It is these comparisons which permit statements such as 'Evelyne is in the top 10 per cent of applicants'.

Some authorities (for example, the BPS, 1980b) suggest that to avoid misunderstanding the name 'test' should be avoided when these requirements are not met. Where appropriate, the word 'scale', 'inventory' or 'questionnaire' should be used rather than 'test'.

CATEGORIES OF PSYCHOLOGICAL TEST

The definition of psychological test encompasses a very wide variety of instruments and many psychologists have sought to categorise them: unfortunately they may be classified in different ways. So many different classifications exist that the classifications themselves need classification into meta-categories. The first of these meta categories is based upon *what* the tests aim to measure. The second meta-category is based upon *how* the tests attempt their measurement. A third meta category is based on the qualifications needed by the *test user*.

Categories Based on What Tests Measure

There are six main categorisations of test based upon what tests aim to measure.

The most obvious categorisation is based upon the *type of psychological characteristic* being gauged. One possible framework was discussed in detail in Chapter 4 on personal specifications. In essence, tests can be classified into tests of (1) mental ability, (2) manual ability, (3) personality, (4) interests and motivation.

A second categorisation divides tests into *analytic versus analogous tests.* Estimating a candidate's suitability can be approached in two ways. Underlying characteristics, such as intelligence or emotional stability, can be analysed and matched to the underlying characteristics required by the job. Tests which seek to do this are termed *analytic* tests and they are at least implicitly based on some theory of human behaviour. This approach requires insight and understanding of the dynamics of action at a basic level, and it carries the enormous advantage that general tests can be constructed and applied in a wide range of circumstances. The disadvantages of the analytical approach are that the insight and understanding may be wrong; abstractions are one step removed from concrete observation; and they may lack face validity in the eyes of some managers and applicants. The alternative approach is to produce *analogous* tests, which do not seek to understand why people differ in their job competence: they merely seek to reflect the job and a person's competence in that job. Seen in this light, work samples, in-baskets, and many situational exercises can be viewed as analogous tests. The big advantage of analogous tests is the apparent clarity of what they are measuring and their high face validity. The big disadvantage is their specificity to a job or group of jobs and all that this entails in terms of developing and validating a multitude of specific tests.

A third classification divides tests into *tests of aptitude versus tests of attainment.* It is a useful over-simplification to think of tests of aptitude as attempting to measure a candidate's 'innate potential' which could be used to predict their performance at a later date. Achievement tests, on the other hand, represent a snapshot of where the candidate is now as a result of both innate potential and environmental factors, such as education or experience. Unfortunately this neat distinction is severely strained in practice. Inherited abilities have to be measured via acquired skills such as speech and writing and consequently there are no pure tests of aptitude. Furthermore, the present attainments of candidates are highly relevant to their future performance and consequently attainment tests can be used as measures of potential. Because of these difficulties Anastasi (1982) writes, 'A useful concept that is coming to replace the traditional categories of aptitude and achievement in psychometrics is that of developed abilities', and she proposes a continuum with course-orientated achievement tests covering narrowly-defined technical skills at one extreme and culture-fair tests of general ability at the other. At this point it becomes clear that the analogous tests, described in the previous classification, map on to the specificity pole of Anastasi's continuum, while analytical tests map on to the generality pole.

A fourth classification of tests according to what they measure divides into *measures of typical performance versus measure of maximum performance*. This distinction is best seen by a comparison of two professors, T and M. Professor T (who shall remain nameless to spare his blushes) is a nice even-tempered fellow who is always pleasantly courteous without becoming overwhelming. Professor M (who shall remain nameless in order to protect the livelihood of one of the authors) is usually rude, irascible and petulant, except when in the presence of research sponsors when he scales the very heights of consideration, tact and human concern. A test of civility where Professor T has the highest score would be a test of typical performance while a test of civility where Professor M was superior would be a test of maximal performance. Many authors, such as Cronbach (1970, p.39), seem to prefer measures of maximal performance that are responses to extreme or unusual situations which are not typical in a day's work. There is some suggestion that measures of maximal performance have slightly higher validities.

Another categorisation according to what tests measure concerns the *level of the test*, and it is mainly used in connection with tests of ability. Most tests used in selection are designed for use with the general population, ranging from the quite dull to the quite brilliant. Yet when candidates are drawn from a special group these tests may not give sufficient discrimination. In practice these considerations apply at the top end of the range where most candidates can be expected to be clever. In theory it also applies at the bottom end of the ability range. A classic example is provided by the AH series of intelligence tests (Heim, Watts and Simmonds, 1970).

A final categorisation, based upon *what* tests measure, is often called the *power–speed continuum* and is also mainly relevant to tests of ability. Some tests have questions which are very easy: an intelligent candidate can answer each question in one or two seconds and an unintelligent candidate can still answer them but will take three or four times longer. These tests have fairly short time limits and the final score is largely determined by the number of questions attempted. Tests of this kind measure speed of thinking. Power tests, on the other hand, tend to have longer time limits and the questions are steeply graded: a few questions are easy, some are average difficulty and some are so hard even quite bright candidates cannot produce the correct answer, no matter how long they take.

Categorisation Based on Method of Measurement

Tests can also be categorised on the basis of the method used to obtain their measures and most of the categories are self-explanatory.

Tests can be divided into *group tests or individual tests*. The vast majority of tests used for selection purposes are group tests and they can be administered simultaneously to several candidates, consequently reducing costs. Group tests are relatively simple to administer and they can also be used in an individual situation. Individual tests require one tester for each applicant and the administration of most individual tests is complex. In industry individual test are only used in extreme situations.

Tests can be categorised into *pencil-and-paper tests* and *apparatus tests*. The majority of tests used in selection are the pencil and paper variety because they are relatively cheap and easy to score. The use of apparatus tests is largely confined to psychomotor abilities, such as manual dexterity. In general, pencil-and-paper tests tend to be group tests, while apparatus tests tend to be individual tests.

The *directness of the method* can be used to categorise tests. Some psychological tests of arithmetical ability or verbal fluency, for example, collect data which is *directly relevant to the characteristic they attempt to measure*. Self-report tests work in a more indirect way via the candidate's perceptions and what he or she is prepared to divulge, and these additional factors increase the possibility of error. For example, the question, 'Are you usually good at organising your work?' may provide a misleading answer in two ways. First, a candidate may not be best judge of his/her own abilities: an executive may be so disorganised that he cannot recognise the trail of havoc and chaos he leaves behind. Second, a candidate may not wish to reveal the truth: only a stupid candidate would be prepared to indict herself by answering 'No' to the question. Very little can be done about candidate's lack of self-insight, but wilful distortion can often be detected by a lie scale embedded in a test. *Projective tests* work in a different way by presenting a candidate with a vague stimulus. The candidate has so little information that they must use their own ideas and thoughts in order to make any response: that is, they project their own characteristics and motives into the vague situation which confronts them. There are two main projective tests: the Rorschach

Ink Blot Test is widely known but, nowadays, it is rarely used; the TAT (Thematic Apperception Test) is occasionally used for selection purposes, mainly in the measurement of motivation.

Categorisations According to Qualifications of Test User

In order to maintain confidentiality of test material, and to avoid incompetence or misuse of tests, they are often divided into categories according to the qualifications needed by the test user. Most publishing companies will only supply test materials to users with appropriate qualification. One scheme (BPS, 1980a) divides tests into four categories. First there are simple tests, such as interest tests. These are tests which are easy to administer, having objective scoring and requiring minimum technical knowledge. Tests in this category may be released to responsible users, such as teachers or personnel officers. Often tests in this category are used in a guidance or a training context. Second, there are relatively straightforward tests of attainment yielding one or two scores which are simple to interpret and administer. Examples of this category are tests of arithmetic, typing ability and some of the simplest measures of intelligence. The competences needed to obtain these tests can be gained from a short course of about one week which covers background theory to tests, administration scoring and test interpretation. The third category consists of more complex tests which may yield a series of subscores that need careful integration and interpretation. The use of these tests requires thorough knowledge of principles underlying testing, together with specific training and wide practical experience. Good examples of this category are Cattell's 16PF test of personality and Bennett, Seashore and Wesman's (1974) Differential Aptitude Test Battery (DATB). The competences needed to use tests in the third category are usually gained from a further course of about a week which is largely devoted to matters of interpretation or from possessing an appropriate degree in psychology. Usually there is a short follow-up of about one day, six months after the initial training to ensure the maintenance of proper standards. The final category consists of very specialised tests requiring extended and specific training, even for psychologists. Individual tests of mental ability require a high degree of professional skill and experience for their proper administration and interpretation (for example, the Wechsler Adult Intelligence Scale (WAIS) devised by Wechsler, 1955) and postgraduate or extended specialised training is usually needed. Some of the projective measures of personality and some tests used in clinical psychology fall into this category.

SPECIFIC PSYCHOLOGICAL TESTS

There are so many tests available that a description of each one is impossible. Consequently this section will only mention those which are significant from a theoretical viewpoint or which are used most frequently in personnel selection.

Tests of Intellectual Ability

Measures of global ability

Although it is hardly used in industrial selection, the WAIS is theoretically important because it is one of the best intelligence scales in existence; it has been called the 'paragon of intelligence tests'. Consequently the WAIS is often used to 'calibrate' other tests. The WAIS consists of 11 subscales which can be used to produce estimates of:

(a) general intelligence
(b) verbal intelligence
(c) performance intelligence

The WAIS is an individual test which requires one highly trained tester for each candidate. This has the advantage of permitting the inclusion of a range of non-pencil-and-paper tasks, and it permits some flexibility in administration. In addition to the wide sampling of skills, the WAIS enjoys excellent standardisation studies which have been conducted in most major countries. Unfortunately the WAIS is expensive to use because, as a complex individual test, it requires about one hour of a highly-trained administrator's time for each candidate.

Raven's Progressive Matrices (RPM: Raven, 1960) is also a very highly-regarded test of mental ability. It is a non-verbal test and is less influenced by culture and linguistic ability than many others. The matrices consist of nine figures cast in a 3 × 3 square. The ninth figure is missing but its contents can be deduced from the sequence of the proceeding eight. The candidate is required to identify the correct item which should be the ninth figure. The questions become progressively harder. There are three versions of the progressive matrices test: the standard matrices, the advanced matrices for superior adults and the coloured matrices for use with children. The RPM can be administered as either a group or individual test, and it is supported by a vast literature of 1000 research papers. It has been argued that the RPM forms one of the purest measures of Spearman's general intelligence *g*. The standard matrices consist of 60 problems and take 25 minutes to administer. In essence, the matrices are power tests. The main weakness of the RPM is the absence of modern norms, especially for US samples. The matrices are occasionally used for selection, especially at skilled operative level.

A survey by Sneath, Thakur and Medjuck (1976) showed that the most popular test of general intelligence in British industry is Heim's (1967, 1968) AH4 test. It is a short test which can be completed in 25 minutes and consists of two parts. Part one involves 65 traditional verbal and numerical items such as 'help is to hinder as permit is to . . . (a) ticket (b) allow (c) prevent (d) forbid' and '10, 26, 37, which number comes next?' Part two involves 65 perceptual and spatial problems. The two subscores can be combined to produce a global score. The AH4 is a broad spectrum test which can be used when little advance information about candidates is available. Its reliability is greater than 0.9 and it shows a correlation of 0.69 with RPM. One of the present authors found that the AH4 produced a correlation for senior managers of 0.70 with the WAIS. T. G. Thurstone and Thurstone's (1952) Test of Mental Alertness has many similarities with the AH4 and can be used as a substitute in appropriate situations. Heim, Watts and Simmonds (1970) have revised the AH4 to produce parallel tests, the AH2 and AH3. The AH range of test of general intelligence is completed by the AH5, AH6 (Arts Graduates) and AH6 (Science, Mathematics, Engineering) which are intended for use with above-average applicants.

The Wonderlic Personnel Test (Wonderlic, 1959) is very useful as a screening device where a quick estimate of mental ability is needed. The 50 items take only 12 minutes to complete. Test-retest reliabilities greater than 0.8 are generally achieved. Several parallel forms are available and there is a large amount of standardisation data.

Batteries of specific mental abilities

Although several of the measures of global ability also provide subscores on numerical, verbal and possibly perceptual abilities, in many situations a more detailed analysis is required. In general, the most important group factors of this kind are spatial ability and mechanical ability as well as numerical and verbal abilities. Several batteries contain tests to measure these and other abilities. Either the complete battery or individual tests can be used.

Probably the best battery of this kind is the DATB developed by Bennett, Seashore and Wesman (1974). In an enthusiastic review of the original battery, Carroll (1959) wrote: 'The authors have done such a thorough and technically satisfactory job that the reviewer finds it hard to make himself appear sufficiently critical.' The DATB consists of eight independent tests:

(a) verbal reasoning;
(b) numerical ability;
(c) abstract reasoning;
(d) clerical speed and accuracy;
(e) mechanical reasoning;
(f) space relations;
(g) Spelling;
(h) language usage.

Most of these tests last about 25 minutes, and the complete battery takes almost four hours. The length of time taken is one of the battery's disadvantages. The battery yields estimates of numerical and verbal reasoning after 60 minutes' testing. Comparable estimates can be obtained after 20 minutes using tests such as the Thurstone Test of Mental Alertness. Clerical speed and accuracy is the shortest test, and takes six minutes using tests such as the Thurstone Test of Mental Alertness. Clerical speed and accuracy is the shortest test which takes six minutes, including the practice items, but this test has a very low reliability. The DATB enjoys the advantage of parallel forms and excellent norms (Hodgkiss, 1979).

A possible alternative to the DATB is Morrisby's (1955) Differential Test Battery which includes tests of:

(a) verbal ability;
(b) numerical ability;
(c) perceptual ability;
(d) shapes;
(e) mechanical ability;
(f) speed.

The Morrisby battery is more time-efficient than the DATB but is more complicated to administer and there are no parallel forms. Standardisation data is also less extensive.

Most government employment services have developed test batteries for specific mental abilities (see Figure 9.1). The United States Employment service has developed the General Aptitude Test battery (GATB) which consists of 12 separately-timed tests. The British Department of Employment has developed the Department of Employment Vocational Aptitude Tests (DEVAT). Both GATB and DEVAT are designed for use with average or lower than average ability groups and are primarily intended for vocational guidance. Neither of the batteries is generally available.

The Flanagan (1960) Industrial Tests constitute a battery of 18 very short tests which attempt to measure:

Inspection	Reading scales	Arithmetic
Vocabulary	Patterns	Comprehension
Components	Expression	Electronics
Precision	Ingenuity	Mechanics
Memory	Assembly	Mathematics
Co-ordination	Tables	Planning

Unfortunately the battery has been heavily criticised on account of the low test reliabilities and the inadequacies of the manual.

Individual tests of specific abilities

There are a large number of tests measuring specific abilities which are not part of a larger battery. Probably the largest group consists of tests of *mechanical ability*. Unfortunately many of these tests seem to be attainment tests which merely reflect the contents of a physics school textbook rather than a more general mechanical aptitude. The main exceptions to this generalisation are Vincent's (1974) Mechanical Diagrams Tests. Both tests give a diagram of a mechanical contraption of levers, pivot, pulleys or gears and require the applicant to forecast the consequence of some movement, such as a lever being pushed or pulled.

There are also several tests of spatial ability. Probably the most popular test of spatial ability is the Minnesota Form Board Test. The 20-minute test consists of 64 problems in which the applicant must match a design with one of five other designs. In some of the more difficult problems parts of the design have been rotated or turned over.

Figure 9.1   Some tests of mental ability

Name of Test	No. of subscores	Numerical	Verbal	Levels
WAIS	10	✓	✓	LAS
Raven's Matrices	0	x	x	LAS
AH4	2			A
AH5	2			S
AH6 (Arts Graduate)	2	?	✓	S
AH6 (Science, Maths, Engineering)	3	✓	✓	S
AH2/3	3	✓	✓	A
Thurstone Test of Mental Alertness	2	✓	✓	A
Wonderlic Test	0	x	x	A
Watson–Glazer Test of Critical Thinking	5	x	x	S
Saville–Holdsworth Critical Reasoning	3	✓	✓	A
Saville–Holdsworth Advanced Battery	7	✓	✓	S
Saville–Holdsworth Personnel Battery	8	✓	✓	A
Saville–Holdsworth Technical Battery	4	✓	✓	AS
16PF B Scale	1	x	x	A

KEY TO LEVEL L = Below average; A = Average; S = Superior

SOME TESTS OF VERBAL ABILITY

National Institute of Industrial Psychology Test 90A/90B	Verbal Scale from Morrisby
Saville–Holdsworth VTS	Verbal Reasoning from DATB

SOME TESTS OF NUMERICAL ABILITY

NIIP EA4, GT66, EA2
Numerical Reasoning from DATB
Numerical Scale from Morrisby
Saville-Holdsworth NT2, NA4
Flanagan Mathematics and Reasoning
Flanagan Arithmetic

SOME TESTS OF MECHANICAL ABILITY

Vincent Mechnical Diagrams
Cox Mechanical Tests
Bennett Mechanical Reasoning (similar to DATB test)
Macquarrie Test for Mechanical Ability
Saville–Holdsworth MT4
Mechanical Ability Test from Morrisby Differential Aptitude Battery
Mechanical Reasoning Test from DATB

Figure 9.1 continued

Figure 9.1 continued

SOME TESTS OF SPATIAL ABILITY

Minnesota Form Board
Minnesota Spacial Relations Test
Guildford–Zimmerman Part V: Spatial Orientation
Spatial Reasoning from DATB
Shapes Test from Morrisby Battery
NIIP Tests
Saville–Holdsworth ST7
Embedded Figures Test

The test is widely respected and Guion (1965) notes, 'the test has a broad record of usefulness in engineering, architecture, military tactics, drafting, machining and . . . spatial imagery'. An alternative measure of spatial ability is the Minnesota Spatial Relations Test which requires equipment, and is essentially an individual test. It consists of a board in which patterns are cut out to form holes. Pieces which fill the holes are placed in front of the applicant in standard positions and the applicant is required to place the pieces in the appropriate hole. Unfortunately, as a test of spatial ability, the Minnesota Spatial Relations Test is inevitably contaminated by factors such as clumsiness.

Tests for Specific Occupations

Some tests of ability have been developed for specific occupations; probably the largest group concerns *clerical occupations*. Often batteries of clerical ability contain tests of numerical and verbal ability plus tests of number and name checking. They may include tests of spelling, comprehension and vocabulary. Typical clerical test batteries are the General Clerical Test (Psychological Corporation, 1944) and the 'Typing and Office Skills Tests (Science Research Association, 1980). An interesting development is a battery developed by Saville-Holdsworth for the selection of word processor operators (1989).

Tests of Temperament

Controversial nature of personality tests

The use of temperament tests is much more controversial than the use of ability tests for several reasons. First, many people feel that there are ethical issues in temperament testing, and so there are. Yet although the quantitive nature of temperament tests brings the issues into much clearer focus, the ethical issues are not restricted to tests. They apply to all means of temperament assessment including interview, references and applications.

A second objective concerns the approach (for example, Cattell, 1965; H. J. Eysenck, 1970) which underlies temperament tests. The trait factor analytic approach to temperament underlies the most commonly used temperament tests, such as Cattell's 16PF (see below). This approach lays emphasis on temperament rather than situational factors as determinants of behaviour. Despite this emphasis, trait theorists such as Cattell do recognise that both personal make-up *and* situation determine behaviour. Nevertheless, many other psychologists – for example, Mischel (1968, 1977) – argue that trait theories do not place enough emphasis on the part that situations play in determining behaviour. Pervin (1980) provides a useful summary of the debate. Recent evidence suggests that, generally, 15 per cent of the variation in behaviour is due to the situation (Funder and Ozer, 1983).

The final objection to temperament tests is pragmatic and rests on the belief that tests are too inaccurate for use as selection devices. Meyer and Bertotti (1956), for example, suggest that the accuracy of measures of temperament is less than the accuracy of measures of interests, abilities or physical characteristics. Whilst this view may be correct, it does not follow that temperament tests are not useful for selection purposes. There are just too many examples where temperament tests have been found useful. An important meta-analysis by Barrick and Mount (1991) suggests that individual scales can have validities of 0.2 and combinations of scales can have validities higher than 0.3. Tett, Jackson and Rothstein (1991) show that when the use of personality tests is guided by proper job analysis the validity rises to 0.38.

Some Personality Tests

Occupational Personality Questionnaire

The Occupational Personality Questionnaire (OPQ) is, perhaps, one of the few tests of temperament which was specifically designed for occupational uses. In the UK it is probably the most frequently used temperament test in selection and assessment.

In fact there are several versions of the test. Some are ipsative. Probably, the most comprehensive is the Concept Five version, which measures 32 facets of temperament thought to be relevant in occupational settings. The 32 facets are grouped into three domains: relationships with people; thinking style; feelings and emotions. Each domain is divided into subdomains. For example, relationships with people is operationalised into nine traits grouped into three subdomains: assertiveness, gregariousness and empathy. There is also a scale to measure social desirability. Eight other versions of the OPQ provide a less detailed picture of temperament which may be more useful in some circumstances. A feature of the OPQ is the willingness of the publishers to devote resources to maintaining up to date norms and an openness to research into the validity and reliability of the test.

Some tests of personality

Occupational Personality Questionnaire
16PE
Edwards Personal Preference Schedule
EPQ.EPI
Myers Briggs Inventory
Gordon Personal Inventory
Gough Adjective Check List
Guildford–Zimerman Temperament Survey
NEO–FFI
Thurstone Temperament Schedule

One of the personality tests more frequently used in selection is the 16PF test (Cattell, Eber and Tasuoka, 1970). It was developed from a statistical analysis which located 16 personality factors from a mass of judgements and measure of personality. The 16 scales were then combined to produce the 16PF test, which takes about 40 minutes to complete. Originally there were two parallel forms (A and B); subsequently two shorter forms (C and D) were produced which take about 20 minutes to complete but which give less accurate measures. Finally, forms E and F were produced to cater for subjects of lower socio-educational attainment.

The scores from the 16 scales are not independent of each other and they can be correlated to produce scores for higher order factors, which correspond well with the 'big five' personality factors described by Digman (1990).

The higher order factors are not simply the sum of the scores on the scales. They *must* be calculated using an appropriate equation given in

Cattell, Eber and Tasuoka (1970). Most of the scales in the 16PF test (forms A and B) have adequate reliabilities except the scales which measure intelligence (B), shrewdness (N) and self control (Q3). However, the reliabilities of all the scales on form C and form D are low and generally appreciably lower than 0.5. Consequently the short forms of the 16PF should not be used for selection purposes.

The 16PF has been extensively used for over 20 years and has a great deal of supporting research. Data has been collected on samples of more than 100 occupations, and typical profiles can be constructed and used for interpretation. Furthermore, equations have been established which use the 16PF scores to produce scores on other factors such as creativity, academic achievement and leadership.

The Eysenck Personality Questionnaire (EPQ)

The EPQ is a short test which takes about 10 minutes to complete. It yields scores on psychoticism, extroversion, neuroticism and a lie scale. Since the extroversion and neuroticism are similar to two of the second order factors on the 16PF the EPQ can be used as a cross check. The existence of the lie scale is a useful feature but, unfortunately, very conscientious candidates often obtain high scores. The EPQ has adequate reliabilities and substantial validity information. A previous version was called the EPI and did not possess a scale to measure psychoticism.

The NEO–FFI Inventory

One of the newest tests of temperament is the NEO-FFI (Neuroticism, Extroversion, Openness Five Factor Inventory) produced by Costa and McCrae (1989). The NEO-FFI is specifically based upon analyses which identify the 'big five' temperament factors: neuroticism, extroversion, openness, agreeableness and conscientiousness. The first three of these aspects have subscales to measure their facets. For example, neuroticism is divided into anxiety, hostility, depression, self-consciousness, impulsiveness and vulnerability. A research base for the NEO-FFI is accumulating but norms are only available for US populations and more studies of occupational validity studies are needed. The NEO-FFI has several forms. One, the NEO inventory, measures only three factors of temperament: neuroticism, extroversion and openness. Another form measures only the five factors of temperament but not their facets. A particularly interesting feature of this suite of tests is the availability of two versions R and S. Form S is a typical self complete questionnaire. In form R a rater completes the questionnaire in respect of the subject. Hogan (1986) also presents a questionnaire based on the five factor model.

Tests of Interests and Motivation

An interest may be defined as a liking for doing something: the performance of an activity which produces its own intrinsic rewards and feeling of happiness and satisfaction. It may follow that if we find our work interesting we will devote more effort to its performance and be prepared to maintain our effort over a longer period. Consequently, interests may form a basis for selection and we should aim to place individuals in jobs where interests and work are congruent.

Unfortunately there is little empirical evidence to support this simple logic. Ghiselli and Brown (1955) suggest that there is only a low relationship between interests and job performance. The main exception to this generalisation concerns sales work where average correlations of 0.32 and 0.34 were obtained. These figures must be interpreted with care because they do not necessarily imply a lack of relationship between interest and proficiency. Consequently interest tests are seldom used for selection purposes.

Some interest tests

APU Occupational Interest Guide
Connolly Occupational Interest Questionnaire
Holland Vocational Preference Inventory
Kuder Preference Record (vocational)
Rothwell–Miller Interest Bank
Saville–Holdsworth Advanced Occupational Interest Inventory
Saville–Holdsworth General Occupational Interest Inventory
Saville–Holdsworth Managerial Interest Inventory
Strong–Campbell Interest Inventory

The Strong–Campbell Interest Inventory (SCII) is a frequently used interest test and it operates in a fundamentally different way from most other interest tests. The inventory consists of 325 items and takes almost an hour to complete. The responses are then matched to the responses of samples from differing occupations. For example, there are scoring keys for farmers, bankers, sales personnel and accountants.

There are 67 scoring keys for male samples and 57 for female samples. While this procedure gives very specific information, scoring is excruciatingly time-consuming, even when only a handful of scoring keys are involved. Any substantial use of the SCII requires computer scoring and involves additional costs and delays.

The occupational basis of the SCII is both a strength and a weakness, and it differentiates the SCII inventories from most other measures of interest which focus upon themes. The latest version includes a modification which also allows the inventory to be scored for six themes: realism, intellectual, artistic, social service, economic and clerical. The scores on the themes can then be related to specific occupations. A banker, for example, would be expected to have high scores on the clerical and the economic themes, whereas an advertising executive would be expected to have a high score on the artistic theme.

A particular feature of the SCII interest tests is the volume of relevant research. Reliabilities are generally high (0.85, 0.82 and 0.75 over 3, 10 and 22 years respectively; Strong 1951; C.P. Campbell, 1977). Both Anastasi (1982) and Guion (1965) report evidence of validity in selection of engineers, bakery shop managers and insurance salesmen.

The Kuder Preference Record is another major interest test and it produces scores in terms of ten interest categories or themes:

(a) outdoor
(b) mechanical
(c) computational
(d) scientific
(e) persuasive
(f) artistic
(g) literary
(h) musical
(i) social service
(j) clerical

The Kuder also contains a validity scale which can be used as a check against carelessness or wilful distortion. Completion takes about 40 minutes and applicants find the test rather tedious. The Kuder is not often used in selection, although Tiffin and Phelan (1953) found that it could be used to identify those who would be likely to leave employment after a short time.

The Rothwell-Miller Interest Blank must represent the best value of all interest tests in terms of information produced per minute of candidate's time. It consists of nine lists of twelve occupations, and subjects are required to rank the occupations according to preference. The Rothwell-Miller Interest Blank takes about 15 minutes to complete and yields scores on the same categories as the Kuder, plus scores for practical and medical interests.

The Holland (1978) Vocational Preference Inventory is based on the view that interests can be thought of as a hexagon with realistic, intellectual, artistic, social, enterprising and conventional interests at the angles. Thus realistic interests are opposite social interests. The test can also be scored for self control, masculinity, status and infrequency. The Holland Vocational Preference Inventory was primarily designed for use in vocational guidance.

With the possible exception of the Strong interest inventories, most interest items have been designed with the 16–21-year-old age groups in view. This may reduce their face validity to older groups. Three recent tests developed by Saville and Holdsworth (1984) are particularly useful in this context. The General Occupational Interest Inventory includes activities from semi-skilled to supervisory levels and is suitable for people whose educational level is average. The Advanced Occupational Interest Inventory includes activities from skilled and supervisory levels to professional and managerial levels and is suitable for people whose educational level is above average. The availability of the two tests should make scores more precise and relevant. A particularly nice feature of both tests is their basis on a systematic analysis of job interests. Job interests are arranged in a hierarchy which starts with three categories that are similar to Fine and Wiley's (1977) job analysis categories of people, data and things. Scoring is tedious, but it provides scores at all points of the hierarchy. Estimates of reliability of 0.72 and above (generally 0.8 or more) have been obtained. Unfortunately validity data is sparse.

Another innovation from Saville and Holdsworth (1983) is the test of the Managerial Interest Inventory. The inventory takes about 20 minutes to administer. Although the scoring is excruciatingly tedious, the test provides scores for interest in 12 management functions and 12 management skills. As an added bonus, the test also gives an index of experience in both the managerial functions and managerial skills. However, the estimates are based on self-report by the subject, and might be virtually useless in a selection context.

Some tests of motivation

Tests of motivation are rarely used in selection and there are very few well recognised tests. Perhaps the most widely used are versions of the TAT. Subjects are shown four vague pictures and are asked to say what is happening in the picture, who the people are, what happened in the past and what will happen in the future. The resulting stories can then be analysed for the motives they contain. The main motives obtained from these tests are the achievement motive (n Ach), the affiliation motive and the power motive. Achievement motivation is probably the most extensively researched motive and detailed scoring systems are available (D. C. McClelland, 1963, 1976). Many authors (see D. C. McClelland and Bradburn, 1957; Smith *et al.*, 1982) have claimed a strong link between achievement motivation and entrepreneurial and managerial success.

One of the most extensive efforts to measure motivation is the Motivation Analysis Test (MAT) developed by Cattell, Horn, Sweeny and Radcliffe (1959). The test attempts to measure two aspects of each facet: conscious motivation (integrated motives) and unconscious motivation (unintegrated motives). The test measures five 'innate' ergs: mating assertiveness, fear, comfort seeking and pugnacity–sadism. It also measures five 'learned' sentiments: self-concept, super ego, career, sweetheart-spouse and home. Thus the test yields 20 motivation scores which are believed to gauge variance not covered by ability and temparament tests. Additional information can be obtained from comparing the integrated and unintegrated scores. For example, if the integrated career score is higher than the unintegrated career score, it might be that the person was once very motivated by his or her career but that motivation has now subsided.

Finally, Rotter's External-Income Locus of Control has been used, but it must be clear that it is not ideal for selection purposes.

OUTLINE OF TEST CONSTRUCTION

Test construction is a complex and technical undertaking which is best left to specialists in the field. As books by Adkins (1974), Gulliksen (1950), Cronbach and Glesser (1965) and Lord and Novick (1968) show, test construction can involve complex statistical models. Consequently, the following simplified description of test construction has two limited objectives: to give insight which will aid the evaluation and use of tests, and to help those who need to liaise and converse with the psychometric mega-beings who actually construct tests. The precise method of construction varies according to the constraints of specific situations, but the 'classic' method usually proceeds in seven major stages.

The first stage is to *define the domain* of a test. Probably the most important point is to define the aims of the test. This is a crucial decision upon which all else is built, and the way that the decision is reached is more an art than a science. Once the aims have been agreed, a specification of the test content can be produced. Generally the content can be divided into two parts: the subject matter and the mental operations. For example, the content of an arithmetic test can involve money, length, weight or time and each of these content categories can be subject to the mental operations of addition, subtraction, multiplication and division, to produce 16 different types of problem. Clear thinking at this stage should help to ensure that the test adequately samples the domain.

Second, it is also necessary to *specify the type of question*. There are two major types of question: open-ended questions, and multiple-choice questions. Open-ended questions can vary from asking for several sentences on a topic (for example, what has been happening to the people in the picture), to the answer to an arithmetic problem (for example, $194 + 78 = ?$). Sometimes a subject is merely asked to fill in a missing word. Open-ended questions have the great advantage that the subject's responses are not limited by the viewpoint of the test constructor, and the subject is required to produce the answer rather than just recognise it. Open-ended questions have the great disadvantage that, except in arithmetical problems, they are very difficult to analyse and score. Multiple-choice questions range from yes/no or true/false questions, to the most usual format consisting of a stem which poses the question, three or more plausible but wrong answers (distracters) and a correct answer. The construction of multiple-choice questions limits the replies a subject can give, and their preparation needs great care. They are, however, easy to score and analyse. The duration and length of the test also need to be specified in advance. Another consideration is the way that subjects will be asked to respond: should they make their marks on the test booklet or would it be appropriate to use separate answer sheets and so reduce costs?

The third stage is to *assemble items* according to the test specification. It must be anticipated that many of these items will not survive subsequent stages of test construction. Initially, about three times the number of final items is needed. Usually at this stage the questions are cast into an open-ended format and the directions for administering the test are drafted.

The fourth stage of test construction is to *try out the large initial pool of items* on a relatively representative population. Care should be taken to include appropriate numbers of minority groups at this stage. If the test is to be timed, a time limit is not imposed at this stage. Instead, subjects are merely asked to mark where they are up to at various points.

The fifth stage consists of an *item analysis* of the responses obtained in the previous stage. At a very minimum this consists of calculating the percentage of the sample who pass each question. Unfortunately the decision of which items to retain and which items to reject is a dilemma. An item has maximum discrimination when it is passed by 50 per cent of subjects, and it would follow that tests should be composed solely of items of average difficulty. However, in an extreme situation this would lead to half of the subjects receiving maximum marks and half receiving minimum marks, with no one in the centre of the distribution. In practice most test constructors avoid questions with very high and very low passes and then systematically sample the intermediate range. An adequate item analysis would investigate discrimination in addition to the difficult item. Items which have high correlations with the total score are retained while those with low correlations are rejected. An excellent discussion of item analysis is given by Guilford and Fruchter (1978).

The sixth stage in constructing a psychological test is *selecting the items* to be included. Usually non-discriminating items are rejected first. Items of appropriate difficulty are selected from those which remain. The items are arranged in an appropriate order, instructions added and the booklets printed. The most frequently used method of arranging questions is the spiral omnibus method which systematically works through all types of easy questions, progressively moving to harder ones. For example, an arithmetic test would start with very easy additions, subtraction, multiplication and divisions and then go on to average addition, subtractions, and so on before finishing on a very difficult division.

The seventh and final stage of constructing a test involves *researching the psychometric properties of the test* on a large representative sample and establishing norms, reliability and validity and, if possible, the fairness of the test.

ADMINISTRATIVE ASPECTS OF TESTS

Decision to use tests

The first administrative decision is whether to use tests in preference to other selection devices. The main advantage of tests is their objectivity and, in most cases, their better predictive ability. However, the use of tests tends to involve a high set-up cost. However, since many applicants can be tested simultaneously, the marginal cost of extra candidates may be quite low.

Choosing among Tests

The first criterion governing the choice of specific tests should be relevant to the items mentioned in the personnel specification, fairness and the psychometric properties (especially reliability and validity). Once these over-riding criteria have been satisfied the following can be considered.

1. *Cost* of booklets, answer sheets, manual and scoring keys.
2. *Delivery time* (several months may elapse between order and delivery).
3. *Training needed for administrators*: its cost and availability.
4. *Time required* for administration.
5. *Time required for scoring* or *cost of scoring*.
6. *Adequacy of manual*, which includes items such as:

   (a) ease of understanding;
   (b) clear statement of purpose of test;
   (c) clear instructions for test administration and scoring;
   (d) clear instructions for scoring of test;
   (e) validity and reliability studies needed for correct interpretation of scores;
   (f) norms for relevant groups. The norms should be based on systematic samples which are larger than 100, and they should be representative of the candidates being tested. Adequate standardisation samples will also include appropriate numbers of minority groups. Ideally, norms which are more than 20 years old should be avoided.

Restrictions on use

The manual should be carefully checked to see that it is appropriate to the candidates concerned and that the vocabulary and examples are appropriate to women and minority groups. The level of test should be chosen so that the range of scores among candidates is at least seven. In some cases it is important to choose tests which will be fair to those with impaired sight or muscle control. If older candidates are to be tested, tests with very short time limits should, if possible, be avoided.

In principle, tests should be chosen so that the most important items on the personnel specification receive 'most' attention. For example, if a personnel specification says that spatial reasoning is an essential characteristic and that ability to deal with stressful situations is a desirable characteristic, it would be appropriate to devote, say, 30 minutes to the former and 15 minutes to the latter. In practice, however, this balance is much more difficult to achieve because the reliability and validity of the test and the other measures which are to be used should be taken into account. A useful procedure is to draw up a matrix with the requirements down the side and measures to be used along the top. The times involved can be entered in the cells. At the also very least, this procedure will identify gaps, and it will allow the global pattern to be evaluated and adjusted.

Test Security

Having decided to use tests, it is important to remember that most tests are supplied on a confidential basis. Tests would quickly lose their value if they became common knowledge and people could look up their answers in advance. In order to maintain test security they should be stored in a locked cabinet to which only registered testers have access. Tests should not be loaned to non-qualified testers and any requests for such a loan should be met with a tactful explanation that tests are provided on a confidential basis and that breach of the confidentiality could have important consequences for the person permitting the loan: registration by test publishers could be withdrawn and disciplinary action could be taken by a professional organisation. Test materials should not be photocopied. At the end of a testing session the number of test booklets should be counted to ensure that candidates do not take booklets away. Breaches of test security should be reported to both the test publisher and the appropriate professional bodies.

Test Administration

Standardisation is a distinctive feature of tests and a part of this standardisation is to ensure that candidates have the same frame of mind when they are taking a test. Administration plays a key role in creating a uniform frame of mind and it merits careful and detailed attention.

Good test administration starts when the candidate is invited to take the tests. The letter of invitation should explain that tests will be used and the part the results will play in the selection process. It is also worth reminding candidates who wear spectacles to bring them along. Good administration also involves advance preparation. Well in advance of the testing session rooms of adequate size should be reserved and supplies of test materials should be checked in case previous candidates have marked question booklets or in case stocks of answers sheets have been depleted. A day or two before the testing session, the test room should be checked for sources of noise and interruption and details of reception, marshalling and routing of candidates should be sent to those concerned. Equipment, especially computer equipment and supplies, should be checked. An introduction and explanations for candidates should be prepared. Several hours before the testing session accommodation should be re-inspected to ensure that tables are properly spaced and that ventilation and heating are in order. Any computer equipment should be rechecked. An additional table should be available where the tester can lay out the materials in the order of administration. It is also helpful to have a table or other arrangements for bags, coats and umbrellas. There should be an adequate supply of water and glasses, ashtrays, pencils, chalk or flip chart, and namebadges or nameplates. It is also essential that a 'DO NOT DISTURB' sign is available for each entrance to the testing room and in some cases a 'QUIET PLEASE, EXAMINATION IN PROGRESS' may be required for adjacent corridors. Half an hour before testing begins materials should be taken to the room, pencils and paper laid out on table and stopwatches checked. Whenever possible, parallel forms of the tests should be taken to the testing room so that if by chance a candidate has recently completed the test, or if the man with the hammer, pneumatic drill and siren strikes yet again, the test can be restarted after dealing with the catastrophe.

Even with the best preparation, unanticipated events occur. The only course of action is to take these events into account during marking. This process will be infinitely easier if a contemporary account is available. Human memory is very fallible and much information is forgotten even after a short interval. Consequently, the use of a test log is essential. It should be prepared in advance and consist of the date, name of testers, list of tests used (in order), and seating plan with candidates names, There should also be plenty of space to record occurrences which may have influenced the candidates. The candidates' behaviour (such as acute anxiety, failure to settle down, attitude to testing, giving up before time) should also be recorded in the test log. Entries in the test log should be made in a discrete way in order not to raise anxiety or distract the applicants. A useful ploy is to delay making an entry for one or two minutes after an occurrence.

A single administrator can usually cope with 8–10 candidates, two administrators can usually cope with up to 25 candidates and three administrators can usually cope with 50 candidates. Where several administrators are involved, one administrator should be formally nominated to act as the main administrator who is responsible for test materials, giving explanations, signals to start work and keeping the time. Assistant administrators should be responsible for distribution of materials, answering individual questions and marking tests. In general, the administrators should arrive at the test room 20 minutes before the start of a testing session.

The main administrator should be responsible for introducing the session and the introduction should be worked out in advance. The introduction is crucially important and often done badly. The introduction must achieve two objectives: it must give the candidates the knowledge they need to complete the test, and it must put them in the right frame of mind. The introduction usually starts with the tester giving his or her name and job title, and the name and job titles of assistants. Then it is customary to welcome the candidates and check that they can hear the instructions absolutely clearly. This is followed by a fairly long explanation of the programme, arrangements for refreshments and estimated finishing time. In group testing sessions, it is usually wise to say that in order not to inconvenience non-smokers, smoking is not allowed but there will be breaks when smoking is possible. The administrator should explicitly ask if candidates need spectacles for reading and check that they are available. Names of candidates without their spectacles should be recorded in the test log. The main administrator then invites general questions and when they have been dealt with, a five-minute break is announced so that candidates can visit the cloakroom or collect spectacles.

When the group reassembles, the administrator needs to induce a frame of mind where the candidates lose any anxiety and develop a desire to do the tests as best as they can. To reduce anxiety the administrator may suggest that candidates might like to take off their jackets to get comfortable and explain that the pencil-and-paper exercises are supplemented by other information such as references, interviews, and so on and they are included in order to be fair to everyone and to try to get as much information as possible (note the avoidance of the word 'test', especially the words 'intelligence test'). Next the candidate is reassured that full instructions will be given, and to ensure that everyone is dealt with fairly the instructions will be read from a card. Always explain that each part of the exercise will be preceded by practice items. Finally, the candidates should be reassured that there are no trick questions and that their results will be strictly confidential. The candidates should now be ready for the instructions for specific tests being used and they should be read verbatim, either from the manual or the instruction card for the test.

When reading instructions make sure that any time limits are clearly stated. Often it is necessary to make it absolutely clear that candidates can take their time over practice items. It may also be useful to demonstrate on a flip chart how candidates may alter answers they have already given. Usually it is important to invite questions. Frequent questions are 'Is there any penalty for guessing?' and 'What should I do if I am not completely certain?' Sometimes, candidates ask what a test is supposed to measure. Give a straightforward reply of one or two sentences (for example, 'the ability to solve problems involving shapes'). Avoid answers which might specifically help some candidates or compromise the purpose of the test. A good ploy is to reply 'That is a very good question but I can't give you an answer now because my answer might possibly influence your results!' It might be possible to add that you will give a full answer when the test is finished. Immediately before the test starts, it is wise to say that, 'Once the test starts, I cannot answer questions and that there should be as little noise or disturbance as possible until the end of the test has been announced.' After a few seconds, tour the room checking that candidates are answering in the correct way. Conduct similar tours every few minutes.

When the testing session has finished ask candidates to remain seated until the books and answer sheets have been collected (this makes it easier to check that all materials are returned). As the answer sheets are collected, double check that they bear a readable name. The candidates should then be thanked for their participation and any subsequent stages of selection should be explained. The materials should then be locked away in a secure place and final entries made in the test log.

Marking Tests

The marking of tests should, in theory, be easy and accurate. All that is needed is a marking key which is placed over the answer sheet and the 'correct' answers counted. In practice there is no room for complacency. Indeed, it is probable that at least 5 per cent of the error variance in a typical validity study arises from poor marking procedures. Fewest mistakes are made on simple attainment tests such as the AH4 and the Thurstone Test of Mental Alertness, where it is only necessary to count the number of correct answers. More mistakes are made on scoring systems which involve subtracting the number of wrong answers or making a correction for guessing. Most mistakes are made with scoring keys which require differential weighting of replies (for example, some boxes have a score of 0, some 1 and some 2). In addition to these largely arithmetical sources of error, there are two other major pitfalls: careless markers frequently include duplicate answers where the candidate gives two replies to a question requiring only one; and careless markers may also wrongly include two answers that have been cancelled by candidates. These errors are particularly prevalent on such tests as the 16PF, where candidates are required to tick or blacken a box. Another source of error arises from carelessness of the candidates where they accidentally omit a line from the answer sheet so that their responses get 'out of sync'. Such errors are easy to locate on tests like the AH4 but are virtually impossible to identify on complex tests such as the 16PF or the SH Managerial Interest Scale. When a sudden change in pattern of answers is encountered the marker should explore the possibility of this type of error and, if appropriate, it should be dealt with by repositioning the answer key and giving full credit for misplaced answers which are correct.

In general, markers should aim for a standard where there is no more than one error in marking a group of seven different answer sheets. The main requirement of good marking is to obey the instructions in the manual exactly. Aim to be as systematic as possible and establish a marking rhythm for each test. First examine the test for multiple answers, or answers which are ambiguous, and highlight them with a coloured pen. Do not give credit for ambiguous answers. Next score the test using the key, looking out for answers written in the wrong place. Always check that subscores have been added and transferred correctly. It is usually preferable to have all marking cross-checked by an independent marker. Finally, it is always important to check that the appropriate norm tables are used in interpreting scores.

Test Profiles

Tests containing three or more subscores usually have a profile sheet. These aid interpretation but they should be filled in correctly. It is wrong simply to join the points of the profile as it implies that the scales are related to each other in some order of magnitude.

Instead a histogram where bars protrude from the average can be used. An even better method is to mark the actual scores on a profile and indicate the standard errors surrounding the scores (see Wainer and Thissen, 1981, and also Figure 9.2).

Code of Practice in Using Tests

Tests can cause anxiety and mislead or put people at a disadvantage if they are wrongly used. Test use *must* be governed by a set of principles designed to preserve their confidentiality and usefulness to the

Figure 9.2   Correct method of drawing psychometric profiles

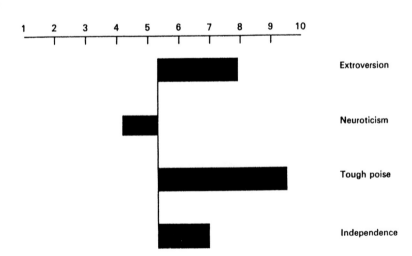

community. The following items represent *some* of the ethical considerations.

1. Tests should only be sold to qualified users.
2. Test confidentiality should be maintained by secure storage and the prevention of 'leakage' by circulation or photocopying.
3. Testing should be carried out under standard conditions.
4. No one should be tested under false pretences: the testee should be informed of the uses to which the results will be put.
5. Test results are confidential and should not be divulged to those who have no right to them or who would not be able to interpret them correctly.
6. If the records are stored on computer, it is usually better that individuals are identified only by number and not by name. Data protection legislation should be strictly followed. If data is stored on a systematic basis, this must usually be registered. Unauthorised access to the data should be prevented by a system of passwords and other security measures. Arrangements should be made to delete information after an appropriate time. In general, tests should not be administered through the mail. The main exceptions to this rule are some simple tests of interest and some ability tests which have been developed for this purpose 'in house' and which are not used for selection by other organisations.
7. People should not be 'coached' for a test.
8. Never use a test which unfairly discriminates against a subgroup in society except, perhaps, as a temporary expedient when the test is less discriminatory than alternative measures.
9. Tests should not be released without adequate research.
10. Tests should not make secret or harmful claims.

Additional aspects of good practice can be obtained from Anastasi (1982); APA (1974 and 1981); USA Government (1978); Division of Occupational Psychology (1983).

TAILORED TESTING

Tailored testing is probably the most significant development in psychological testing in the last two decades. As we shall see later, it holds the promise that an applicant can call an employment office, be seated at a computer terminal and visual display unit (VDU), answer

40 to 50 questions within 10–15 minutes, and be classified as accurately as if he or she had completed a much longer test battery. Tailored testing usually incorporates the principles of item response theory (see Chapter 6).

In essence, tailored testing is based on the notion that a test score is determined by very few items: those items in the difficulty band which lies above the 'floor' where all the answers are correct, and below the ceiling where all the answers are incorrect. The difficulty band is where some answers are correct and some are incorrect. In traditional tests where questions are ordered in level of difficulty, a great deal of time is wasted getting to the correct difficulty band and answering questions which are far too easy. Probably the best review of tailored testing is by Kilcross (1976), who describes a number of approaches to tailored testing.

Flexilevel tests probably form the simplest method which is based on paper and pencil. Questions are arranged in two columns: the first column contains the easier questions and the second contains the harder questions. Across the top of the page is a question of average difficulty and depending upon the answer to this question, the candidate works down either the easy column or the hard column. Betz and Weiss (1975) compared this method with a conventional test and found marginally higher reliability (0.84 versus 0.80), and validity (0.91 versus 0.89), for the flexilevel test.

The next level of complication in tailored testing is to use *two-stage procedures*. For example, candidates are first given a routing test of say, 10 items. On the basis of their scores on this test, they are given a subsequent test of, say, 20 items of the second test.

Flexilevel tests and two-stage tests represent the limit of what is feasible with conventional pencil-and-paper technology (see Lord, 1971). More complex methods have been attempted but they run the risk of involving complex instructions which baffle the candidate and produce invalid test results. In a selection context this might not matter since employers usually seek the most competent candidates and research suggests that it is the less able candidate who is most likely to produce an invalid test result. However, there are equal opportunity implications since minority groups with language difficulties may also produce an above average number of invalid results.

The practical use of tailored testing has been transformed by changes in computer technology. It is now possible to buy a personal computer with high resolution graphics and memories of over 640k for less than the weekly labour costs of a professional employee and even a small company can obtain the benefits of the more advanced techniques of tailored testing. One of the more sophisticated designs are the *branching tests*. For example, a candidate sitting at a VDU may be asked a question at the 50 per cent level of difficulty. If the answer is incorrect he or she is asked a question at the 25 per cent level and so on. Branching tests of this kind are very efficient, but there is the danger that on the basis of one question the candidate may be routed wrongly, and there may be a tendency for the route to 'oscillate' widely as the program seeks appropriate items. To overcome these problems it has been suggested that there should be several questions at each node of the test.

The most sophisticated approach to tailored testing involves probability calculations and *item finding* using item response theory (see Chapter 6). This approach has many advantages. Urry (1977) points out that it is possible to decide in advance how precise the estimate of a candidate's ability must be and to continue testing until this level of precision has been obtained. The item selection approach also has profound implication for test construction. The unit of test construction becomes the item which can be linked to a difficulty level. Thus item banking becomes a real possibility in which a store of thousands of questions, whose difficulty level, reliability and discrimination indices are known, is set up (see Hambleton, Swaminathan, Cook, Eignor and Gifford, 1978).

Tailored testing is very successful when applied to ability tests. It is economical and requires only a third to a half of the testing time of conventional paper-and-pencil testing. Further, the results may be slightly more valid: clever candidates are not given the chance to slip up on easy questions and poor candidates are not given the chance to guess difficult questions. As Urry (1977) indicates, there are still more practical advantages:

(a) walk-in testing could be available in every personnel office;
(b) scores and reports of candidates' suitability for a range of jobs could be computed within seconds at the end of the test;
(c) administration of the test would be completely standardised by the computer, thus reducing the training needed for personnel staff;
(d) increased confidentiality of tests since each candidate is only exposed to a few items.

The use of computers could produce a genre of tests using the colour movement of the video screen. For example, to test strategic ability, a scenario could be established where a chief fire fighter has to reduce the damage caused by forest fires. On the video screen he or she is given a map of the forest, an inventory of resources and the location of the villages. A fire is started in some area and the candidate is required to deploy resources. The situation becomes dynamic, the fire spreads and other fires erupt. The fire fighter needs constantly to adjust the strategy and the computer times and records the decisions that are made (Putz-Osterloh, in press).

As computer and information technology improves, the possibilities become almost endless and could revolutionise test publishing. Instead of maintaining stocks of tests and sometimes being short of *the* test which is required for a specific occasion, companies might simply telephone their local viewdata computer and download the tailored test they require. The results would be uploaded to the computer thus improving the background data on the items used and enhancing the reliability and validity of the results. In a really brave new world of tailored testing, test construction would be international. There would be no major obstacle to organisations in Wyoming, Winnipeg, Woomera and Whaley Bridge using and contributing to the same data band.

Bias of Tests

Racial bias of tests

Many of the investigations under this heading have not been concerned with bias *per se*, but with the rather different topic of differential validity. Differential validity exists when a test or other measure is valid for the majority group but not for the minority group, and vice versa. Differential validity is always important from the viewpoint of accurate selection, but it is only partially relevant to bias in selection. There are circumstances where using a test which is valid for whites and not valid for blacks is, racially, quite fair. Bartlett and O'Leary (1969) examine six possible types of differential validity and find four of them to be fair.

Concern about the consequences of differential validity escalated during the 1960s in response to highly publicised court cases such as the Motorola case, and psychologists such as Berdie (1971) suggested that tests have been misused because psychologists have failed to take account of the differences in validity that tests have for different populations. Subsequent analysis and research have indicated that such fears of differential validity are confounded. A classic analysis by Boem (1972) examined 160 validity coefficients derived from diverse samples of medical technicians, craftsmen, clerical workers, administrators, welders, and so on, and found only 33 examples of single group validity; they further concluded that these instances of single group validity appear to be related to the use of ratings as criteria and to the use of small samples. Gael and Grant (1972) examined service representatives and concluded that the validity coefficients for black and white applicants were comparable, and that common test standards could be used to evaluate minority and non-minority job applicants. Ruch (1972) also re-analysed studies of differential validity.

The empirical finding that differential validity is rare was extended by conceptual developments. Schmidt and Hunter (1978) point out that many of the studies of differential validity have used very small samples, especially for the minority groups. Consequently, the correlations based on these small samples are very unstable and fluctuate within a wide range. It follows that many of the low correlations for minority groups are merely random fluctuations of correlations similar to those obtained for the majority group (Schmidt, Berner and Hunter, 1973; Hunter and Schmidt, 1978). In an extremely rigorous analysis of 866 validity studies comparing blacks and whites, involving control over statistical artefacts and a combined sample size of 185 487 data points, Hunter, Schmidt and Hunter (1979) concluded that there is no apparent evidence of differential validity. Furthermore, they could find no evidence to support the hypothesis that differential validity is more likely to arise when subjective criteria are used. In order to avoid the artefacts introduced by the use of small samples, investigators should clearly consult tables giving appropriate sample sizes for investigations of this kind (for example, Trattner and O'Leary, 1980).

Unfortunately, the fact that differential validity rarely exists does not completely settle the question of racial bias in tests. Validity coefficients rely essentially upon correlations, and correlations merely indicate that the pattern of the results are similar: there may be absolute differences. Since the absence of differential validity can co-exist with certain types of bias, alternative types of evidence must be considered.

Earlier, in Chapter 8, it was noted that the internal consistency of a test can be used as evidence of bias. Jensen (1977) undertook an internal consistency analysis of the Wonderlic Personnel Test (a measure of intelligence). He compared the rank order of the questions of the test according to the percentage of each group passing each question, the assumption being that if some of the items were unfair to blacks, they would appear much lower down the list. On the basis of the results he concluded that the Wonderlic shows very little evidence of cultural bias.

Probably the best type of evidence of bias is to regress test scores against criterion data. A number of studies have employed this strategy. Ruch (1972) re-analysed 20 validity studies to check regression coefficients for blacks and whites. He found that 64 per cent of the regressions did not show any significant differences compared with the 86 per cent (or slightly less) which would be expected to be free from significant differences by chance alone. A re-analysis by Jensen (1980) indicated that there was rarely any difference in either the slope or the standard error of the regression, but there was a significant and consistent bias for the intercepts. He goes on to note that the white intercept is usually higher than that for blacks and consequently if the regression equation for whites is used to predict the criterion measure for blacks, the average performance of the blacks will be over predicted.

A landmark study was conducted by J.T. Campbell, Crooks, Mahoney and Rock (1973). The six-year study involved 1400 government workers employed in jobs where there were objective criteria and sufficient numbers of blacks to provide adequate samples. Again it was found that the minority group's performance is over-predicted when the formulae for a majority group is used. These are not isolated results. Similar findings have also been obtained by Guinn, Tupes and Aley (1970), Foley (1971) and Thomas (1975). In a slightly different context of college selection Linn (1973) reviewed the regression equations used for selection in 22 racially-integrated colleges. He found that the college performance of blacks was over predicted in 18 cases and in no college was their performance underpredicted.

Sex bias of tests

There is much less information concerning the sex bias of tests. In terms of differential validity it has been consistently found that validity coefficients for women are nearly always slightly higher than the validity coefficients for men. Initially this finding emerged from studies in educational settings (for example, Seashore, 1962; Stanley, 1967). More recently, Schmitt, Mellon and Bylenga (1978) collected 6219 validity (from employment settings) pairs which had been published in three leading journals. In employment settings, it was found that the validity coefficients of males tended to be higher by 0.038. Of course, this difference is very small.

Arnold, Rauschenberger, Soubel and Guion (1982) used physical tests, such as lifting 34 kg bags, shovelling slag, climbing on a ladder and carrying 23 kg bags in order to predict success as steelworkers. They found higher validities for females. They also undertook a regression analysis and noted that a combined regression line would result in a slight bias against men. A study by Bickel, Hammel and O'Connell (1975) showed that, contrary to first impressions, there was a small but statistically significant selection bias in favour of women at the University of California in Berkeley.

Tests and bias against older or handicapped people

Very little research has been conducted into the age bias of tests even though a prima facie case could be made out that older applicants would produce lower performance in tests than on job performance. The situation concerning bias against handicapped people is even more confused since so much would depend upon the nature of the handicap. For example, there seems no reason why intelligence tests should be biased against epileptics, but they may be biased against people with defective vision or motor co-ordination. Consequently, separate studies would be needed for each type of handicap, and the difficulties in obtaining adequate samples are quite formidable.

10 Traditional Selection Procedures

INTERVIEWS

Interviews are a very common method of selection. Industry must spend enormous amounts of money each year paying interviewers' expenses and providing accommodation, yet there is evidence that some of the money is not particularly well spent. Psychologists have known for more than half a century that some interviews have relatively little value. For example, in 1929 Hollingsworth conducted a study in which 12 experienced sales managers arrived at independent personnel selection decisions. The results were appalling. One candidate was ranked first by one interviewer and last by another. A second candidate was ranked both sixth and fifty-sixth.

The major purpose of any selection interview is, of course, to identify the most appropriate candidate for the job in question, but interviews can and do fulfil other important functions. These might include providing the candidate with information about the organisation and promoting good public relations. The additional functions of interviews are mentioned later in this chapter. To begin with, however, discussion will focus on the selection function of interviews.

Traditional and Modern Selection Interviews

It is important to emphasise a point alluded to above: all interviews are not the same. In fact research in the last 10 years or so has shown that it is very important to distinguish between traditional *psychological* interviews (following a rather loose structure and concentrating on identifying characteristics of the candidate thought to be important in the job), and *highly structured job-related* interviews, such as situational interviews (Latham, Saari, Pursell and Campion, 1980). Some of the material concerning interviews presented in this chapter is derived from research on traditional interviews, although much of the more recent work on interviewing has concentrated on highly structured, job-related forms of interviewing. This has been an irresistible and sensible trend since the discovery that these kinds of interviews produce better predictive validity (see Weisner and Cronshaw, 1988).

In essence, the selection function of interviews can be divided into two parts: obtaining reliable and valid data about applicants, and using this information to arrive at a decision. In some organisations these two aspects are dealt with by different people. Personnel specialists, for example, may focus on collecting data and line managers may concentrate on decision-making.

Like any other selection method, interviews need to be both reliable and valid. Interview reliability revolves around two main issues: first, the extent to which different interviewers agree in their evaluation of candidates (inter-judge reliability) and, second, the extent to which an interviewer makes the same assessment of the same candidate on different occasions (intra-judge reliability).

Although there are some studies that demonstrate high inter-judge reliability (for example, Latham *et al.*, 1980), most of the evidence is consistent (for example, Ulrich and Trumbo, 1965) and suggests, that for traditional interviews, inter-judge reliability is not high but the reliability of structured interviews is acceptable (Weekley and Gier, 1987; M. A. Campion, Pursell and Brown, 1988; Maurer and Fay, 1988; Robertson, 1990). Intra-judge reliability is often reasonably good but there are obvious complicating factors, such as the influence of memory and bias.

In general terms, studies of predictive validity suggest that traditional selection interviews do not provide particularly useful methods for predicting future job performance. The mean validity coefficient is less than +0.2 (see Reilly and Chao, 1982; Arvey and Campion, 1982). Despite this rather gloomy background research, the traditional interview is still used widely (Shackleton and Newell, 1991).

Obtaining Data and Information about Applicants

To obtain accurate information, the following are necessary.

1. The interviewer must have a clear grasp of the characteristics the applicants need in order to be able to perform the job (based on job analysis).
2. The interviewer must be able to 'question' the applicants in a way that is likely to produce information. He or she should not miss any major areas.

3. The interviewee must be prepared and able to give information required. Most interviewees are not enthusiastic about divulging unfavourable information and many interviewees are not able to put into words their experience and capabilities.
4. All candidates should be given an equal opportunity.

Many experienced interviewers make use of structured interview guides, either semi-structured, where certain broad subject areas are covered, or structured interviews, where the interviewer follows a prescribed list of questions. It seems likely that a structured guide provides the interviewer with a better basis for meeting the conditions outlined above. Following a guide will help to ensure, for example, that interviewers do not omit any major areas of information. It may provide an interviewer with a better opportunity to give relevant information and also reduce the likelihood of distortion or bias. In fact, although there is little evidence to support the superiority of one interview structure over any other, the available evidence does suggest that the use of structured formats is beneficial (Weisner and Cronshaw, 1988; Wright, Lichenfels and Pursell, 1989).

Structured Interviews

Several different formats have been developed for structured interview formats. One successful format was developed by Latham *et al.* (1980); their procedure, known as situational interviewing, has been used successfully in subsequent research in the USA (Latham and Saari, 1984; Weekley and Gier, 1987) and UK (Robertson, Gratton and Rout, 1990). Other approaches to structured interviewing include behaviour description interviews (see Janz, 1989) and an approach reported by M. A. Campion, Pursell and Brown (1988). Campion, Pursell and Brown (1988) provide an overview of the technique, most of which can be applied to all successful structured interviews. The first three features are of particular importance.

The first step is to *develop questions based on job analysis*. The results of meta-analytic studies of employment interviews have made it clear that interviews based on job analysis have better validity than those not based on job analysis (see Harris, 1989). Clearly one of the major benefits of conducting a thorough job analysis prior to developing selection procedures (such as interview questions) is to help to ensure that the content of the job and the main competencies required for successful job performance are adequately reflected in the selection procedure. The kind of questions used in the different interview approaches may vary. For example, the situational interview approach uses questions that ask candidates how they *would* behave in various realistic job situations. In contrast to the situational interview which asks about future behaviour, the questions in behaviour description interviews focus on past behaviour. The second feature of structured interviewing identified by M. A. Campion, Pursell and Brown (1988) involves ensuring that *each candidate is asked the same questions*. Although this is generally true, some of the approaches require that candidates are asked standardised, rather than identical questions. For example, the interviewers in the Robertson, Gratton and Rout (1990) study selected specific questions from a bank of questions within a predetermined set of categories (based on job analysis). All candidates were asked the same number of standardised questions from each category, but not precisely the same questions.

Step three involves anchoring the rating scales for scoring answers with examples and illustrations. Developing a structured interview does not merely involve preparing a set of suitable questions, based on job analysis; it is also important to provide interviewers with a *systematic scoring procedure* to maximise the reliability and validity of their judgements about candidates. Some investigators have developed rating scales using the procedure for BARS (P. L. Smith and Kendall, 1963). Whatever procedure is used to develop the rating scale it is important to ensure consistency and objectivity of scoring. Frequent checks on reliability (including inter-rater reliability) are highly desirable. Indeed a further point made by M. A. Campion, Pursell and Brown (1988) is that a panel of interviewers should be used to rate and record candidates' performance. They suggest that the panel should independently rate and record candidates' replies during the interview. This procedure would provide a continuing check on inter-interviewer reliability. Other points made by Campion *et al.* (1988) are that the whole interview process should be administered consistently to all candidates, and that special attention should be given to job-relatedness, fairness and documentation of the procedures.

In the absence of a clear procedure like the one outlined above, interviewers are likely to behave inconsistently and in a manner that is less likely to lead to good decision-making. Even when interviewers make some attempt to follow a structure and question the candidate about specific job-related issues, they do not necessarily use the interview to *obtain* information: often they spend more time talking *at* the interviewee and *giving* information. Daniels and Otis (1950) found that interviewees talked for only about 30 per cent of the time.

Even when interviewers are clear on the qualities needed for good job performance, follow a sensible structure and give the candidates a chance to speak, the candidates may not be prepared to give accurate replies. Weiss and Davis (1960) checked the replies of interviewees with their former employers and other factual sources. The accuracy depended on the subject area of the question, but even in those areas where accuracy was greatest (such as job title and pay), about a fifth of candidates give misleading replies. Not all of the discrepancies are due to distortion and lying on the part of the candidates: their memory may be faulty and some of the employers may not have been able to give accurate replies. Nevertheless, if most candidates upgraded themselves by the same extent, the effect would cancel out and would not influence the selection decision. However, some candidates may seriously distort the answers they give.

Interviewing as a Social Process

An interview can be described as a conversation with a purpose. In other words, it is rather like many of the social interactions that we take part in but with some particular constraints and purposes of its own. Herriot (1981, p. 165) described it as follows:

> The selection interview is a rule-governed social interaction with clearly defined reciprocal roles allocated to both parties. For example, it is considered appropriate for the interviewer to take charge of the situation and to ask questions of the applicant. The applicant is expected to wait until invited to do so before asking questions.

Using the framework of attribution theory (for example, Kelley and Michela, 1980), Herriot argued that the frequently observed low validities of employment interviews can in part be explained by the fact that the interviewer and interviewee may not have a common understanding of their roles, and/or the interviewer may misinterpret the candidate's behaviour. In essence, attribution theory focuses on the way we make judgements of others and provides a number of principles to help understand how such judgements take place.

According to attribution theory, an important feature that determines the view that we develop of another person is their 'in-role' or 'out-of-role' behaviour. Someone behaving in-role is merely behaving in a way that is appropriate to the situation. Thus their behaviour can be attributed more to the circumstances (even impatient people stand in queues sometimes) than to any personal characteristics they may have. When someone behaves out-of-role, however, it may be more appropriate to attribute their behaviour to *them* rather than to the *situation*. Ross (1977) referred to an important and pervasive attribution error that people are prone to make. In essence it involves attributing too much of the cause of behaviour to personal factors and too little to the situation. Herriot (1981, p. 168) showed how this might apply to the selection interview:

> When we apply this bias to the selection interview it would result in the drawing of dispositional inferences from in-role behaviour. In other words the good interviewee (who obeys the rules of the interview as seen by the interviewer) becomes the good applicant.
>
> Furthermore, out-of-role behaviour may be taken to indicate a bad applicant, rather than treated as valuable data appropriate to dispositional attribution in general.

What Herriot (1981, 1989) and other writers (for example, Lewis, 1980) have drawn attention to is the important fact that an interview is an interactive social process and is potentially subject to all of the associated problems of faulty communications and judgement by both parties. As such it is a personnel selection technique that is different in many important ways from other techniques, such as psychological tests.

Training Interviewers

The idea that experience alone can produce good interviewers or that most people are 'naturally' good judges of others is not supported by research evidence (for example, Carlson, 1967). Even 'commonsense' is sometimes not as helpful as it may seem as far as interviews are concerned. Dipboye, Fontenelle and Garner (1984), for example, have shown that it is *not* always helpful to preview the information on a candidate before conducting an employment interview.

In an attempt to maximise the quality of selection interviews, many organisations attempt to ensure that their interviewers receive some form of systematic training. It is difficult to generalise about the benefits of all interview training but, in as much as it is possible to draw general conclusions, it seems that interview training that involves opportunities for practice, discussion and feedback can be effective in improving interview performance. Howard and his colleagues (Howard and Dailey, 1979; Howard, Dailey and Gulanick, 1979) have examined the value of the five-day interview training courses that involve a mixture of practice, discussion, demonstration and feedback, and the evidence that they present suggests that these courses are effective. Other researchers have also investigated the impact of training on interviewer performance and produced mixed results. Dougherty, Ebert and Callender (1986) found that training appeared to produce significant improvements in the validity of interviewers' judgements. On the other hand, Maurer and Fay (1988) found that training did not improve inter-rater reliability.

The most common format for interview training courses involves trainees in conducting role play interviews at various stages. Frequently their performance is recorded on videotape and played back to them together with feedback from the trainer and other trainees. It is rare for trainees to be shown an example of an interview being conducted in a 'model' fashion. Recent research work seems to suggest that the format of role play followed by feedback may be less effective than a format involving the use of model interviewers.

In the context of interview training the value of modelling remains unproven. Maybe interview trainers lack the courage, commitment or skill (or all three) to produce and use the model videotapes! In other areas, particularly supervisory training, behaviourial modelling has produced some extremely impressive results (for example, A. P. Goldstein and Sorcher, 1974; Latham and Saari, 1979; Decker, 1982; J. S. Russel, Wexley and Hunter, 1984). Robertson (1989) has provided a review of the work on behaviour-modelling training.

In an attempt to help interviewers do a better job a variety of 'how to interview' guides exist (for example, J. M. Smith, 1982), and many courses are based on the sort of advice given in these guides. Many of the 'how to interview' courses and books are useful and cover ground that seems to be important in the development of interviewing skills (for example, types of questions to use, encouraging candidates to talk, common judgemental errors and how to avoid them). Despite the likely value of such training it is worth noting Arvey and Campion's (1982, p. 317) stricture: 'There is a dearth of guidelines and suggestions concerning the improvement of interview effectiveness based on *research* findings. Instead many guidelines, suggestions, how to interview workshops and techniques are founded on intuition, beliefs and what seems more comfortable, rather than on research results.' Arvey and Campion made their point in 1982. Since then some solid *research* findings have produced clear guidance on how to improve selection interviews. These findings have shown quite clearly that highly structured, job related interviews produce improved validity.

Behaviour and Decision-Making during the Interview

Some fairly systematic information exists concerning what takes place during real life traditional employment interviews and what links exist between behaviour during the interview and the outcome (for example, accept/reject decisions). Hollandsworth, Kazelskis, Stevens and Dressel (1979) identified three different types of communication that are important in interviews. These are *verbal* behaviour (that is, what is said), *non-verbal* behaviour (for example, gestures, eye movement) and *articulative* behaviour (for example, loudness of voice, fluency of speech). Several studies have shown that non-verbal and articulative behaviour seem to be important in interview settings, although many of these studies have been conducted in simulated rather than real interviews.

A study by Forbes and Jackson (1980) looked at the links between the non-verbal behaviour of candidates and selection decisions in real life interviews. In interviews where the candidate was subsequently rejected there was more gaze avoidance and eye wandering on the part of the candidate; there was also less smiling and head movement compared with 'accept' interviews. Accept interviews were also characterised by higher levels of eye contact. This research is interesting and informative but one must be careful not to draw erroneous conclusions about the *causes* and effects involved. It is not clear, for instance, whether lack of eye contact causes subsequent rejection or whether an awareness of possible subsequent rejection on the part of the candidate, the interviewer, or both *leads* to a lack of eye contact.

Parsons and Liden (1984) found that speech patterns showed a link with interview ratings, even when objective information was taken into account. In an interesting study Gifford, Ng and Wilkinson (1985) investigated the extent to which interviewers made use of non-verbal cues to draw inferences about candidates' motivation and social skills.

Hollandsworth *et al.* (1979) investigated the relative importance of various aspects of verbal, non-verbal and articulative behaviour. In some real-life interviews, interviewers were asked if they would select each candidate. Their responses would vary along a four-point scale (not a chance; probably not; probably; definitely).

The most important variable, in terms of its links with post-interview decision, was 'appropriateness of content', followed by 'fluency of speech'; 'composure' came next and 'personal appearance' was also important, but to a lesser extent. What this study demonstrates fairly clearly is that *what* the candidate says is of major importance. Despite this finding it is also clear that the non-verbal behaviour of candidates does affect interviewer decisions. N. Anderson and Shackleton (1990) studied the links between interviewers' impressions of candidates' personality and non-verbal behaviour and outcome decisions. The impressions of non-verbal behaviour studied included eye contact, hand gestures, head movements, posture, postural changes and facial expressions and the interviewers' impressions of candidates' personalities included ratings of boring-interesting and dominant–submissive. They found that interviewers' impressions of candidates' personalities were related to the candidates' non-verbal behaviour and that interviewers' outcome decisions were, in turn, related to their impressions of candidate personality. They also found that interviewers' impression formation was affected by personal liking for the candidate and the extent to which the candidate was seen as 'similar to me (the interviewer)'.

Keenan and Wedderburn (1980) presented some data on the content of discussions during real-life (graduate selection) interviews. Somewhat surprisingly, their study revealed that data concerned with academic aspects of university life (for example, a knowledge of subjects studied) were not extensively discussed. These are issues that the interviewees probably expected to be dealt with in detail, and with which they might have felt more comfortable. As Herriot and Rothwell (1981) have shown, there appear to be considerable differences between applicants' expectations of what will be covered in the interview and by whom, and their actual experience. Keenan and Wedderburn (1980) divided the topics discussed into six general categories:

(a) family and school background;
(b) university life (non-academic aspects);
(c) university (academic aspects);
(d) knowledge of job and company;
(e) extra-curricular activities;
(f) personal circumstances and requirements.

The most popular area for discussion was knowledge of job and company. As Keenan and Wedderburn suggested, it could well be that this is the area where *interviewers* feel most at ease; thus, rather than spreading the discussion across a range of potential topics, the interviewers focus the discussion on the topic that is most comfortable for them. It is interesting to note that knowledge of the job and company is the topic that produces most anxiety on the part of the candidates.

When unstructured interviews are used and interviewers have the freedom to compose and ask their own questions, a number of potential difficulties emerge when they are expected to interpret or weight information and come to a decision.

First, it is very difficult for interviewers to remember all the information obtained in an interview. Research suggests that, at the close of the interview, the interviewer has forgotten much of the information obtained, particularly when an unstructured approach is used.

Second, many interviewers make a decision before all the information has been obtained. Springbett (1958) suggested that interviewers make up their minds in the first four minutes and then spend the remainder of the time looking for information which supports their snap judgement. The idea that interviewers make snap judgements has recently been rejected (Buckley and Eder 1988). The whole issue of confirmatory bias in interviewers' strategy has been investigated in more recent studies (see Sackett, 1982; McDonald and Hakel, 1985; Dipboye and Macan, 1988; Binning, Goldstein, Garcia and Scattaregia, 1988). Taken overall the research has not found consistent support for confirmatory bias although one study (Binning *et al.*, 1988) did find evidence of some bias. These results do not, however, show that initial impressions have no influence. Indeed a related but separate stream of research has shown just how important first impressions of candidates can be. Work by Dipboye and his colleagues (see Dipboye, Fontenelle and Garner, 1984; Dipboye, Stramler and Fontenelle, 1984) has shown that previewing candidates' application forms has an effect (often adverse) on subsequent interviewer behaviour and information recall. Indeed Dipboye and his colleagues propose that, if the purpose of the interview is to make a selection decision, it is better *not* to preview candidates' application forms.

Third, there is the problem of differing standards. Some interviewers are hard to please and others are very 'soft touches'.

Fourth, there is the problem of how interviewers weight and integrate the information available to them. Hakel, Dobmay and Dunnette (1970) suggested that where selectors had information concerning scholastic standing, business experience and interests and abilities, selectors gave most weight to scholastic standing. Keenan (1976) suggested that interviewers of undergraduate students organise information under four headings:

(a)   motivation to succeed;
(b)   knowledge about the job;
(c)   quality of university references;
(d)   academic performance.

Some research has suggested that interviewers tend to give too much weight to negative information, and some work has suggested that interviewers tend to emphasise any behaviour which is unexpected (Bolsher and Springbett, 1961). Recent research (such as Rowe, 1989) has focused on explaining why interviewers give more weight to unfavourable information.

Although in some respects most interviewers behave in similar ways there are also differences between interviewers and although little is known about the characteristics of good interviewers research has suggested that some people are better than others (Dougherty, Ebert and Callender, 1986). There is also clear evidence to suggest that interviewers do behave differently and respond to applicants selectively. Applicants who are perceived to be better qualified (before the interview) are likely to be treated differently from applicants perceived to have less impressive qualifications. Macau and Dipboye (1988), for example, found differences in the number and difficulty of questions asked.

Bias of Interviews

Interviews are essentially interactive occasions which result in subjective judgements. In theory, interviews could be more prone to conscious and subconscious bias than tests. In practice, findings concerning interview bias are not easily organised into a logical sequence. Although a regression approach is technically feasible, it has not been widely used. Since interview judgements are usually global judgements, the internal consistency approach is not possible and most investigators have, therefore, been forced to use the experimental approach.

Racial bias of interviews

Reilly and Chao (1982) attempted to bring together evidence of bias in interviews. Interviews might also be expected to give rise to bias since the subjective impressions of the interviewer are often decisive. After reviewing 12 studies Reilly and Chao conclude, 'Nor is there any evidence that interviews will have less adverse impact than tests.'

Sex bias of interviews

Interviews differ from most other methods of selection because physical attractiveness may be taken into account. Heilman and Saruwatari (1979) and Heilman (1980) investigated the possible bias of attractiveness by asking 45 college students to evaluate application forms and photographs of men and women applicants for either a clerical or management position. Male candidates who were 'attractive' always tended to obtain higher evaluations, but with female candidates the situation was more complex. When attractive women were applying for clerical jobs, they obtained higher ratings, but when attractive women were applying for managerial jobs, they obtained lower ratings than the unattractive women. There is evidence that the sex bias is strongly influenced by the context, especially the proportion of women applicants. Heilman suggests that when less than 25 per cent of the applicants are women, there is a greater level of bias against women. A further contextual factor is the type of interviewer. It is surprising that no authoritative study could be located which attempted to establish whether female interviewers also give lower ratings to female interviewees. A final contextual influence is the personality of the interviewer. Work by Simas and McCarrey (1979) suggests that 'high authoritarian' selectors were more likely to offer jobs to men, and this was true for both male and female personnel officers.

Disability bias of interviews

There is also a paucity of information concerning bias against disabled people. Arvey's (1979) review supported the notion that disabled applicants are usually given credit for higher motivation, but they are less likely to be given job offers. Stone and Sawatzki (1980) produced taped interviews of applicants who had a psychiatric disability or a

physical disability or no disability; applicants who had had two
nervous breakdowns were less likely to be offered jobs.

Additional Functions of Interviewers

It is important to remember that there are two main parties to every
interview: the interviewer(s) and the candidate. In many interviews the
candidate will be gaining important information concerning the job
and the organisation, and on the basis of this and other relevant
information will decide whether to accept the appointment or not (if an
offer is made). Not all post-interview job offers are accepted by
candidates, and in many cases it seems likely that information gleaned
by candidates at the interview is crucial in their decision-making. As
Murphy (1986) has shown, when preferred candidates reject job offers
this can have a damaging effect on the utility (see Chapter 12) of the
selection procedure.

The decision to apply for a job and, if it is offered, to accept or reject
it, involves some self-examination and an attempt to compare one's
own abilities, experiences and preferences with the requirements and
opportunities of the job on offer. Inevitably this matching is sometimes
not as efficient as might be hoped, resulting in labour turnover and
costs to the organisation and individual concerned. Interviews provide
one opportunity to improve this match by giving candidates realistic
information about the job and organisation in question.

Some investigators have studied the effects of more extensive
attempts to provide RJPs. The evidence (see Reilly, Blood, Brown
and Maletsa, 1981) suggests that RJPs have little impact on turnover.

Reilly *et al.* suggested that the main advantage of RJPs lies in
communicating a favourable organisational image (see Popovich and
Wanous, 1982). Tenopyr and Oeltjen (1982, p. 586) made the following
comments:

> It can be concluded that it would be unfair to expect too much from
> RJPs. Their primary objective should be to take much of the
> discussion of job content out of the employment interview, which is
> not the best place to inform applicants about the job anyway, since
> interviewers often are not a credible source of information.

Research by Dean and Wanous (1984) assessed the effects of three
types of preview (realistically specific, realistically general and no
preview). They found that overall job survival rates were not related to

type of preview but that the *rate* at which turnover occurred was significantly different.

The characteristics of the interviewer and his or her behaviour during the interview are often cited as important influences on candidates' intentions to accept or reject job offers. A number of studies have examined this issue and early research (see Schmitt and Coyle, 1976) did seem to suggest that interviewer characteristics/ behaviour did have an impact on candidates' intentions. More recent studies (mostly focusing on initial recruitment 'milk-round' interviews on American university campuses) have failed to find a strong effect due to interviewer behaviour or characteristics. The complicating factor in this research is that the effects of perceived attributes of the organisation or job on offer are difficult to separate from effects on candidates' intentions that are a direct result of the interviewer. In some field studies where attempts have been made to separate these factors clearly (see Powell, 1984) direct effects due to interviewers have not been observed, though some studies have found an effect (see Harris and Fink, 1987). Further work is needed to clarify the impact that interviewers have on candidates. It seems to be the case that candidates perceive interviewers differently (Fletcher, 1983). Fletcher and Spencer (1984) found that interviewees of both sexes felt that they would be less willing to talk about certain topics (such as family life) or behave in certain ways (for example, disagreeing) with male interviewers. Young and Heneman (1986) found that the interviewers' personality was related to the candidates' perception of how likely they were to receive a job offer. As noted above, whether candidates' perceptions of interviewers then influence their job acceptance intentions is unclear.

Interview Validity Reconsidered

Research on the validity of employment interviews has passed through a number of phases. Initially the inconsistent research evidence and frequently low validities observed in research studies led to the pessimistic conclusion that interview validity was low. During the 1980s, triggered by the work of Hunter, Schmidt and colleagues (for example, Hunter, Schmidt and Jackson, 1982) researchers became much more aware of the possibility that statistical artefacts (sampling error, unreliability, range restriction) could be limiting the observed validities of many selection procedures, including interviews. More recent meta-analytic research (Weisner and Cronshaw, 1988) has shown that even unstructured interviews may have better validity than previously thought. These meta-analyses and other empirical research (see Janz, 1982; Orpen, 1985) have also made clear that structured interviews provide better predictions of subsequent job behaviour than traditional, unstructured interviews. Dreher, Ash and Hancock (1988) have proposed that, despite the recent more optimistic view of interview validity, further improved estimates of validity may be forthcoming. They argue that the traditional research design ignores the fact that validity may differ for different interviewers. Most validation studies collapse data across interviewers and, as research cited earlier has shown, there is some evidence to show that some interviewers are better than others. Dreher, Ash and Hancock argue that more sophisticated research designs and analytical procedures are needed to provide a clearer view of the validity of employment interviewing.

REFERENCES

In his review of the literature on reference reports in personnel selection, Muchinsky (1979) pointed out that, 'Of all the more commonly used personnel selection devices, reference reports are the most underresearched' (p. 287). He concluded that over 80 per cent of the respondents requested reference checks as part of their selection procedures. Whilst these studies show that references are frequently *requested* by organisations, they do not show whether they are *used* by organisations when making personnel selection decisions. References might be used to fulfil at least two different functions: first, they can be used to confirm information provided by the applicant; second, they can be used to obtain views on the previous work performance or personal characteristics of the applicant. In the writers' experience some organisations take up references only after an employment offer has been made. References taken at this stage are used (probably) to confirm self-report information and as a last-minute check that the candidate is not grossly unsuitable. References taken up at this stage are clearly not being used to influence decisions. A more recent review of the research on references (Dobson, 1989) has shown that there has been no upsurge of interest in research into the validity of references. The evidence that is available (Reilly and Chao, 1982; Hunter and Hunter, 1984) has shown that references provide poor levels of predictive validity.

Reilly and Chao reviewed seven different studies examining the validity of references and showed that validity coefficients greater than + 0.2 were rare. They calculated that the average validity coefficient for the studies considered was + 0.14. In addition to fairly low validity coefficients there are other drawbacks associated with the use of references for selection purposes. Like self-assessments, references appear to be prone to leniency errors. Browning (1968), for example, used a rating scale to obtain information and found that all of the mean ratings obtained were above 3 on a 4-point scale.

References should be used, if they are used at all, to identify a small proportion of people who should not be considered further. Many organisations do, of course, take up references early in the selection process. Reference checks are often elicited from previous employers but many other sources are used as referees and reference requests take a variety of forms, varying from a pre-prepared form to an open-ended invitation to provide information about the candidate.

Obtaining references may also be a problem; J.N. Mosel and Goheen (1959), for example, reported a response rate of 56 per cent. Although Carroll and Nash (1972) eventually obtained a return rate of 85 per cent, a previous effort produced a return of only 35 per cent. Several practical questions concerning the collection and use of references are also important and, although some guidance can be found in the existing literature, it is clear that more research is needed before definitive answers are available. Mehrabian (1965) and Wiens, Jackson, Manaugh and Matarazza (1969) have suggested that there is a link between the referee's attitude to the candidate and the length of a reference. In a simulation study Wiens *et al.* found a difference in length of references for 'liked' and 'disliked' candidates. Referees who 'liked' a candidate tended to write longer references. The differences in length were still apparent when specific instructions, 'you are to discuss his (her) character, intelligence, ability and perseverance at work' (p. 265), were given.

Other practical questions include whether previous employers provide more valid references than other referees, the form in which references should be collected, and how the resulting data are scored or interpreted. Most research studies focus on references obtained from previous employers. Although it seems sensible to expect employers' references to be more soundly based, there is little evidence to support this expectation.

References can be obtained using an open-ended format or, as seems more common in research on references, a predetermined format is used, such as ratings on various dimensions (Browning, 1968), forced-choice questionnaire format (Carroll and Nash, 1972) or a checklist. It is also possible to use telephone rather than written reference checks. Again, clear evidence on the superiority of one form of reference over another is not yet available.

After reviewing much of the literature Reilly and Chao concluded that: 'The reference check has relatively low validity in employment settings. Even if validity were higher, the utility of reference checks would seem to be limited, because of low reliability, leniency error and poor response rates by previous employers' (p. 38).

Bias of References

References, like interview judgements, offer a great deal of scope for both direct and indirect bias, but Reilly and Chao (1982) could only find one empirical investigation of the phenomena. They report that 1.9 per cent of black applicants received negative references compared to 0.9 per cent of white applicants. As the sample sizes were large these differences were statistically significant, but the practical significance was negligible since the acceptance rate for blacks was 99 per cent of the acceptance rate for whites. In terms of predictive validity, reference checks were marginally valid for both black and white groups.

11 Modern Selection Procedures

WORK-SAMPLE TESTS

The use of some form of test is a feature of many personnel selection procedures. Often these tests take the form of a pencil-and-paper psychological test (for example, general intelligence, numerical ability, aptitude or personality). To the designer of the personnel selection procedure the rationale for using the chosen tests will be perfectly clear. In a well-designed scheme, job analysis and other preparatory work will have identified the psychological characteristics that are thought to be good predictors of successful job performance. Tests will then have been selected to identify the candidates who display these desired characteristics. From the point of view of the candidates, however, the justification for the chosen tests may well be less clear. Often candidates are asked to display behaviour that is rather different from the behaviour that they will eventually be expected to display at work. Thus an applicant for a job as a machine operator may be expected to take tests of general intelligence, numerical aptitude and mechanical aptitude. The potential machine operator may well not be asked to operate any machinery.

Wernimont and Campbell (1968) have commented on this traditional method of choosing predictors. They note that there seems to be an implicit or explicit insistence among applied psychologists that predictors should be somehow different from criteria. Further, Wernimont and Campbell argue that for effective selection it would be more appropriate to make use of predictors that are not different from criteria. They argue in favour of using predictors that are realistic samples of behaviour and are actually as similar to criteria as possible. Asher and Sciarrino (1974) have made a very similar point arguing for what they describe as point-to-point correspondence between predictors and criteria. In other words, the behaviour a predictor requires of the candidate and the conditions under which the candidate is expected to display this behaviour should be as similar as possible to the criterion (that is, actual work behaviour).

Over the past 25 years or so researchers have deliberately attempted to produce valid predictors that are as similar as possible to the desired criterion behaviours. Rather than using psychological tests or other 'signs' of behaviour, this research has explored the extent to which realistic 'samples' of work behaviour can be used as predictors of subsequent job performance. This approach – 'work sampling' – involves identifying a task or set of tasks representative of the job in question, and using these tasks for pre-employment testing. Figure 11.1 provides a comparison of work-sampling and 'traditional' approaches.

Figure 11.1 Work-sampling and 'traditional' approaches

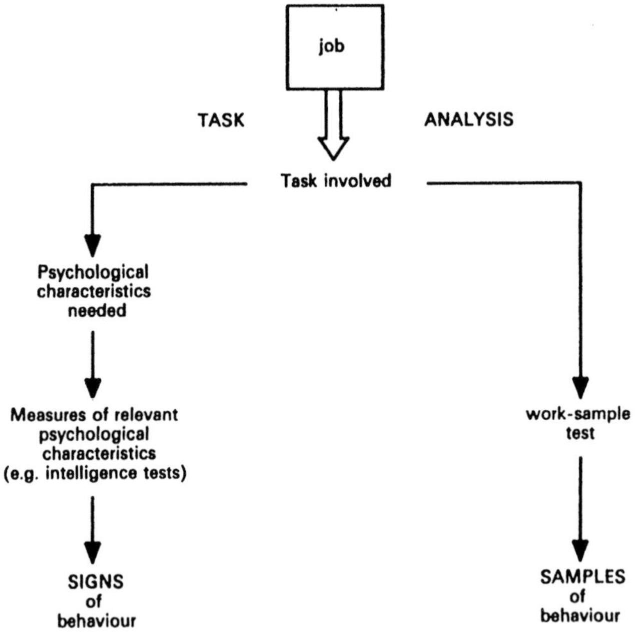

Types of Work-Sample Test

Work-sample tests have been developed and used for a wide range of different occupational areas. In the context of the current discussion it is informative to examine two issues: what types of work-sample test have been developed, and to what extent do work-sample tests provide valid predictors of future work performance? In their review of work-sample tests, Asher and Sciarrino (1974) identified two main categories of tests, motor and verbal. A test was identified as 'motor' if the task was a physical manipulation of things (for example, tracing electrical circuits, operating a sewing machine, making a tooth from plaster or repairing a gearbox), and was designated 'verbal' if 'there was a problem situation that was primarily language oriented or people oriented'. In their review, Robertson and Kandola (1982) proposed a more comprehensive four-category system of work sample tests.

1. *Psychomotor.* This category is much the same as Asher and Sciarrino's (1974) 'motor' category and involves the manipulation of objects: for example, carving something out of chalk, typing, stitching a piece of cloth or using a sewing-machine.
2. *Job-related information.* Tests in this category examine the amount of information a person holds about a particular job. They are usually pencil-and-paper tests and, although not work-sample tests in the simulation sense, they test applicant knowledge in areas thought to be directly relevant to work performance.
3. *Individual, situational decision-making.* Here the applicant is expected to take decisions similar to those taken in the job. This can be done more or less realistically by using in-tray exercises, for example, or more abstractly by presenting the applicant with a series of hypothetical situations and asking how he or she would respond.
4. *Group discussions/decision-making.* Tests of this sort involve two or more people being put together to discuss a particular topic and their performance in the discussion is evaluated. They are used widely for jobs where an individual's contribution within a group setting is an important determinant of job success.

Psychomotor tests

In general, researchers and practitioners have devoted more attention to psychomotor work-sample tests than to the other three types. Psychomotor work sample tests also appear to have been the most successful form of work-sample test. For any type of work-sample test one of the most important stages in the development of the test is the identification of a suitable task(s) to form the basis. Clearly, if the task(s) that form the basis for the work sample are chosen badly the predictive value of the work-sample exercise will be severely diminished.

A good example of the development and use of a psychomotor work-sample test is provided by J. E. Campion (1972) who produced a test for maintenance mechanics. To develop the test Campion followed a procedure based on earlier work by P. L. Smith and Kendall (1963). Campion's procedure involved five stages.

1. *Stage 1* Job experts produced a list of all tasks conducted by maintenance mechanics and indicated the frequency of performance and importance of each task.
2. *Stage 2* Job experts with experience of screening applicants for maintenance mechanics' jobs, plus a personnel specialist, produced a second list of tasks related to the previous work experience that typical applicants would have had.
3. *Stage 3* The experts identified the major dimensions of work behaviour (for example, use of tools, accuracy of work) that they felt discriminated between effective and ineffective performance on the job. Then, each expert independently identified some critical behavioural incidents (Flanagan, 1954) to illustrate actual performance on each major dimension. At the end of stage 3 the experts pooled their information and discussed and reconciled differences of opinion.
4. *Stage 4* In this stage the information produced in stages 1–3 was used to determine which tasks should be used as work samples. To ensure that the tasks chosen were representative of the normal job of a maintenance mechanic, and appropriate for applicants for the job, only those tasks that were common to stages 1 and 2 of the procedure were considered. The tasks chosen were also specifically relevant to the major dimensions of work behaviour identified during stage 3. Tasks finally selected included disassembling and repairing a motor and installing a pulley and belts.
5. *Stage 5* In the final stage the tasks were analysed in detail to identify the various approaches that might be followed by an applicant, and scoring weights were assigned based on expert judgements.

The work-sample test resulting from this procedure was used in a concurrent validity study. The work-sample test results showed a much better relationship with a criterion measure of overall mechanical ability than pencil-and-paper aptitude tests. The most popular example of a psychomotor work-sample test is probably the typing test (for example, West and Bolanovich, 1963; R. A. Ash, 1980) but many other investigators have developed and validated psychomotor work-sample tests for a wide range of jobs. An example of the development of a content-valid work-sample test is given in Schmitt and Ostroff (1986).

Job-related information

In the strict sense, tests in this category are not work-sample tests since they examine the job-related knowledge that an applicant holds, but do not call for the performance of a work sample. Job-related knowledge tests have been shown to have good predictive validity (see Hunter and Hunter, 1984).

Individual, situational decision-making

Individual, situational decision-making tests involve placing applicants in circumstances that simulate, as closely as possible, the real job. The simulations can take a variety of forms. They include psychomotor simulators (for example, for pilots or air traffic controllers) and realistic in-tray exercises where candidates are given a limited amount of time to deal with the contents of a typical in-tray for the job in question. For managerial and administrative jobs the most common form of situational decision-making test is probably the in-tray exercise.

In-tray exercises

A typical in-tray attempts to sample the contents of an executive's in-tray and includes letters, memoranda, hand-written notes, internal company reports, telephone messages and so on. Usually a fixed time is allowed for completion (often 1–1½ hours) and briefing notes are provided describing the background to the job and company and making it clear that no one is available for the candidate to consult. A selection of the contents of an in-tray for department managers in a large manufacturing company is given in Figure 11.2 (Moss, 1984). In common with most other work-sample tests the scoring of in-trays is usually conducted by people with an expert knowledge of the job, although the value of their assessments is likely to be improved by training in the techniques of assessment (Richards and Jafee, 1972;

Frank and Whipple, 1978). Following Frederiksen, Saunders and Wand (1957), R. W. T. Gill outlined two steps involved in evaluating a candidate's performance: (1) an agreed prior classification of the in-tray items is established (for example, irrelevant items, key items, and so on) and (2) evaluation of action first on key papers, and next on the other ones. Gill noted that the available evidence suggested that in-tray performance evaluations are usually related to two major dimensions: supervision (a human-relations dimension) and planning/administration (an intellectual dimension). Other studies of the constructs measured by in-trays have also been conducted (for instance, Tett and Jackson, 1990).

Figure 11.2   Selected contents from a departmental manager's in-tray exercise

---

1   Memo from personnel manager concerning an outbreak of dermatitis caused by solvents.

2   Memo from sales manager to confirm a meeting.

3   Memo (handwritten) from a foreman concerning a disagreement with inspection over the quality of a product.

4   Letter from a customer concerning late delivery of an order.

5   Memo from a foreman pointing out a shortage of bolts needed for a current job.

6   Memo from the general manager placing restrictions on purchasing.

7   Memo from work study manager concerning erratic bonus earnings.

Note: Altogether the in-tray exercise contains 20 letters and memoranda.
Source: Moss (1984).

As far as predicting future work performance is concerned, the in-tray appears to have a useful and unique contribution to make. Wollowick and McNamara (1969) found that in-tray exercises contributed a unique element to the prediction of managerial success. Other researchers (such as Bray and Grant, 1966; Meyer, 1970; Brass and Oldham, 1976; Kesselman, Lopez and Lopez, 1982) have shown that in-tray exercises provided good predictive validity. Although in-tray exercises have shown reasonably good predictive validity this does not mean that there is a clear understanding of how they provide reasonably accurate predictions of future performance. The basis of in-tray exercises is that candidates attempt tasks that are similar to the tasks involved in the target job. Assessors observe the candidates' performance and make judgements about candidates' managerial performance on a number of key dimensions (for example, problem-solving, organising and planning, delegation). This seems straightforward; however, a problem has arisen with in-trays and other assessment centre type exercises. Essentially the problem arises because the construct (convergent/discriminant) validity (see Chapter 7) of in-trays and other assessment centre exercises are not good. In plain English, it is not clear *what* these exercises are measuring. A study by Brannick, Michaels and Baker (1989) examined the construct validity of in-tray scores and found little evidence for convergent or discriminant validity. They utilised alternate forms of an in-tray and expected to find high correlations of the dimensions across the alternate forms (since the same managerial performance dimension was being measured in both). They found rather poor correlations. Their results call into question the validity of inferences about managerial traits derived from in-tray scores. In fact this problem of poor construct validity has been observed with assessment centres in general and is discussed more fully later in this chapter.

Group discussions/decision-making

Group discussion techniques seem to have been used almost entirely for the assessment of managerial potential within industry, commerce and the armed services. One of the most popular discussion exercises is the leaderless group discussion (LGD). An example of an LGD is provided in Dulewicz and Fletcher (1982, p. 199) who used the exercise as part of an assessment centre for Standard Telephones and Cables/ITT (UK):

> Committee exercise: Six participants form an appointments committee set up to fill a vacancy within Geo-Systems Division. They are each given written details of a candidate to propose for the job; they, as a group, are instructed to ensure that the best person is appointed to the job. However, each individual is told to try as hard as possible to get his own candidate selected. The candidates are allocated at random, and each has roughly the same number of strengths and weaknesses. The participants in turn present the case for their own candidate for up to four minutes. Then there is an unconstrained discussion for 40 minutes before (usually though not always) deciding on an appointee.

Unfortunately, although LGDs are used frequently it is not possible to draw unequivocal conclusions about the validity of LGDs. The main reason for this is that although LGDs are used often in assessment centres, it is rare to find studies that focus on the validity of specific components of assessment centres. In an early influential paper, Bass (1954) suggested that LGDs may have some value in assessing leadership potential, but he also provided some important warnings. For example, he emphasised that LGDs must attempt as far as possible to approximate the real situation and that observers should assess the behaviour of candidates and not attempt to infer differences in personality traits amongst candidates.

As well as leaderless groups, it is also common to find group exercises where candidates (often in turn) are appointed specifically to take the lead in group problem-solving exercises (see Gardner and Williams, 1973) although it is probably more appropriate to classify problem-solving exercises such as these (frequently used by the armed services selection boards) as 'situational decision-making' rather than 'group discussion' exercises. Taken overall, group discussion techniques seem to display reasonable validity, although direct evidence is not extensive.

The reliability of LGDs varies depending on the type of reliability being considered. Inter-rater reliability is reasonably good (Gatewood, Thornton and Hennessey, 1990; A. Jones, 1981). Gatewood, Thornton and Henessey have shown that although inter-rater reliability is high, alternate form reliability is much less good. This is not a minor technical failing but has important implications for assessment centre practice. Gatewood, Thornton and Hennessey speculated that the low reliability that they observed across two different LGD problems may be caused by differences in the composition of the two groups and/or differences in the problems assigned to the LGDs. As they point out, the common procedure in assessment centres is to place participants in an LGD and make no allowances or adjustments for the composition of the group. Possible influences on measurement accuracy due to problem content or group composition are not considered when assessment centre scoring procedures are designed, despite the fact that they may have significant effects on candidates' behaviour.

Assessing trainability

Much of the literature on work-sample testing focuses on people who are already trained and able to do the job, and the function of the test is to identify the most suitable candidate. Often the problem is not to select from a pool of ready-trained candidates, but to choose candidates who are suitable for training. Various methods have been adopted to predict trainability, including the use of standard pencil-and-paper psychological tests (see Ghiselli, 1973). The progress of trainees during the early stages of training has also been investigated as a predictor of later training performance, with some success (for example, Gordon and Cohen, 1973). A practical problem with using early training performance as a predictor is that it is still necessary to select trainees in some way and the psychological and financial costs involved in training and then rejecting unsuitable candidates may be considerable.

Over the last 20 years or so investigators have made use of work-sample tests to predict training success. Siegal and Bergman (1975, p. 326) have described the general format for work-sample-based predictors of trainability, 'The job seeker is trained to perform a sample of tasks involved in the job for which he is an applicant and, immediately following the training, his ability to perform these tasks is measured'. In the UK the earliest work-sample trainability tests were developed by Downs (see Downs, 1968).

The essential difference between a normal work sample and a trainability test is that the trainability test incorporates a structured and controlled learning period. For this reason such tests have been described as taking a 'job learning' or 'miniaturised training' approach to performance prediction. In many cases trainability tests also involve the systematic observation of *how* things are done as well as what is done.

Downs (1968) reported the development of carpentry and welding tests. The carpentry test involved making a half-lap T-joint and the welding test involved making several straight runs on mild steel. Since this early work, a variety of work-sample trainability tests (mostly psychomotor) have been developed, both in the UK and the USA. Robertson and Downs (1979, 1989) have provided reviews of the UK work, and Siegal (1983) provided a brief review together with an example of how these techniques have been developed in the USA. Tests used vary in length from 10 to 15 minutes to two hours or so. Work-sample trainability tests exist for many craft trades – for example, bricklaying (Figure 11.3), centre lathe-turning and capstan operating (see, for example, Robertson and Mindel, 1980) – and for various other jobs such as dentistry (Deubert, Smith, Downs and Berry, 1975) and sewing-machining (Downs, 1973).

Figure 11.3 Bricklaying trainability test

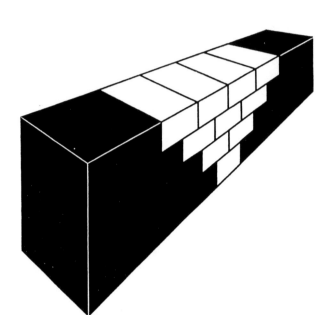

(The candidate is asked to build the unshaded section of the wall.)

Source: Robertson and Mindel (1980).

Guidance on the development and use of work-sample trainability tests is provided in Downs (1977). Most work-sample trainability tests developed so far have been concerned with psychomotor skills, but it seems likely that the approach could be of more general use. Robertson and Downs (1979) provided some advice on the factors that might need to be considered in any wider application.

As far as validity is concerned, the evidence for work-sample trainability tests is quite good. This evidence has been reviewed and summarised, using meta-analysis techniques, by Robertson and Downs (1989). The results showed that work-sample trainability tests predicted short-term training success best of all, with mean validity coefficients in excess of 0.4. Work-sample trainability tests also predicted job performance. Robertson and Downs found that longer-term predictive validities were generally less high than those obtained from shorter follow-up periods, but the longer-term validities showed less variability across studies. A very interesting, important, but currently unresolved, question concerns the extent to which work-sample tests and pencil-and-paper tests predict overlapping or independent aspects of criterion performance. In essence, if work-sample tests and pencil-and-paper tests predict overlapping aspects of criterion space, it is pointless to use both in a selection procedure. If, however, they predict independent aspects of criterion space, used together they could produce significant improvements in predictive validity. Future studies using both work-sample tests and pencil-and-paper tests on the same sample of people could examine the extent to which they predict independent aspects of criteria.

Benefits and Limitations of Work-Sample Tests

Applicants

From the applicants' viewpoint, realistic work-sample tests may have advantages over traditional psychological tests. For a work-sample test, applicants are expected to perform some activities which very closely resemble the job for which they have applied and which they presumably feel competent to carry out or be trained to carry out: that is, the tests have high face validity. The high face validity of work-sample tests may be beneficial.

One likely benefit of a work-sample test is that candidates themselves are provided with an opportunity to assess their own potential for the job. Downs, Farr and Colbeck (1978) reported the use of a trainability test with applicants for employment as sewing-machinists. Candidates were not selected on the basis of their test performance; all candidates were offered jobs. No fewer than 90 per cent of people graded A (the highest grade) started work whereas only slightly over 23 per cent of those graded E began work. Work-sample tests have the potential to help the selectors and applicants to come to a decision. Work-sample tests may in fact represent the most effective way of providing candidates with a useful and realistic job preview. They may also be used, and frequently are, in assessment centre settings to provide candidates with feedback about various aspects of their job-related performance.

A second likely benefit of work-sample tests, in terms of applicant reaction, is that they may encourage positive attitudes on the part of the applicants. To a large extent this positive attitude may be a function of the high face validity of work-sample tests. Cascio and Phillips (1979) provided some evidence suggesting that the clear link between a typical work-sample test and the work itself is an important asset. In their study applicants were being assessed for both initial hiring and for promotion. When conventional tests were being used as part of these procedures, 5–10 per cent of job applicants, and 20 per cent of applicants for promotion, sent in complaints about the way that they had been tested. In their 17-month study of work-sample tests no complaints were received.

Organisations

The benefits of a work-sample approach to personnel selection are clear and have been discussed earlier in this chapter. When looked at from the perspective of the organisation these benefits need to be balanced against the limitations and difficulties associated with work-sample tests.

Work-sample tests are often more time-consuming to administer than traditional psychological tests, and they are unquestionably more demanding in terms of resources. Since work-sample tests are designed to involve the core activities of jobs, they must of necessity incorporate into their format a requirement for some of the equipment and materials. An in-tray exercise designed to sample parts of an executive job will usually need little more than a room, paper, writing equipment, a desk and perhaps a telephone. By contrast, where manual skills are involved, special equipment and premises may be needed. A work-sample test for a bricklayer requires bricks, mortar, tools and the space to build a small section of wall. Tests for other craft trades (for example, capstan setting, centre lathe-operating or welding) require considerable and expensive equipment, machinery and premises. Not only can work-sample tests be costly in terms of machinery, materials, equipment and premises; they are also costly in terms of human resources. For most work-sample tests it seems sensible to have evaluators who are skilled performers of the job in question. Although there is no conclusive research support, this has been the practice of many researchers and practitioners. Organisations will often find it costly or inconvenient to release skilled performers. The evaluator is required to observe and assess the quality of the candidate's performance as he or she carries out the work sample and it is often difficult for one person to administer work-sample tests, simultaneously, to more than about three candidates. By contrast, with many traditional psychological tests a qualified tester may be able to administer a group test to ten or more candidates simultaneously.

Work-sample tests are related to specific jobs, and as such will need to be redesigned and validated as jobs change. Although this is true for all selection instruments, it may be more time-consuming and expensive to redesign and validate a work-sample test than it is to redesign and validate a battery of pencil-and-paper psychological tests. Further, there is a great variety of ready-to-use, standardised pencil-and-paper tests, but relatively few ready-made work-sample tests. In many cases it is fairly unlikely that a ready-made work-sample test will show sufficient similarity to the jobs conducted within an organisation.

Against the problems and limitations of work-sample tests, it should be borne in mind that such tests show good validities, appear to have the potential to reduce adverse impact and improve fairness (see Chapter 8), provide a realistic preview of the job, aid self-selection and are well received by applicants. The choice of when and where to use work-sample tests should be made on the basis of the likely balance of benefits and drawbacks.

ASSESSMENT CENTRES

In almost all selection situations, it is not sensible to base decisions on one predictor only (say, an interview) or even on one type of predictor only (say, a battery of psychological tests). When several predictors are used together the fundamental aim should be to ensure that the predictors provide information on different aspects of candidates' performance. In other words, predictors should not duplicate each other (it is pointless to measure the same factor twice), but they should complement each other. For example, a group discussion exercise might provide information concerning a managerial candidate's interpersonal skills, and psychological tests could be used to provide information on intelligence and aptitudes.

One popular and successful method of managerial selection and placement that makes use of many different predictors is the assessment centre approach.

The assessment centre method involves getting groups of candidates together (often about 6–8 people) and involving them in a variety of tests, interviews and work-sample exercises. Candidates are generally assessed by senior managers (plus, sometimes, a psychologist). The candidates may be either candidates for initial selection to an organisation or existing employees where future promotion and development within the organisation are being assessed, although the two types of candidate are not normally mixed within the same group. Assessment centres extend for a period of about two or three days, though they may be as long as a week or as short as one day. Detailed information on the research base for assessment centres and the development and use of assessment centre procedures can be found in Ungerson (1974), Moses and Byham (1977), Thornton and Byham (1982) and Woodruffe (1990).

The fundamental building block of an assessment centre is the development of a set of dimensions that are thought to be indicative of managerial potential for the jobs and organisation in question. These dimensions are derived from a comprehensive study of jobs under examination, usually employing a job analysis technique (see Chapter 2), interviews with experienced managers and a study of dimensions found to be successful in other assessment centre programmes. The dimensions (recently in the UK the term competence has been used to replace dimension; see Boam and Sparrow, 1992) typically arrived at include factors such as oral communication skill, leadership, problem analysis, planning and organising.

Assessment centres vary in the number of different dimensions that are evaluated (anything from about 7 to more than 20). One very influential assessment programme, American Telephone & Telegraph company (AT & T) uses between 8 and 25 dimensions depending on the level being assessed (Crooks, 1977). A published catalogue of assessment centre dimensions (Development Dimensions, 1975) contains a list of 26 representative dimensions commonly employed by organisations.

Jeswald (1977) provided some criteria that might be helpful in arriving at a final list of assessment dimensions. He emphasised, for example, that assessment dimensions should be defined in behavioural terms. 'For example "oral communication skills" can be defined in terms of eye contact, enunciation, voice modulation, gestures, etc. Certain other concepts, such as "character" or "maturity" may be too vague to permit reliable observation' (p. 59).

During an assessment centre evaluation, candidates are assessed on the basis of their performance on several tests and exercises; each test is designed to examine specific dimensions. Exercises used in assessment centres include interviews, in-tray (in-basket) exercises, group discussions, role-plays (for example, manager–subordinate interviews), simulated decision-making and judgement exercises, and pencil-and-paper psychological tests. Figure 11.4 provides examples of the dimensions assessed by two of the exercises in an assessment centre designed for potential first-line managers, and Figure 11.5 provides an illustration of how the information derived from an assessment centre might be utilised.

Figure 11.4   Dimensions assessed by two assessment centre exercises

---

Background Interview

Background interviews are conducted with each candidate by assessors who are specially trained. The interviews are primarily to assess the following dimensions:

Oral communication skill	Initiative
Oral presentation skill	Independence
Written communication skill	Planning and organisation
Stress tolerance	Delegation and control
Career ambition	Problem analysis
Leadership	Judgement
Sensitivity	Decisiveness
Flexibility	Reading and understanding
Tenacity	

In-Basket Exercise

The in-basket exercise simulates the problems a newly-appointed foreman might encounter. The in-basket contains 14 items and takes 1½ hours to complete. During the assessment day each participant is interviewed for one hour relative to his or her performance on the in-basket.

The following dimensions are assessed from the in-basket performance:

Oral communication skill	Planning and organisation
Written communication skill	Delegation and control
Stress tolerance	Problem analysis
Leadership	Judgement
Sensitivity	Decisiveness
Flexibility	Reading and understanding
Initiative	

Source: Crooks (1977).

Figure 11.5   The flow of assessment centre information

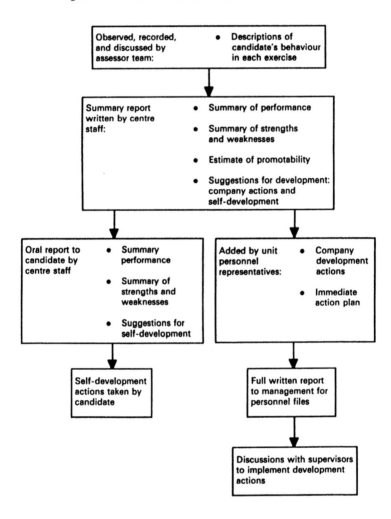

Most organisations using assessment centres recognise that a considerable amount of effort should go into the training of assessors for assessment centre programmes. Although there is no clear concensus on the format, content and duration of this training, some useful discussion of the issues can be found in Byham (1977) and Frank and Whipple (1978). Useful guidance on training people to rate and assess others can also be found in Latham and Wexley (1981). Fay and Latham (1982) provided an illustration of the benefits that training can have in reducing errors for various different types of rating scales. They provided suggestions on the objectives a rating training programme should seek. These include the acceptance by trainee assessors of the following points:

(a) performance related dimensions are often correlated (this has often been found to be the case for assessment centre dimensions); in other words a person who is good at one thing is often good at others;
(b) ratings that show a high proportion of positive scores are not necessarily an indication of leniency error;
(c) ratings should not necessarily form a normal distribution with most people scoring in the middle of the range and equal numbers above and below the middle, with few very high or low scores;
(d) it is not necessarily an error when a ratee is given the same score on many scales.

Benefits, limitations and validity

The use of assessment centres is widespread and appears to be increasing in the UK. In 1986 Robertson and Makin reported that a little over 20 per cent of their survey sample of 108 British organisations used assessment centre type exercises for managerial selection. More recently Shackleton and Newell (1991) found that 60 per cent of their sample of UK organisations utilised assessment centres.

In terms of predictive validity the evidence concerning assessment centres is broadly positive. Several large-scale validation studies and a meta-analysis which included most of the published studies (Gaugler, Rosenthal, Thornton and Bentson, 1987) have revealed positive validity coefficients. The mean validity coefficients for assessment centres and various criteria (such as job performance, potential, training performance and career advancement) obtained by Gaugler *et al.* was 0.29. When adjusted to correct for statistical artefacts this became 0.37. A mean validity, derived from meta-analysis (see Chapter 7), of about 0.3 does not imply that individual studies will not have produced noticeably smaller or larger validity coefficients than this (see, for example Feltham, 1987). The results of meta-analysis for assessment centres do, however, suggest that in general assessment centres will work reasonably well.

Although assessment centres predict various criteria reasonably well there are still several important questions that need to be resolved. The most important unresolved questions concern: (1) the factors that moderate assessment centre validity from one situation to another and (2) the reasons behind good predictive validity of assessment centres. As far as the first question is concerned the work of Gaugler *et al.* showed that, even after correcting for statistical artefacts, there was still substantial variation in the validity coefficients across different studies. This suggests that other factors may be moderating the validity of assessment centres from one setting to another (see Chapter 7). Gaugler *et al.* examined their data to assess the possible moderating effects of several factors (psychologists as opposed to managers as assessors, days of assessor training, ratio of assessors to assessees). The results of their moderator analysis provide interesting reading and show that several factors moderated the validity of assessment centres. Figure 11.6 lists some of the factors investigated and whether or not they were found to be related to validity.

Somewhat surprisingly although the use of psychologists as assessors is associated with better validity, Gaugler *et al.* found no link with length of assessor training. They conducted their analysis based on research reports and could not assess the quality of training: perhaps this, rather than length, is the important feature here. The results obtained for both women and ethnic minorities are interesting but need to be viewed with caution in the UK/European context, since the civil rights situation in the USA (where most of the studies used in the meta-analysis were done) is unique in many respects. Studies have confirmed the finding that assessment centre validity can vary from one setting to another. Schmitt, Schneider and Cohen (1990) found that the type of assessor used, the centre's administrative arrangement and prior assessor-assessee contact all moderated the validity coefficients. Cumulatively these studies of assessment centre validity underline the point that the mere use of a technique, such as an assessment centre, is no guarantee of validity. As Schmitt, Schneider and Cohen put it:

assessment centers work when they are operationalized as they were intended. That is, raters are selected and trained appropriately and efforts to maintain quality control in the implementation of the center are made on a continuous basis. When the center becomes a fad or a way to legitimize the actions of an organization, it would seem that center validity deteriorates. (p. 11)

Figure 11.6 Some of the factors moderating the validity of assessment centres

	Moderator: ✓ or x
Number of different types of exercises used	✓ More exercises give better validity
Number of days of assessor training	x
High proportion of women in the assessee group	✓ High proportion of women linked with better validity
Small proportion of ethnic minority group members in the assessee group	✓ Low proportion of minorities linked with better validity
Use of psychologists versus managers	✓ Use of psychologists linked with better validity
Ratio of assessees to assessors	x
Use of peer evaluation in the assessment process	✓ Peer evaluation associated with better validity

An important study by Sackett and Dreher (1982) raised some concerns about the second issue, the measurement properties of assessment centres. The significance of their study arises from the design and conceptual basis of assessment centres. Assessment centres are designed, after job analysis, to provide a series of exercises which allow trained assessors to judge candidates' capabilities on a set of job-relevant dimensions (competences).

The exercises are a vehicle to enable assessors to make judgements about candidates' competences. If assessment centres are working as designed they should display certain psychometric properties. The key properties concern the convergent and discriminant validity (D. T. Campbell and Fiske, 1959) of the assessment dimensions. Briefly, if assessment dimensions show convergent validity the correlations of candidates' performance on the same dimension across different exercises (monotrait-heteromethod correlations) should be fairly high; these correlations should certainly be higher than the correlations of *different* assessment dimensions in the same exercise (heterotrait-monomethod correlations). Finally a factor analysis of the assessment data should reveal factors interpretable in terms of the assessment dimensions (see Chapter 7).

Sackett and Dreher's original study and several replications, including one using UK data (Robertson, Gratton and Sharpley, 1987), have shown that the convergent/discriminant validity and factor structure of assessment centre data are not as they should be. The important and troubling implication of this line of research is that assessment centres are not providing interpretable and valid measures of dimensions (competences). In fact, *within* exercise correlations are usually higher (across different dimensions) than the intercorrelations of the same dimension *across* exercises. Similarly, the factor structures of assessment centre results do not produce clear dimension-related factors; in fact, factors are often more closely linked to exercises than dimensions. In short, although assessment centres predict job behaviour quite well we do not have a clear view of *what* they are measuring and thus no clear understanding of *why* they predict. Technically, the criterion-related validity of assessment centres is established but the construct validity is not.

More recent work has shown that changes in the assessment process, such as the use of behaviour checklists, can improve construct validity (Reilly, Henry and Smither, 1990), and that limiting the number of dimensions assessed improves accuracy (Gaugler and Thornton, 1989). Nevertheless the puzzle of assessment centre validity remains (Klimoski and Brickner, 1987).

BIOGRAPHICAL DATA (BIODATA)

Many studies have demonstrated that various important aspects of work performance can be predicted with the aid of biographical information (Asher, 1972; Drakely, 1989). In most selection situations there is a readily available source of biographical information about candidates: their application forms. Even the most rudimentary application forms provide some basic biographical data such as age, marital status, number of previous jobs and time spent in previous jobs. In its simplest form, using biographical data to assist in selection decisions is relatively straightforward. The basic procedure is to collect biographical data (using application forms, for example), examine the links with successful job performance, and use the links to make future selection decisions.

In some circumstances the use of biographical data in personnel selection may involve an approach to the problem of predicting a candidate's work performance that is rather different from the approach used when other selection methods are utilised. When using selection procedures such as interviews or psychological tests, the specific areas to be examined in the interview or tests are normally derived from a systematic analysis of the job in question, and there is a clear link between the nature of tasks involved in the job and the selection criteria used. When biographical data are used the link between the job and the criteria used for selection may sometimes be much less clear. Specific types of biographical data may be chosen not because they have any clear relationship with the tasks involved in the job but because on a statistical basis they are good predictors of future performance, although (as later sections in this chapter will show) reliance on statistical, rather than psychological, evidence may not be good practice.

The use of biographical data in personnel selection may, at first sight, seem to represent an extreme form of actuarial prediction, where selection decisions are influenced purely on the basis of statistical links between predictors and criteria.

Although biographical data can be used in this way, some work (for example, Owens, 1976) demonstrates that biographical data may represent much more than a collection of isolated items of information about a person's life. This work is discussed later in this chapter.

Using Biographical Data for Selection

In order to examine the use of biographical data in personnel selection it makes sense to identify the two main ways in which such data are collected: application forms and biographical questionnaires. The difference between these two data sources is largely a matter of quantity. A typical application form (application blank) will request a fairly limited amount of information from candidates, and will cover items of personal information such as age, marital status and education and employment history.

It is rare for an application form to ask for much more than rudimentary biographical information. A biographical questionnaire, by contrast, is specifically designed to provide detailed life-history information, often containing a large number of questions. Biographical questionnaires with over 100 items are not unusual (for example, A. S. Levine and Zachert, 1951; Baehr and Williams, 1967; Rawls and Rawls, 1968; Owens, 1971).

To some extent the distinction between application forms and biographical questionnaires is rather artificial and is further complicated by the fact that biographical data can be collected in a wide variety of ways, including structured interviews.

Studies using biodata to predict subsequent job behaviour have been successful. Reviews by Reilly and Chao (1982), Hunter and Hunter (1984) and Schmitt, Gooding, Noe and Kirsh (1984), summarising the research on biodata, have shown strong evidence for the criterion-related validity of biodata. These reviews show that biodata are good at predicting most criteria including productivity (a mean validity coefficient of 0.46: Reilly and Chao) and job performance (a mean validity of 0.37: Hunter and Hunter). In fact, the results concerning biodata show that, for most criteria, biodata are among the best predictors. Even for turnover, which is a particularly difficult criterion to predict, biodata produced better criterion-related validity (mean validity = 0.21; Schmitt *et al.*) than other predictors.

An illustrative study involving the use of an application form to collect data is that of J. N. McClelland and Rhodes (1969). They investigated the use of biographical data to predict the job success of hospital aides and orderlies. The following biographical information was obtained from application forms:

(a) age;
(b) marital status;
(c) number of dependents;
(d) education in years;
(e) health impairment (the absence or presence of any disability, other than spectacles);
(f) average tenure on past jobs;
(g) related experience (number of years in previous jobs in related fields);
(h) salary difference between present and last job;
(i) restriction on hours available for duty;
(j) number of months resident in local area.

McClelland and Rhodes also used a 'clinical' personality questionnaire – the Minnesota Multiphasic Personality Inventory (MMPI)
– to attempt to predict job success. They found that both types of
predictor (that is, the biographical questionnaire and the MMPI)
helped to predict job performance. They noted that: 'In general the
findings of this study are similar to many in which a sampling of
biographical data, a personality measure or both, have been used to
predict job performance criteria . . . *Biographical items were more
important than MMPI scores for predicting composite job performance*' (pp. 53–4).

More recent studies involving the use of biodata are Drakely,
Herriot and Jones (1988) and Mitchell and Klimoski (1982). There are,
however, various criticisms and unresolved questions that may be
asked concerning biodata, and Owens (1976) provides a thorough
review. One of the more important issues concerns the accuracy of
biodata. In other words, when people report on their life history and
current circumstances, how do we know that the information is
accurate? They may be lying and memory may be at fault. As Owens
notes, there is not a great deal of evidence available concerning this
question. J. L. Mosel and Cozan (1952) checked records of applications
for employment and found high agreement between application claims
and verifications by past employers on weekly wages, duration of
employment and job duties. With one exception all correlations were
0.90 or over. I. L. Goldstein (1971), however, produced data suggesting
that substantial falsification may occur. Another, in many ways more
important, problem with the use of biodata has been succinctly
summarised by Owens (1976, p. 625):

Research involving biodata has been subject to more or less constant
criticism on the basis that quite good prediction is achieved, but that
it is accompanied by modest, if existent, gains in understanding.
There has also appeared to be a not unreasonable feeling that
research in this area has been somewhat insular, neither seeking nor
defining its relationship to the larger body of psychology. Thus
Guilford (1959) has quite properly observed that biodata research
has been characterized by an empirical shotgun approach to
prediction, largely devoid of both theory and generality. Similarly,
Dunnette (1962) reviewed selected biodata applications to the
problem of predicting managerial and executive success and stressed
the need for moving beyond simple prediction to a greater emphasis
on the finding of causal relationships.

Some work on biodata, in particular that of Owens and his associates (Owens, 1976; Owens and Schoenfeld, 1979; Neiner and Owens, 1982), has focused on attempts to develop a much more coherent and theoretically sound basis for the use of biodata as a predictor of performance. Owens points out the intuitively appealing basis on which biodata rests. He argued that, in essence, biodata provides a measure or indicator of previous behaviour: that is, it provides, 'A postmortem view of the development of the individual – an inverted pyramid of many recent and a few remote events the validity of which is limited chiefly by the insight of its author and by the memory and intention of the respondent' (1976, p. 625). He then asserted, as many psychologists before him have asserted, that the best predictor of a person's future behaviour is what he or she has done in the past.

Thus Owens argued that biodata represent not merely a few isolated items of information about a person, but a much richer source of data which, if interpreted sensitively and insightfully, represents an alternative, factually-based, view of a person's life so far, and which may be used to make predictions about the person's future life in a rational and coherent way. Current research is focusing on the methods used for collecting biographical data (Eberhardt and Muchinsky, 1982) and on investigating Owen's proposal that biodata can provide a coherent view of individual development over time (for example, Neiner and Owens). A good example of this work is C.J. Russell, Mattson, Devlin and Atwater (1990). These researchers generated biodata items by collecting retrospective life history essays from a relevant sample of people. The resulting biodata scales predicted peer ratings of leadership as well as performance ratings in the US military. Perhaps more importantly, for this line of research the results were interpreted within a framework suggesting that the original essays and thus the biodata items represented developmental life experiences that were causally linked to subsequent behaviour. Mumford, Stokes, Owens and Sparks (1991) have provided the most detailed model so far linking human development to biodata. Although use of the term 'biodata' suggests that the kinds of items used in biodata questionnaires would focus on verifiable and objective (often referred to as hard) information such as examinations passed, it is actually quite common for biodata questionnaires to include less objective (soft) items asking, for example if respondents felt homesick when away from home as a child or if they would enjoy conducting scientific experiments. With items like these it is increasingly difficult to decide where biodata end and personality testing begins.

Racial Bias of Application Blanks

Reilly and Chao (1982) considered the racial bias of application blanks. They indicated that decisions based on biodata could be expected to be biased because many personal history and background data are related to gender, age and race. Moreover, the choice of items for a selection system using biodata might favour items which are valid but which work at the direct expense of minority groups. Pace and Schoenfeldt (1977) found, for example, that having a Detroit address was negatively correlated with a certain criterion. But, since more blacks lived in the city than in the suburbs, this particular item was likely to have had an adverse impact. However, after reviewing 11 studies of application blanks, Reilly and Chao concluded that where two groups differ only slightly in their performance on criteria, biodata may result in minimal adverse impact.

Probably the best study investigating the bias of résumés is by McIntyre, Moberg and Poser (1980). They mailed résumés to a carefully constructed sample of companies. They then compared responses and found 86 instances of black favouritism and 52 instances of white favouritism. In other words, there was evidence of bias *in favour* of black applicants. More detailed analysis indicated that black applicants are the beneficiary of favouritism in every region of the USA except the west, in every job category sampled except those applying for electrical engineering positions, and in organisations of all sizes. This is not an isolated result. Other investigations (Wexley and Nemeroff, 1974; Rand and Wexley, 1975; Haefner, 1977) have found little evidence of unfavourable evaluations being given to black candidates. Newman (1978) found a definite trend for larger companies to discriminate *in favour* of blacks.

Sex Bias of Application Blanks

There is fairly strong evidence that interviews and application blanks can be used in a way that is biased against women (Reilly and Chao, 1982). A review by Arvey (1979) showed that there is a consistent tendency for females to be given lower evaluations than men, even when they have similar or identical qualifications. This is particularly true when the jobs are considered to be masculine in nature. Haefner (1977) showed that males tended to be given half a grade more on a five point grading scale. McIntyre, Moberg and Posner (1980) also found that employers preferred male applications over females and on average took 2.6 days longer to reply to speculative applications made by women.

Age Bias of Application Blanks

The age bias of the application blank has received relatively little attention, but from the material available there appears to be a strong, pervasive bias against older workers. Haefner (1977), using a set of carefully controlled stimuli, compared the racial, sex and age bias of 286 employers in Illinois. He found that the age bias was roughly the same size as the sex bias (half a scale point on a five point scale). Rosen and Jerdee (1976) examined the stereotypes of undergraduate students towards 60-year-old workers and found that they were rated lower on performance capacity and potential for development, but higher on stability.

12 Other Selection Methods

The methods for personnel selection described in earlier chapters have covered the methods in common use, including more recently developed ones. The methods described in this chapter are in general not widely used, and most of them do not have well-established levels of criterion-related validity. They are nevertheless worth discussing, either because they may be particularly useful in certain situations (such as self-assessment) or because they are interesting and controversial (for example, handwriting analysis and astrology).

SELF-ASSESSMENT

Most decisions concerning initial selection are made by personnel specialists and other members of the organisation who are senior to the person assessed. This is clearly sensible in many respects but the person with most knowledge of the applicant – the candidate himself or herself – is excluded.

Many reviews of the value of self-assessment in industrial and organisational settings (see Thornton, 1980; Reilly and Chao, 1982; Schmitt and Robertson, 1990) conclude that there is little to recommend its use. The criticisms of self-assessments centre on three main issues (see E. L. Levine, Flory and Ash, 1977): first, people may produce an inflated (lenient) picture of their own abilities; second, people are unable to make accurate or reliable self-assessments; third, leniency and low reliability will lead to poor validity.

Leniency

The evidence supports the idea that self-assessments are lenient. R. A. Ash (1980), for example, found consistent over-estimates of typing ability (51.4 words/minute) against a tested mean (39.6 words/minute). In fact, with the notable exception of Heneman (1974), all of the relevant research reviewed by Thornton (1980), Tenopyr and Oeltjen (1982) and Reilly and Chao (1982) showed consistent over-estimates in self-assessment. However, it should be remembered that leniency effects can also occur in non self-assessments. Makin and Robertson

(1983) argued that the degree of leniency in judgements will be influenced by the purpose to which the assessments will be put.

Accuracy and Validity

It is possible to assess the accuracy of self-assessments by, for example, comparing self-assessments with the assessments made by other people (see Thornton, 1980). Such studies have produced mixed results, although most show some relationships between self and other assessments. Harris and Schaubroeck (1988) conducted a meta-analysis of all the articles they could find in the occupational psychology literature over the last 15–30 years (depending on the source used). They found modest mean correlations for self-supervisor (0.22, corrected for sampling error; 0.35 corrected for other artifacts) and self-peer ratings (0.24, 0.36). They also found higher agreement in self-supervisor and self-peer ratings in blue collar jobs compared to managerial jobs. The level of agreement between peers and supervisors was somewhat higher than self-supervisor or peer supervisor (mean validity coefficient corrected for sampling error = 0.48; corrected for other statistical artefacts = 0.62). These comparisons are based on two sets of ratings and merely indicate the extent to which the views of two people correspond. The 'acid' test for accuracy of self-assessments involves comparing a self-assessment with some objective measure of performance rather than subjective ratings.

Some research has directly compared self-appraisal with objective performance measures, (for example, De Nisi and Shaw, 1977; E. L. Levine, Flory and Ash, 1977; Ekpo-Ufot, 1979; Primoff, 1980). R. A. Ash (1980) compared self-assessments with objective measures for various forms of typing ability. The results showed that peoples' self-assessments corresponded more closely with objective assessments when the factor being assessed was straightforward and well understood (for example, for simple copy-typing ability there was a correlation coefficient of 0.59). For more complex skills (for example, typing tables) the self and objective assessments correspond less well (a correlation coefficient of 0.07).

Relatively few studies have examined the value of self-assessments in selection situations. Reilly and Chao (1982) reviewed eight studies, four of which involved attempts to estimate the predictive validity of self-assessments. Reilly and Chao (1982, p. 32) made the following comments: 'Although several studies reported positive results, only three studies included validity coefficients with overall criteria. Based on these limited data (three independent coefficients, total N = 545) an average weighted validity of .15 was calculated.'

More recent studies have not produced particularly encouraging results for self-ratings. G. Fox and Dinur (1988) obtained confirmation of the leniency of self-ratings when they compared self, peer and supervisor ratings. In their meta-analysis Harris and Schaubroeck (1988) found that on average self-ratings were over half a standard deviation higher than supervisors' ratings. George and Smith (1988) used self-ratings to predict the job performance, absenteeism and turnover of seasonal workers in a food processing company. Like Fox and Dinur, George and Smith found that respondents inflated their assessment of their own performance. Fahr, Werbel and Bedeian (1988) studied academics in the USA. Although their results showed better levels of agreement between self and supervisor ratings the study suffered from methodological problems, since other raters had access to individuals' self-ratings at the time of the study.

It has been suggested (see above) that the accuracy of self-assessment will be influenced by the use to which the assessments will be put. Fox and Dinur went some way towards exploring this by telling their respondents that their ratings would be compared with assessments from other sources (Mabe and West, 1982, suggested that this particular action should improve accuracy). Fox and Dinur did not find that this affected the predictive accuracy of self-ratings. In their study of seasonal workers George and Smith explored the hypothesis that self-assessments based on experiential job information will be more accurate. This hypothesis was not supported.

Self-Efficacy

A final and distinctive area of work involving self-assessments is worth mentioning. Some investigators have used Bandura's (1977, 1986) social learning theory as a basis for the development of a particular kind of self-assessment. Social learning theory defines the concept of self-efficacy as, 'the conviction that one can successfully execute the behaviour required to produce the outcomes' (Bandura, Adams and Beyer, 1977, p. 126). In conceptual terms (Bandura, 1986) self-efficacy is clearly distinguished from general self-confidence, and specific methodologies have been developed for the design of scales to measure self-efficacy (see Moe and Zeiss, 1982). The literature on self-efficacy within the personnel selection field is as yet quite small, but does show promise. Several studies have shown that self-efficacy scores are predictive of work behaviour. Barling and Beattie (1983) and Lee and Gillen (1989) found self-efficacy to be predictive of sales performance. In a simulation study Bandura and Wood (1989) found that self-efficacy predicted the performance of a managerial group. Frayne and Latham (1987) showed that self-efficacy was related to attendance at work and Stumpf, Brief and Hartman (1987) used self-efficacy scores to predict successfully interviewer performance in job interviews. Taken overall the strong theoretical base and empirical success of this work suggest that self-efficacy theory may provide a valid and reliable way of developing self-assessments.

Bias of Self-Assessment

The general tendency of the evidence collected by Reilly and Chao (1982) is that blacks tend to give themselves higher ratings than whites, but these differences were not always significant. However, one study found that the majority group tended to give themselves higher ratings on typing ability and that these estimates were more valid than the lower estimates of the minority group.

PEER EVALUATION

As far as initial selection to an organisation is concerned, peer-evaluation is likely to be of little value. It is clearly impossible for an employer to obtain peer assessments of a candidate who is coming from outside the organisation. For promotion decisions within organisations peer evaluations show reasonably high levels of validity (Lewin and Zwany, 1976; Reilly and Chao, 1982) though there are many problems concerning, for instance, friendship patterns with the peer group. Kane and Lawler (1978) reviewed some of the techniques that can be used for peer evaluation. As Reilly and Chao pointed out, perhaps the crucial factor in the success of a peer evaluation system is acceptance of the system by participants. Cederblom and Lounsbury (1980) found that most participants in such a system favoured its discontinuation. More recently McEvoy and Buller (1987), working with hourly paid personnel in a food processing plant, found better levels of acceptance for peer appraisal.

Peer ratings show much better agreement with supervisor's ratings than self-ratings do. Harris and Schaubroeck (1988) found a mean correlation of 0.48 (corrected for sampling error only) and 0.62

(corrected for other artefacts). Interestingly Harris and Schaubroeck found slightly better peer-supervisor agreement for trait (0.64) compared with behavioural (0.53) ratings, when most psychological principles would lead us to expect the opposite.

Bias of Peer Evaluations

Reilly and Chao (1982) could locate no studies specifically relating to the fairness of peer evaluations. However, they found some studies concerning the average ratings given by peers to different ethnic groups. As we have seen earlier in this chapter, a difference in average scores does not necessarily imply bias. Two points emerge from studies: first, special training programmes and situations may reduce or perhaps eliminate racial prejudice. However, racial bias is generally to be expected in peer evaluations. Second, bias in peer evaluations can work both ways. Members of a given race tend to evaluate same race peers higher.

Amazingly there appears to be no evidence concerning the potential sex bias involved in peer ratings.

GRAPHOLOGY

Most of us feel that we are able to recognise our own handwriting and also the handwriting of close friends and relatives, suggesting that there is something individualistic and different about each person's handwriting. Perhaps, like finger prints, no two people's handwriting is the same. It is a relatively small step from this to suggest that it might be possible to draw inferences about someone's personal characteristics by examining his or her handwriting. Graphology – that is, handwriting analysis – is the examination of the features of handwriting in which the analyst draws inferences about the writer. It has been estimated that 85 per cent of continental European companies use graphology to help with personnel decisions (reported in Klimoski and Rafaeli, 1983).

Despite its widespread popularity in some countries (Shackleton and Newell, 1991), the evidence for the predictive validity of handwriting analysis in personnel selection (and other) situations is not great. A starting point in considering the value of handwriting in personnel selection is to examine the extent to which handwriting varies or remains stable. Several studies (O. L. Harvey, 1934; Walner, 1975) have been conducted to assess the consistency of script features, and by and large the evidence suggests that handwriting is stable over time, although there is also evidence to suggest that in certain circumstances handwriting does vary. Loewenthal (1975), for example, found that the handwriting of a group of students differed from normal when they were told to produce an example of their 'best' handwriting as if they were applying for a job. Downey (1919) observed variations in handwriting which seem to show some links with variations in mood and health. Predictably, perhaps, Wing and Baddely (1978) found reliable variations in handwriting after the consumption of alcohol! Loewenthal (1975) has demonstrated that handwriting can be faked. Students who were asked to fake the handwriting of methodical and original people produced samples that were reliably judged as such. In short then, although it may be possible to fake handwriting and some variations may be caused by situational and emotional factors, it seems that the important features of a person's handwriting are reasonably consistent over time. Loewenthal (1982, p. 91) presents an interesting view on this fundamental consistency:

> In spite of variations, handwriting can usually be identified correctly as coming from a particular individual . . . There are some people who, sadly, because of disablement, must use mouth or feet to write with; and yet, regardless of the limb used to guide the pen, a given individual produces writing that is characteristically his. Handwriting is not so much handwriting as brain-writing.

Methods of Analysis

Like many others who attempt to assess human characteristics, graphologists do not adopt a single approach, although certain common features of handwriting are recognised as significant by most analysts. Klimoski and Rafaeli (1983) cited Patterson (1976), who identified 12 features that are typically examined by graphologists, including size, slant, width, regularity, pressure and form of connection.

Loewenthal (1982) outlined two major forms of handwriting analysis (graphoanalysis): the single feature approach which involves the examination of specific features (for example, size, letter slant) of handwriting and single aspects of personality, and the total approach where several features are combined and related to personality, and an attempt is made to view handwriting as a whole rather than focus on individual features.

Klimoski and Rafaeli identified three approaches: the trait approach and the Gestalt approach which seem to correspond with Loewenthal's single feature and total approach respectively, and the graphoanalysis approach, founded by Bunker in 1929, which focuses on the study of individual features but which also emphasises that people must be studied as a whole. Research to examine the validity of handwriting analysis is beset with problems, including a lack of detail concerning the training and experience of the analysts involved, lack of information on the approach/method of analysis used, and a lack of control over the type of material used for analysis.

In a particularly well-controlled study, Rafaeli and Klimoski found that graphologists using the same method of analysis showed some agreement in their analyses of sample scripts and that the agreement was no worse when graphologists using different methods were compared. Klimoski and Rafaeli (1983, p. 195) concluded that, 'Although different methods of handwriting analysis are unique, they do represent some unified framework of personality analysis.'

Some graphologists, for example, prefer to work from copied material, while others like to use spontaneous scripts of an autobiographical nature where the candidates àre asked to write something about themselves. Clearly the content of an autobiographical piece of writing may provide information over and above the cues provided in the nature of the handwriting itself. As the previous chapter has shown, autobiographical data can provide a good basis for predicting future behaviour.

Rafaeli and Klimoski examined the effects the content of the handwriting had on analysis. They asked handwriting experts to examine two types of scripts, 'neutral' descriptions of houses, and 'autobiographical' material written by the people being assessed. Contrary to their predictions, script content had little effect on the graphologists' assessments.

The Validity of Handwriting Analysis

The evidence is rather limited but it implies that handwriting analysis is a reasonably reliable method of assessment and is not influenced by script content or the procedure adopted. The evidence for validity, however, provides less encouragement for the graphology enthusiast.

Studies reviewed by Klimoski and Rafaeli (1983) provided rather mixed findings, sometimes offering no support for the validity of graphology as a measure of personality (see D. Rosenthal and Lines 1972), and sometimes offering some support (see Lemke and Kirchner, 1971).

Studies looking at the validity of graphology in work situations are also ambiguous. Zdep and Weaver (1967: life assurance agents) and Sonneman and Kerman (1962: executives) provided some positive findings, but Klimoski and Rafaeli criticised both investigations on methodological grounds.

Other studies (such as Jansen, 1973) offered no support for handwriting analysis as a predictor of work-related criteria. In Rafaeli and Klimoski's (1983) study, practising graphologists were paid to provide assessments of American real estate sales personnel. An objective index of performance and supervisor's ratings were used as criterion measures. The data offered no support for the validity of the graphologists' assessments. Ben-Shakhar, Bar-Hillel, Bille, Ben-Abba and Flug (1986) conducted two experiments to assess the validity of graphologists' analyses. In the first study they showed that although graphologists obtained small, positive validities, so did non graphologists using the same data. The second study showed that graphologists could not predict a writer's profession at a level better than chance. Ben-Shakhar (1989) reported the results of a meta-analysis of 17 studies which found average correlations between inferences based on handwriting analysis and job proficiency and training criteria of between 0.14 and 0.19. These results were for a mixed group including graphologists, but also psychologists and lay persons. The graphologists did not do better than the other groups; in fact they did consistently worse than the psychologists. Ben-Shakhar (1989) concluded that, 'Clearly the small validities obtained by graphologists can be accounted for simply by the possibility that biographical and other information contained in the script is used, or at least influences the graphological assessment' (p. 475). At least one other investigator (Nevo, 1988) did not draw the same conclusion as Ben-Shakhar and has argued that the work of Ben Shakhar *et al.* (1986) can be reinterpreted to show that graphology does have small but statistically significant validity. Even Nevo (1988) however noted that, 'it is doubtful whether graphology is to be recommended as a device for the selection of personnel' (p. 94). The unflattering research evidence on graphology has not prevented over 75 per cent of French organisations using it some of the time for managerial selection (Shackleton and Newell, 1991).

ASTROLOGY

Most people have some knowledge of astrology and appreciate that it involves attempts to relate human behaviour and characteristics to the position and movements of the stars and planets. To some people such a notion seems perfectly reasonable; to others it seems quite ludicrous. Much of the evidence offering support for this fundamental notion is far from clear-cut. What is clear is that no one has yet provided evidence enabling the notion to be conclusively rejected or validated.

Astrology is little used for personnel selection purposes. Some sources provide advice on using astrological techniques in vocational settings (Luntz, 1962); however, surveys in the UK and Europe indicate that it is used by less than 1 per cent of organisations. There is scientific evidence concerning the extent to which astrological methods can produce valid predictions relating to a person's work behaviour. In essence, astrology involves two separate but related acts. First the astrologer constructs a horoscope (basically a map of the heavens at the time of birth), and second the astrologer interprets the horoscope.

Constructing a Map

Whilst individual astrologers might differ on some details, the procedures for constructing the map appear to be fairly common. The starting point for the construction of a horoscope is the place, date and time of birth of the person concerned. Most people are familiar with the 12 signs of the zodiac and many can also remember their own sign and that of some close friends and relatives. Unlike the generalised astrological information provided in the popular press, 'serious' astrology involves a very specific horoscope for an individual person and takes into account much more than the relevant sign of the zodiac. Various textbooks provide outlines of how the procedure is conducted. H. J. Eysenck and Nias (1982) have provided an overview, and more information is given in Parker and Parker (1975).

Interpeting the Map

The interpretation of astrological data involves a subjective, holistic and intuitive act rather than straightforward and systematic inference. The following passage from a committed astrologer (Macleod, 1982) illustrates this:

The astrologer uses intuition. The chart has been studied and enters the subconscious, where it picks up the rules and structures of astrology acquired by time-consuming study of the tradition. The details are then synthesized by the brain in much the same way as they are synthesized by· the computer. However, the astrologer is now able to leave the mind free to sense the entirety of the chart, the pattern, and the potential within it. Feedback is now dependent upon the unique situation of the astrologer, the consciousness of the astrologer, and the astrologer's act of judgement which requires perception and active imagination. Intuition is used to interpret what cannot be measured by technique alone. Intuition refuses to be pinned down and placed under the microscope so that we can examine how it functions.

In other words, she is arguing that astrology may be difficult to investigate with the methods of traditional scientific enquiry. (Supporters of various other 'unscientific' pursuits make the same claims). Whilst there may be some truth in such a point of view, it is equally fair to state that assertion alone is not enough to demonstrate the validity of a method or procedure. Astrology, like other methods of selection, must be investigated in a way that at least minimises the possible influence of chance factors, self-fulfilling prophesies and other artefacts.

When carefully-controlled studies of astrology are conducted the results do not provide unequivocal support for the proponents of astrology; on the other hand, the evidence is such that many (though by no means all) scientists are prepared at least to suspend judgement for the time being. The most notable source of scientific evidence comes from the work of a French psychologist, Michel Gauquelin (see Gauquelin, 1978, 1980). Gauquelin has conducted extensive work examining the links between various factors, such as occupation, character, sporting prowess and astrological characteristics.

Some of Gauquelin's early work concentrated on the links between astrological factors and occupational groups. One early study used a sample of over 500 eminent French medical practitioners. The results showed that when compared with a control group drawn at random from the electoral register, the eminent doctors were more likely to have been born when Mars or Saturn had just risen or just passed the midheaven. Several other positive results have emerged from Gauquelin's work linking occupations with planetary positions, including, for instance, fairly large samples of successful artists (over 5000) and scientists (over 3500).

Gauquelin has also produced data showing links between personality characteristics and planetary positions. One study (Gauquelin, Gauquelin and Eysenck, 1979) revealed links between extroversion/introversion and planetary positions at birth. H. J. Eysenck and Nias (1982) argued that results linking personality with planetary position at birth show that it is personality rather than occupation that is important. The link with successful members of occupational groups occurs because certain personality types tend to be successful in certain occupational areas.

By and large Gauquelin's research is carefully designed and fully documented. A review of the available work, including the Gauquelins' work, is provided in Eysenck and Nias. On balance the evidence seems to suggest that there are some statistically significant relationships between the positions of heavenly bodies and some aspects of human behaviour that are consistent with astrological thought, although many astrological ideas are not supported by data. Overall, the work seems to provide some evidence for what Eysenck and Nias (1982) described as a 'connection between the affairs of man and the position of the planets at the time of birth' (p. 209).

It is also clear that, despite the support provided for astrology by Gauquelin's work, most orthodox scientists remain sceptical. Eysenck and Nias provided a description and evaluation of the reaction of the scientific community to Gauquelin's work.

Despite the availability of some evidence to support astrology it must also be pointed out that even when evidence appears to be strong there may be alternative explanations of the results that do not invoke astrological ideas. For example, one possible explanation of some of the apparently significant results involves using the idea of a self-fulfilling prophecy. Many people are aware of some of the various supposed links between astrological factors and occupational factors, some even get vocational guidance from astrologers. It is possible that knowledge of astrology (however slight) might influence peoples' occupational choices.

Indeed two studies referred to by Nias (1982) illustrate this point rather well. One study (Mayo, White and Eysenck, 1977) examined the link between the personality characteristic, extroversion/introversion, and signs of the zodiac. According to some astrological predictions people born under odd-numbered signs of the zodiac (such as Aries and Gemini) should display extrovert characteristics, and those born under even-numbered signs (such as Taurus and Cancer) should be more introverted. The results from the research did indeed produce the predicted pattern. Nias, however, reported two other studies where, for people who were less familiar with astrology or did not believe in it, no such relationship was observed. In general, however, it seems unlikely that Gauquelin's research can be dismissed entirely by this or any other currently available alternative explanation.

Within the specific context of personnel selection one final comment is in order. Even for research where evidence to support astrological ideas has been produced, the magnitude of the observed effect is rather small and would not provide a basis for powerful predictions of employment success, although the predictive value of astrological data may be quite unique and different from that obtained with other predictors. It is also, of course, true that if planetary influences on human behaviour are eventually accepted, a significant new phase in our understanding of human behaviour will have been attained.

HONESTY TESTS

Employee theft is of considerable concern in industries such as retailing, health care and manufacturing, and a number of questionnaires have been designed with the aim of predicting which employees are likely to be dishonest. The questionnaires adopt one of two main approaches. First, there are questionnaires which ask candidates if they have engaged in certain activities: for example, 'Have you ever stolen anything worth more than £5 from a previous employer?' or 'Have you ever had a conviction for theft?' Second, there are questionnaires which ask about candidates' opinions concerning dishonest practices: for example, 'Should a person be fired if caught stealing from an employer?' or, 'What percentage of people take more than £1 per week from their employer?'

Considering that honesty testing is a fairly new development, there is surprisingly plentiful evidence about how good it is. Sackett and Harris (1984) reviewed studies of ten different tests. One study, for example, looked at workers collecting donations for charities. It was found that those selected by the test collected, on average, $18 per day more than those with lower scores. Sackett and Harris argued a case that compelling evidence of the validity of honesty tests has not yet been produced, but they also noted that what stands out is the consistency of positive findings across tests and across validation situations. They also indicated that there seem to be few equal opportunity implications for these types of test.

Good information is available concerning one test, the Personnel Selection Inventory Dishonesty Scale. It is a scale which attempts to measure three aspects of undesirable behaviours: dishonesty, violence and emotional instability, and alcohol and drug use. A meta-analysis of a combined sample of 1806 applicants conducted by McDaniel and Jones (1986) indicated that the dishonesty scale has a validity of 0.5. This is probably an over-estimate of the scale's validity in operational settings since some of the subjects were students and the replies were anonymous. Furthermore, in some cases the subjects knew that independent evidence of their honesty was available. From the data supplied by McDaniel and Jones, it would appear that when these influences are taken into account the validity would be about 0.33.

ACCOMPLISHMENT RECORDS

Accomplishment records require considerable preparation. First the job is analysed, and then a simple form is drawn up and candidates are asked to state their previous accomplishments in each of the key areas. Finally, the statements are scored with a rating scale which gives specific examples of accomplishments at different levels (BARS). Initial results indicate that the method is highly reliable, and validity correlations of 0.25–0.47 were obtained against subsequent performance.

FUTURE AUTOBIOGRAPHIES

Most methods of selection use either past performance, such as experience, or current performance, such as tests, to predict future performance. It is probably apposite to end this chapter by briefly describing one measure which also looks into the future.

It starts with a notion from careers psychology: we all have some idea of what we would like to be and that our lives are a process of moving to our ideal. It follows that if we want to know how someone will behave in the future we need to find out their ideals. Perhaps the best example of future autobiographies is the work by Tullar and Barrett (1976).

Salesmen wrote a future autobiography stating what they would be doing five years from that date. Each future autobiography was then scored on three dimensions which were: (1) the extent to which he saw himself as the main determinant of his future; (2) the extent to which he saw life as a series of long term demands requiring effort; and (3) the extent to which he had a detailed and complex view of the future. The ratings were correlated with performance judgements provided by the salesmen's managers. The ratings of complexity were not particularly good and provided correlations of about 0.17. However, ratings for demand and self-determination seemed to offer some promise and yielded correlations of about 0.26 and 0.39 respectively. Such correlations are not particularly high and they are based on a tiny sample, but they may well be particularly important because they may measure aspects which are not covered by other methods of selection.

Part IV
Evaluation

13 Making a Decision and Estimating the Value of Selection

CLINICAL VERSUS ACTUARIAL

Whatever methods are employed to obtain data from candidates, the information must be used to choose the candidate who will be offered the job. The many ways of making this choice can be divided into two main types: clinical and actuarial.

As its name implies the *clinical* method follows the medical model in which an expert, or at least an experienced practitioner, reviews the available information, and the choice is made on the basis of their experience and expertise. The *actuarial* method follows the model of insurance assessment where various factors are quantified and then put in a formula which predicts the level of risk.

The main question is, which approach is the most accurate? Although the outcome is hard to generalise, the actuarial approach seems to offer the advantages of consistency and accuracy (see Meehl, 1954). Sawyer (1966) provided a more recent comparison of clinical as opposed to actuarial prediction and concluded that although clinical prediction, in some studies, could equal the statistical method, there was no case where the clinical method was actually superior. Nevertheless, the clinical approach may be best in extreme situations because the formulae used by the actuaries are based on samples which contain only a few extreme cases and therefore they produce a less solid base for decisions in special situations.

It seems clear that the actuarial method is superior to the clinical method, but the superiority is rarely more than 10 per cent. This means that when the actuarial method is not available, the clinical method should not be discounted.

ACTUARIAL APPROACHES

In a very simple situation where there is only one score and only one vacancy, the choice of candidate is straightforward: where everything

255

else is equal, the applicant with the highest score is offered the job. This is called 'top down' selection, and it will always produce the best probability of success even when the differences between candidates are small. However, if there is more than one score the scores must be combined in some way.

Simple Method

In a slightly more rigorous approach, the selector goes through the personnel specification and eliminates those candidates who do not have all the essential characteristics. The surviving candidates are then reconsidered and awarded a grade on, say, a six-point scale for each of the requirements (essential and desirable) on the personnel specification. The grades are then summed and, other things being equal, the candidate with the highest score is offered the job. In essence the selector using this simple system is using an actuarial approach. Suppose the personnel specification calls for qualities of verbal intelligence, assertiveness, conscientiousness and imagination, the implicit formula is:

predicted   =   (1 × verbal intelligence) + (1 × assertiveness)
suitability   + (1 × conscientiousness) + (1 × imagination)

It must be noted that the simple approach requires measures to be on the same scale (for example, a sten scale).

Weighting Scores

The simple method has the disadvantage that all items on the personnel specification are equally important. If this is not the case, it is necessary to multiply the items by an appropriate weighting. For example, it might be decided that verbal intelligence and conscientiousness are three times as important as imagination, and assertiveness is twice as important. The formula would then be: $ps = k + 3v + 3c + 2a + 1i$:

predicted   =   3 + (3 × verbal: intelligence) +
suitability   (3 × conscientiousness) +
                      (2 × assertiveness) + (1 × imagination)

The k represents a constant (in this case 3) which is usually needed to bring the mean to a particular desired level.

Multiple Regression Approach

In most situations, using judgement, discussion and advice to determine these weights is the only practical course of action. However, under certain circumstances they can be obtained with much greater precision. If follow-up data are available for a sample of 100 or more applicants, it is possible to use the statistical procedure of multiple regression (see Guilford and Fruchter, 1978). In essence, multiple regression tries to establish the exact combination of selection measures which produces the best prediction of a candidate's suitability.

Guion (1965) quotes two studies which compared the efficiency of the multiple regression approach and more simple weighting approaches. Lawshe and Schucker (1959) used three separate samples and found that the average success in identifying 'hits' for the weighting approach was 68 per cent, and the average success for the multiple regression approach was 66 per cent. Similarly Trattner (1963), studying a series of 12 different jobs, found that multiple regression produced slightly poorer estimates than a simple weighting approach. These results are surprising because, in theory, the multiple regression approach should produce optimum solutions. One possible explanation is that, in practice, imperfections in the test and minor violations of statistical assumptions mean that the power of the multiple regression approach is not used to the full.

Use of Minimum Cut-Off Points

The multiple regression approach is very powerful but it makes an important assumption: deficiencies in some characteristics can be compensated for by strengths in others. For example, it might be that a slightly dull branch manager can make up for his relative stupidity by being extremely conscientious. Undoubtedly, compensation of this kind is possible, but perhaps only up to a point. Probably some minimum level of intelligence is needed below which a person cannot cope, no matter how conscientious they are. Companies often use these cut-off points and their use is implicit in the rejection of candidates who do not meet the 'essential' requirements in the personnel specification.

Profile Similarity Approaches

An alternative ploy is to look at the profile of the scores on the different measures and compare it with a standard profile. The technique is useful when hard criteria are not available. The first stage is usually to establish the standard profile by collecting data on a sample of competent present employees. Each candidate's profile can be superimposed on to the standard profile and an estimate of the difference made. The candidate with the smallest difference is offered the job. Instead of relying on subjective estimates, it is better to calculate and sum the differences to provide an inverse index of similarity. Since large differences are usually more important than small differences, the customary practice is to square all differences before calculating the total. Figure 13.1 shows some of the complications which can arise with the profile similarity approach. The example is purely hypothetical and uses only four scores, but it shows that correlations should not be used in profile matching. Correlations are sensitive to shape rather than absolute differences. As the second example in Figure 13.1 shows, it is possible to obtain a high correlation even when massive absolute differences are present. On the other hand, distance measures are insensitive to the shape. Cattell, Eber and Tasuoka's (1970) pattern similarity coefficient produces an index which may be interpreted as an ordinary correlation but it is essentially a distance measure.

The use of data from present employees can produce difficulties. The sample of present employees will usually contain a mixture of good, bad and indifferent workers, so the average profile may not provide a good means of selecting out the worst employees. Similarly, present workers reflect, in part, the job requirements five years ago rather than present-day needs. Indeed, the company may have decided to instal a selection system in order to break away from the pattern set by its current employees. These problems can be overcome by using only 'ideal' or 'recent' employees in the sample for the standard profile, but only the very largest organisation will have enough employees for this strategy.

MULTIPLE VACANCIES FOR ONE JOB

When there is only one vacancy the decision-making is quite straightforward; other things being equal, the candidate with the highest combined mark derived from simple weighting or multiple regression or profile similarity is offered the job. However, if the company has a steady stream of vacancies and candidates the question becomes: will this particular candidate meet the standard, or should I wait for the next? To answer this type of question it will be necessary to

Figure 13.1   Complications in profile matching

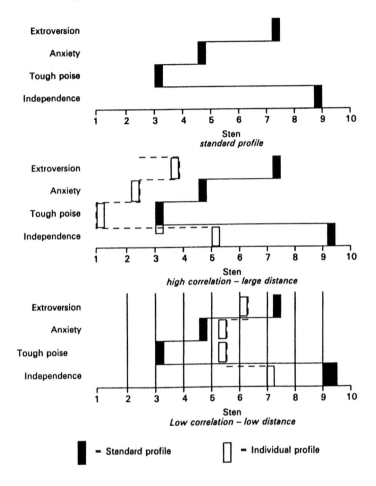

compare the predictor score with the criterion. The process is best demonstrated from a Belgian electronics assembly plant making ULMA fault detectors. The company administers a psychological test and arrives at a score for each applicant. It employs all 20 people and follows up their performance six months later. The work-study department has established that an efficient worker can assemble an average of 100 ULMA fault detectors per hour. The data on the test scores and the job performance are cast into a scattergram as shown in Figure 13.2. A minimum score is needed so that if an applicant calls

Figure 13.2 Relating predictors to performance using a scattergram

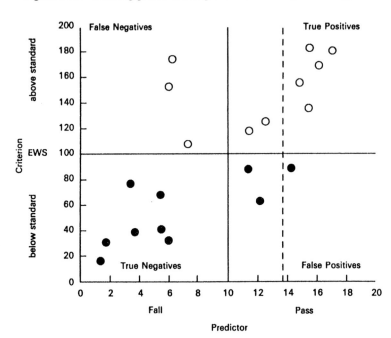

and undertakes the test, he or she can be given an answer fairly quickly. The problem is: how can this minimum score be set? A great deal depends on the number of applicants and the number of employees needed. In the example, the company estimates it receives 20 applications per year and that next year it will need seven 'good' ULMA assemblers. What minimum score could it use? The question can be answered by sliding a vertical ruler across the scattergram and counting the number of true positives. The minimum score should be the predictor score at which the true positives equal the number of employees required. In this case the answer is a score of 10. If only five 'good' assemblers are needed, the minimum score would be 14. In a real example, of course, a much larger sample would be needed.

An alternative approach is to plot a trend line which has as many points above as below (actually, the squares of the distances above and below the line should cancel out exactly if the trend line is perfect). The trend line can then be used to establish the test score most likely to produce an EWS (Efficient Worker Standard) of 100. This score can then be used as a cutting point.

MULTIPLE VACANCIES FOR SEVERAL JOBS

Deciding on cutting scores seems complex, but it merely scratches the surface. A part of the over-simplification reflects a concentration upon recruitment when the situation actually involves both recruitment and placement. This is particularly true of large organisations. For example, an international accountancy organisation recruits over 100 graduates each year, and subjects them to a two-year training programme. People react to this programme in different ways: some find it challenging, others find it frustrating. Some of those who are challenged rise to the occasion, others rest on their laurels. Some who are frustrated work hard and overcome their frustration, others give up. The company needs hard-working, achievement-orientated accountants for those clients who are ambitious and in the ascendancy. The company also needs relaxed, complacent, tolerant accountants for clients who are disorganised or stolid. The problem is to select the right people and then place them in the appropriate situation. This process is more complex. The complexity is probably best illustrated by Dunnette's (1963a) selection model. Dunnette's model is too imprecise to have a direct practical impact, but it is useful in reminding us that decisions are rarely as straightforward as they seem. A more statistical examination of some of these issues is given by Cronbach and Glesser (1965).

ESTIMATING THE MONETARY VALUE OF SELECTION

Quadrant Analysis

Quadrant analysis is the simplest method of estimating the utility of a selection system. It is most useful with a predictor with a clear pass/fail mark and a clear standard for the criterion. Criterion and predictor data are cast into a scattergram as in Figure 13.2 and a vertical line is drawn at the pass/fail mark while a horizontal line is drawn at the criterion standard. The first step is to establish the chance level of success by the number who perform above the criterion in the total sample. In Figure 13.2 the chance level is 50 per cent. The next step is to find out how many pass the test *and* turn out to be 'good' workers. This is divided by the number who pass the test. In this example, 70 per cent of those above the pass mark are also satisfactory workers. Consequently the use of the predictor has increased the percentage of acceptable workers by 20 per cent. Often it is more convenient to consider the percentage improvement in selection by relating the improvement to the baseline figure (that is, $20/50 \times 100 = 40$ per cent). It is worth noting that the percentage improvement in selection is strongly influenced by the position of the pass/fail mark.

If the company in the example had fewer vacancies it could raise the pass mark to 14 and only one-sixth of candidates would prove unsuccessful at the job. The percentage improvement in selection would be 66 per cent ($33/50 \times 100$). This example clearly demonstrates an important principle in selection: the usefulness of a selection method is strongly influenced by the number of applicants the company can afford to reject. A low selection ratio in which only a small proportion of applicants are offered jobs nearly always leads to improved efficiency of selection.

An example of quadrant analysis is given by Sneath, Tahkur and Medjuck (1976) in which a large New York underwriting firm administered the Card Punch Operators Aptitude Test (CPOAT) to a sample of 41. At the same time they collected information from supervisors which enabled the company to classify the operators as above average or below average. The results are given in Figure 13.3. Without using the test, 51 per cent ($21/41 \times 100$) of the company's workers were satisfactory. But by using the test 71 per cent of the workers were satisfactory ($15/21 \times 100$) and this represents an improvement in selection of 25 per cent. The correlation between test and criteria was 0.71.

Sneath's case study demonstrates that it is not necessary to plot a scattergram in order to calculate the efficiency of a selection device: it is possible to use simple frequency counts. It also demonstrates that the relationship between predictor and criteria can be expressed accurately as a correlation coefficient (however, it should be noted that in many cases the *tetrachoric* correlation, the *phi* coefficient or the *point biserial* correlation should be employed in preference to the more usual product moment correlation: see Guilford and Fruchter, 1978).

Expectancy Charts

The data from Sneath's case study can be expressed in another way: 70 per cent of candidates who pass the test can be expected to be good

Figure 13.3 CPOAT grades and efficiency of selection

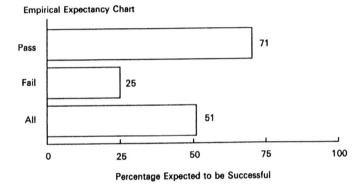

Frequency Count

		Below standard	Above standard	Combined
Predictor	Pass	6	15	21
	Fail	15	5	20

Empirical Expectancy Chart

Pass	71
Fail	25
All	51

Percentage Expected to be Successful

Source: Based on Sneath, Takhur and Medjack (1976).

operators, whereas only 25 per cent of candidates who fail the test can be expected to be good operators. On the basis of the frequency counts an empirical expectancy chart may be constructed and used as a basis for subsequent employment decisions. The use of expectancy charts was pioneered by Lawshe and Bolda (1958) and Lawshe, Bolda, Brune and Auclair (1958: see Appendix III).

Unfortunately, empirical expectancy charts are tedious to construct; they do not make the maximum use of the available data; and due to sampling errors they sometimes produce anomalous results (see Albright, Glennon and Smith, 1963, p. 93). These problems led Lawshe and co-workers to advocate the use of theoretical expectancy charts. First, it is necessary to obtain a correlation coefficient. Second, the selection ratio is computed. Finally, the table is used to identify the proportion of applicants who pass the selection procedure who would also be successful in the job. For example, in Sneath's case study, a correlation of 0.71 was obtained between the score on the

CPOAT and evaluation by their superiors. The company was satisfied with approximately 50 per cent of its employees. If the company used the test with a selection ratio of 50 per cent, then in theory it could expect it would be satisfied with 75 (extrapolated as halfway between the figures of 70 and 80 given by the B and C categories in Table C of Appendix III) per cent of its new employees (approximately what was obtained in practice). If the company selected only one applicant in five, it could expect to be satisfied with 90 per cent of its new employees, whereas if it accepted nine out of ten applicants, it could expect to be satisfied with only 55 per cent of its new employees.

Expectancy Tables and the Money Value

Expectancy calculations may be tedious, but they are extremely important in deciding whether a selection system is worthwhile. For example, a pilot study of 100 policemen in a local police force indicated that there was a correlation of 0.33 between scores on the 16PF test and success in the two-year training programme. It was found that 70 per cent of recruits successfully completed the course. To ensure a supply of 150 successful recruits each year, the police force needed to engage 215 cadets.

The question arose, would it be worth using the 16PF when the initial set-up costs, including the training of 12 testers and supply of test materials, would be about 18 000 ecus, and the annual cost would be about 18 000 ecus to screen about 2000 applicants per year? Expectancy tables can be used to answer this type of question. Turning to the section of the table where 70 per cent of employees are considered superior, it is possible to locate the theoretical expectancy for a correlation of 0.30 and a selection ratio of 0.2.

Using these parameters, 84 per cent of recruits could be expected to succeed if they were chosen on the basis of the 16PF test. Only 179 applicants would be needed to ensure 150 qualified policemen, representing a saving of 36 recruits per year.

Each wasted recruit costs 6000 ecus and the saving of 36 recruits represented a total saving of 216 000 ecus per year. In itself this would represent a return of over 600 per cent in the first year. This is a conservative estimate since the correlation was rounded down and it was assumed most of the costs (such as accommodation and instructors' time) could not be deployed elsewhere. Furthermore, there was no correction for attenuation of the criteria or the restriction of range. When these factors are taken into account the saving rises to over 370 000 ecus per year.

Limitations of Expectancy Tables

The use of expectancy tables in computing the monetary value of any selection system provides an acceptable basis for many decisions. However, the approach has its limitations. The tables usually produce a conservative estimate. The expectancy tables over-simplify the situation by dividing employees into successful and unsuccessful groups. A great deal of information is wasted by assuming all unsuccessful recruits are worthless and all successful recruits are equally productive. In fact, there is often a wide range of productivity even in successful recruits. Another important disadvantage is the arbitrary nature of the line between success and failure. This has a strong influence on the final monetary value. For example, suppose an employer uses a selection device with a validity of 0.5 and a selection ratio of 0.2 . If one manager judges that 50 per cent of employees are satisfactory, then the percentage improvement in selection will be 56 per cent (28/50). On the other hand, if another manager feels that only 30 per cent of employees are satisfactory the percentage improvement is 93 per cent (28/30).

ADVANCED METHODS OF CALCULATING MONETARY VALUE

Naylor–Shine Table and Jarratt's Table

Naylor and Shine (1965) attempted to overcome these difficulties by presenting a new set of tables where performance is assumed to be continuous, and they calculated the percentage improvement in productivity for different combinations of validity, selection ratio and spread of performance. Ghiselli and Brown (1955) attempted to simplify the use of the tables by devising the nomograph shown in Figure 13.4. In order to use the nomograph the selection ratio is located on the bottom axis and a line is projected up to the appropriate validity coefficient. The line is projected horizontally to the scale, giving the appropriate ratio of best to poorest worker and the percentage gain obtained. Jarratt's (1948) table is more complex. It

Figure 13.4 Ghiselli–Brown nomograph for estimating improvement in productivity from selection

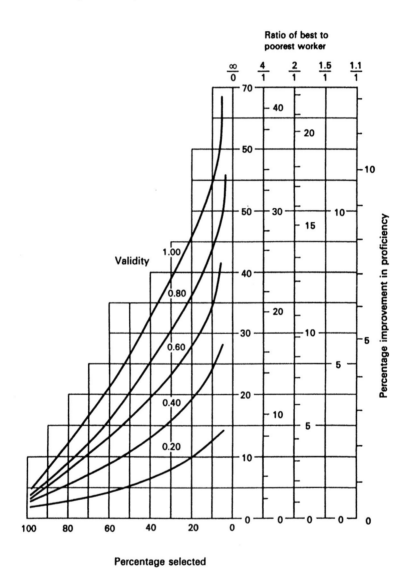

Percentage selected

requires knowledge of the standard deviation and the mean productivity of workers.

Both methods share several advantages: they are more precise and avoid the arbitrary decision between success and failure by acknowledging that productivity is a continuum rather than a dichotomy. A major disadvantage is that objective indices of productivity are not available for many jobs. But perhaps the main disadvantage of both the Naylor–Shine and Jarratt tables is that they finish just one stop short. They do not calculate the monetary value of selection. Whilst percentage improvement in efficiency is much more useful in decision-making than the usual jargon of psychologists (correlations, t statistics, F statistics, and so on), most managers are used to making decisions based upon money estimates.

Schmidt and Hunter's Decision Theoretic Equations

The work on utility theory was started in the 1950s and 1960s by Brogden but it remained a theoretical development until practical applications were identified by Hunter and Schmidt (1982). The method proceeds in five main stages. For the purposes of explanation we will imagine the calculations for the selection of salespeople who earn, on average, 20 000 ecus per year.

Stage 1: Selection at random

The first stage is to work out what would happen if selectors worked at random choosing employees with a pin. Elementary statistics predict that the output of a group of workers would form a normal, bell-shaped distribution, as shown in Figure 13.5, in which most salespeople would produce sales to the value of about 20 000 ecus, with a few producing much smaller sales and a few much larger sales. In order to describe the normal distribution two parameters are needed: the central point of the distribution (*the mean*) and a measure of spread (*the standard deviation*). The height of the curve at any given point on the bottom axis is known as the *ordinate*.

Stage 2: Perfect selection

The second stage is to work out what would happen if we were able to select employees with perfect accuracy. A lot depends on the selection ratio. If there are 10 applicants to every job the selection ratio is 0.1; if there are three applicants to every job the selection ratio is 0.33.

Figure 13.5   Selection at random

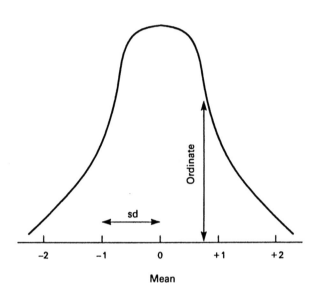

Obviously, if we were able to select with perfect accuracy we would select from the extreme right of the normal curve: that is, if we had a selection ratio of 0.33 we would select the top third of the distribution (the shaded part of Figure 13.6).

Statistics tables can be used to tell us where to draw the borderline between accepts and rejects. For example, the table in Appendix I shows that for a selection ratio of 0.33 we would need to draw the dividing line 0.43 standard deviations above the mean and that the ordinate at this point is 0.36.

The question arises, 'What is the average performance of those people in the shaded area (the selectees)?' This could be answered by drawing the diagram on graph paper and counting squares. This process is tedious and inaccurate. It is better to calculate the average productivity using the formula:

$$\text{average performance} = \frac{\text{ordinate}}{\text{selection ratio}}$$

Figure 13.6 Perfect selection

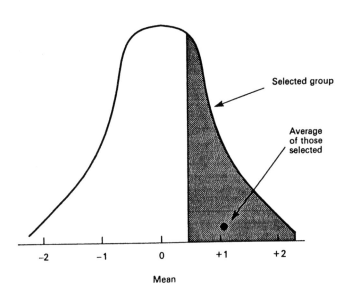

Thus, if the selection ratio is one-third and we can choose with perfect accuracy, the average output of the employees we select will be 1.09 standard deviations above average (0.36/0.33).

Stage 3: Selection in practice

It is obvious that we can never select perfectly. The figure from the previous stage is the theoretical maximum. It needs to be scaled down. The scaling down factor is the validity coefficient. This can be obtained by a specifically designed study or it can be estimated from the results of the meta-analyses. For the purposes of explanation, let us suppose that the company intends to select its salespersons on the basis of a selection procedure which meta analysis suggests has a validity of about 0.5. So, in practice, we would expect that selecting salespersons with this method and a selection ratio of one-third would raise the average performance of the salespersons by 0.55 standard deviations (1.09 × 0.5).

Stage 4: Conversion into money terms

Results in terms of standard deviations cut no ice with organisational decision-makers. Consequently, conversion of the results into money terms is a crucial step. It hangs on the question, 'How much is a standard deviation worth?' The question can be answered in three ways.

First, the accounts department can be asked to cost the output of a sample of 50–100 incumbents and the standard deviation can be computed. In the case of some operative occupations where there is a standard product whose market value is known this may be feasible. However, in many jobs (especially professional or managerial jobs) establishing the value of the finished product may be almost impossible. Further, this method cannot be used when there are only a few people in the job. The method is rarely attempted.

A second way of establishing the cash value of the standard deviation of performance is to ask experts to judge the value (Hunter and Schmidt, 1982). Typically, a group of ten or a dozen supervisors are asked to estimate the value of an average worker (50th percentile). Next they are asked to estimate the value of a good worker who is better than 85 per cent of workers. Finally, they are asked to estimate the value of a poor worker who is worse than 85 per cent of workers. The consensus figures for all the supervisors in the sample are calculated. As it happens, the 85th percentile is almost exactly one standard deviation from the mean, so it is easy to use the three estimates (mean, top 85 per cent and bottom 85 per cent) to calculate the money value of a standard deviation of performance. Even this procedure is time-consuming and there may not be enough supervisors available to form an acceptable sample of judges.

A third way of estimating the money value of the standard deviation is the 40 per cent rule. It was noticed that when the other methods were used they tended to give a figure which was 40 per cent of the wages. Thus, it seems reasonable to adopt this ratio as a general rule of thumb. Consequently, if a salesperson is earning 20 000 ecus per year, the monetary value of the standard deviation of performance is likely to be about 8000 ecus.

Once the value of the standard deviation of performance has been established it is easy to convert the improvement in standard deviation terms into an improvement in money terms. In our example the improvement in standard deviation terms was 0.55. Consequently, the improvement in money terms will be 4400 ecus per year (8000 × 0.55).

Subsequent research suggests that the 40 per cent rule is a very rough average; for operative jobs the percentage is nearer 20 while for high level jobs it is over 60.

Stage 5: Value per workgroup

Individuals rarely stay with an organisation for exactly one year, and selection systems are rarely used on just one person. The calculations need to be adjusted to reflect these facts. In our example, the average salesperson stays with the organisation for 1.5 years and the selection system is used to select 10 salespersons. This means that the improvement in money terms is 6600 ecus per individual or 66 000 ecus for all 10 salespeople (1.5 × 10 × 4400).

Stage 6: Taking costs into account

Selection systems do not appear out of thin air, and neither are they given free by test publishers and consultants. The processes of selection consume the time of the personnel department, and the expenses paid to applicants can mount up to a king's ransom. All of this must be set against the benefits. In the hypothetical example, the costs may well be 600 ecus per candidate and it was necessary to screen 30 applicants in order to obtain 10 successful ones. The total costs of 18 000 ecus must be subtracted from the benefit to reveal a net benefit of 48 000 ecus.

For most purposes the figure produced at the end of stage 5 will be quite adequate. It will be comparable to the estimates bandied by other functions as they make their bids for resources. It can form the basis for further calculation of the ratios such as 'rate of return on capital' or 'payback period', which decision-makers use when allocating resources.

However, two notes of caution are needed: this method of calculation is not appropriate in certain circumstances and, in fact, the calculations need to be refined further.

Refining the Utility Estimates

The huge savings indicated by utility analyses are probably an over-estimate. John Boudreau points out they need to be adjusted for three additional factors which may have a marked effect on the result of the calculation (perhaps reducing it by 80 per cent). These additional factors need to be handled with care. They apply to all organisational investments and it would be stupid and unfair for the personnel function to include them when production and data processing do not include them in theirs. The three additional factors are variable costs, inflation and taxes.

Variable costs need to be taken into account because good workers generally incur more expenditure than poor workers. This is most clearly seen in the case of sales representatives. A good representative will spend more time 'on the road' and will have higher travel claims. He or she will use more brochures and the extra business generated will probably mean a higher level of stock needs to be maintained. These extra costs must be subtracted from the extra sales revenue that a good representative achieves.

Inflation must also be taken into account. Most selection costs are 'upfront' at the point of engagement, whilst the benefits of having a more able work force accumulate over a number of years. Inflation means that today's money is almost certain to be worth several percentage points more than tomorrow's money.

Most organisations pay *tax*. The government will cream off a slice of any benefit. Organisations exempt from tax should note the implications of tax exemption: because some of the benefit is not syphoned off, good selection is particularly cost-effective in organisations which do not pay tax.

The calculation of these effects is not particularly new; the financial department in most organisations can be asked to provide the appropriate expertise.

Utility Analysis and Human Resource Management

Perhaps one of the most exciting prospects is the role which utility analysis will have in enabling the personnel function to manage an organisation's human resources more effectively. At present, personnel managers have to make many subjective decisions. Faced with a decision on how to use a windfall budget of 100 000 ecus, how does a personnel manager decide between the many possible options, such as a wider advertising campaign for operatives, the introduction of situational interviews for clerical staff, or establishing assessment centres for management? Utility analysis can be used to guide these decisions in a quantitative way.

For example, Boudreau and Rynes (1985) looked at a decision which might face one organisation: should they spend money developing an advertising campaign and a biodata key which could be used to score application forms, or should they employ a recruitment agency and then interview those forwarded? Both strategies have advantages and disadvantages. Press advertising is likely to attract many moderately suitable candidates, but screening application forms is quite a good method of selection. The recruitment agency, on the other hand, seems likely to attract a better pool of candidates, but the interview is a poor way of selecting among them. Faced with this choice, a personnel manager must usually rely on intuition and experience. Like all human intuition and experience this can be very subjective. Utility analysis can be used to work out the costs and benefits so that an informed decision can be made. In the particular circumstances envisaged by Boudreau and Rynes the use of the recruitment agency appeared to be the superior strategy. In practice, the utility of other combinations needs to be examined.

Utility analysis can be used to work out the sensitivity or the robustness of recruitment strategies. Decisions need to be made in anticipation of the future. Often the future does not conform to expectations. Utility analysis can be used to see how easily a selection strategy can be blown off course. For example, a company may design a selection system on the assumption that the labour market remains fairly favourable at a selection ratio of four applicants for every job. However, labour markets can change. So, the organisation repeats the calculations assuming an improvement in the labour market to, say, six applicants per job. It also repeats the calculations assuming a deteriorating market where it will need to accept one out of every two applicants. If necessary it could also vary the expected length of service or the numbers likely to be recruited. In this way, decision-making can become very sophisticated and the company may not choose the selection method or strategy which yields the highest value; instead it may choose the selection strategy which produces the surest results.

A final implication needs to be noted. The methods of utility analysis are beginning to be applied to other personnel techniques such as training, participation and incentive schemes. The available data do not allow any firm comparisons to be drawn. But, looking at the horizon, there are indications that selection is one of the most cost-effective techniques. Using these techniques, Hunter and Schmidt (1982) attempted to assess the dollar value of using the Programmer Aptitude Test to select 600 computer programmers per year. A saving of at least $5.6 million was indicated. Bravely, Hunter and Schmidt went on to extrapolate these findings to the employment of programmers in the whole USA and concluded that, under the most conservative assumptions, a saving of $93 million is possible. They suggest that such a high level of gain is not atypical and that in 1982 new selection procedures could save $600 per checkout clerk, $540 per adding-machine operative, $348 per production worker, $1020 per clerical worker and $424 per nursing aide. Independent corroboration is offered by Arnold, Rauschenberger, Soubel and Guion (1982), who used a simple measure of strength, an arm dynamometer, to predict the productivity of steelworkers; the test had an average utility of $5000 per year for each employee selected. During the fiscal year of 1979 the company hired 1853 entry-level workers. The average tenure of a new hire is about one year. Based on this information, the estimated yearly utility of the test would be £9.1 million.

14 The Impact of Assessment, Selection and Feedback on Candidates

IMPACT ON CANDIDATES

In a sense, the classical view of the personnel selection process implies that making an assessment of someone is a psychologically neutral procedure, which has no impact on the person being assessed. However, there *is* some evidence to suggest that being assessed (even without feedback) could be an important event for someone and may have some psychological impact; for example, Schmitt, Ford and Stults (1986) have shown that being exposed to at least some selection methods may bring about small changes in self-perception. When assessment is coupled with feedback and a selection/promotion decision, the possibility of impact on candidates is enhanced.

The topic has been identified as a research need for some time (see Thornton and Byham, 1982; Dreher and Sackett, 1983; Smith and Robertson, 1989). Research that has been done may be divided into two main categories: exploring candidates' reactions to assessment and selection, and work focused on the actual psychological impact of the assessment procedure or decision on candidates.

Work in the first category, exploring candidates' reactions to assessment and selection, has centred on particular selection techniques. Several studies have explored candidates' reactions to assessment centres (see Bourgeois, Leim, Slivinsk and Grant, 1975; Dodd, 1977; Teel and Dubois, 1983; Robertson, Iles, Gratton and Sharpley, 1991). It is difficult, in this kind of research, to separate the reactions to the assessment procedure from reactions to the selection decision, and in general candidates react less well to the procedure if the decision is negative as far as they are concerned. This is not a universal finding, however, and some of the research cited above provides examples of situations where successful and unsuccessful candidates have reacted in similar ways to the assessment process.

This suggests that it is possible to design assessment procedures so that even unsuccessful candidates are content with the procedure adopted.

Although most of the work on candidates' reactions to assessment has looked at assessment centres, other procedures have also received attention. M. S. Taylor and Bergman (1987) and Harris and Fink (1987) looked at reactions to USA campus interviews and Robertson *et al.* (1991) looked at structured, situational interviews.

A relatively small amount of research has moved beyond examining candidates' reactions and looked at psychological impact. Noe and Schmitt (1986) found that trainees' reactions to assessment helped to predict their satisfaction with subsequent training. Noe and Steffy (1987) found that candidates' subsequent career exploratory behaviour was related to the favourability of earlier assessment. Robertson *et al.* (1991) found links between post-assessment work and organisation attitudes/intentions and features of the assessment process (such as candidates' success or failure).

Avoiding Negative Impact

This line of research into the impact of personnel selection and assessment on candidates is in its early stages and few clear conclusions are possible. It is, nevertheless, possible to use the research evidence and some rules of thumb about good practice to generate a brief set of guidelines. Assessment centres have a reasonably good track record in identifying managerial talent and are used in many organisations to help identify potential. Individuals who participate in assessment or development centres and do not get positive feedback, promotion or development may find the experience demotivating and reduce their commitment to the organisation. Clearly selection decisions must be taken. Organisations cannot promote all internal candidates; indeed, at some stage in their career most people are likely to be given the explicit or implicit message that further progression is unlikely. Maximising the benefit and minimising the damage of selection and assessment procedures may be dependent on the procedures used, how they are used and how feedback is delivered to participants. There are at least four principles that may help to get the most positive impact from selection and assessment procedures.

The first principle of *using valid and reliable methods* is important in the sense of maximising the likelihood of good decisions and providing a basis for accurate feedback. Candidates, perhaps more than anyone, are in a position to recognise the accuracy and fairness of decisions and feedback. Educating both assessors and candidates by *providing them with some grasp of the research* on different methods is the second sound principle and should help to ensure that both groups understand the limitations of assessment techniques and develop realistic expectations about what can be achieved. The third principle of *valuing solid performers* as well as high fliers is not well established in many corporate cultures; instead, the notion that being successful in the organisation involves continuous, upward job progression is the norm. Only relatively small numbers of people can live up to this concept of success and anything other than more-or-less continuous progress may produce negative feelings. Assessment events and procedures may provide a focus and sharpen these negative feelings unless it is clear that being successful and being valued by the organisation is more complex than merely being promoted to the next level of seniority or being assigned to the 'fast-track'. Fourth, *give developmental rather than judgemental feedback*. The issue of feedback is so important that it requires a section of its own.

FEEDBACK TO CANDIDATES

The question of feedback to candidates is a very important one which an organisation should think through with care.

At a simplistic level it is possible to follow the strategy of always giving as much feedback as possible. This has the advantage of being open and honest: it is usually successful when the feedback is overwhelmingly positive. However, there may be difficulties with unsuccessful candidates and where the feedback is negative: argument and perhaps litigation can result. Perhaps the ideal situation would be to provide feedback plus proper counselling but, of course, this option is very expensive and, in organisational terms, may not represent the best use of personnel resources. Full feedback can also compromise the security and often the fairness of the selection procedure.

These difficulties lead some organisations to adopt the opposite policy of giving no feedback, or perhaps only the most general indication. This policy has excellent defensive qualities. It is also cheap and maintains the confidentiality of the selection procedures. However, many candidates find it intensely unsatisfactory: it gives the impression of being arbitrary and secretive.

Other organisations adopt an intermediate strategy of providing feedback up to a point but making it clear that further feedback is not available. Generally, feedback of this kind starts with a general indication of the level of the candidature (for example, 'You were an excellent candidate and please contact us again . . . ', 'You were a good candidate', or 'we feel that your strengths would be best appreciated in other jobs where . . . '. The feedback then goes on to indicate the one or two most positive aspects of the application plus tactful references to one or two negative features which may be euphemistically referred to as 'development points'.

With internal applicants, the question of feedback is particularly acute and, if it is badly handled, it may cause the person to leave or arouse general discontent. In the worst case scenario, it results in years of suboptimal performance because an able but rejected candidate 'switches off'. In most circumstances, feedback to internal candidates should be on a one-to-one basis and a meeting should be offered at the time when the rejection is made known. The meeting needs to have an ample allowance of time. Often, a good start is to ask the ex-candidate what they thought about the selection procedures used. It is a relatively neutral topic and it allows any misunderstandings about procedures, which could form the basis for discontent, to be cleared up. The middle part of the session is probably best devoted to feedback itself. One format is to sandwich negative feedback in between positive feedback at the start and finish of this phase. Evidence from Fletcher and Williams (1976) suggests that no more than two negative points should be made. In many cases, it is appropriate to end the meeting with a problem-solving phase in which the candidate is encouraged to adopt a positive strategy which meets their own and the organisation's needs. In this way the feedback takes on a developmental mode, as recommended in the previous section.

Practical Aspects of Feedback to Candidates

Establishing an appropriate tone

Generally, the purpose and expected length of the feedback session should be indicated in advance and the session itself can start with a cheery question such as 'How did you find the tests?' This achieves a number of functions: it gives the candidate an opportunity to introduce things that are worrying him or her or explain things which may have affected their performance; it allows the selector to judge the mood of the person and perhaps the approach to be used; finally, a question of this kind sets the tone that the person is expected, right from the start, to participate and not be a passive recipient of information. This tone should be maintained throughout the feedback session by providing the person with pauses and opportunities to ask questions, to clarify understanding and to comment on the methods of selection. At various points, particularly before moving on to a new set of information – or before drawing together conclusions, or exploring the implications – the candidate's views on the accuracy of the results should be elicited. Often all that is needed is a question: 'Do you think that is a fair picture or is there something that is not quite right?'

Establishing information

When providing feedback, the golden rule is that the information transmitted by the selector is less important than the impression left in the mind of the recipient. A long-winded, technical report can sometimes only serve to confuse. The knowledge and the state of mind of the recipient must be taken into account. In general this means that the names of scales must be given in lay terms which are accurate and meaningful. For example, when reporting the scores on the WAIS it would, under most circumstances, be silly to refer to 'digit span'. It would probably be better to use the term 'short-term memory'. When giving information on more than a few scores, it is generally better to provide profiles and visual aids. Whenever possible the profiles should be designed in a way that the inter-relationships between scales and the precision of measurement are made clear by using proximity, boxes, arrows and perhaps colour.

Two other aspects often help to establish understanding. In most circumstances the same scoring system should be used throughout. It is confusing to present one set of scores as stens, another set as quotients and another set as T scores. It is usually best to standardise on one or two: perhaps stens and percentiles. The sequence in which information is given can also aid understanding. One strategy is to work from the global to the specific. For example, in feeding back the WAIS results, it is probably more meaningful to start with the 'Full Scale Score', then consider the verbal and non-verbal scores, and only then consider the scores on the individual scales. This approach often aids understanding but it is against the grain for the many psychologists who, quite logically and properly when arriving at *their* analysis, build up from the specific to the more general.

Written feedback to candidates

It is permissible to be a little more technical when providing written feedback to candidates because technical sections can be re-read until their meaning is understood. Generally, a written report should contain some explanation of why particular measures have been used. For example, a report could contain the following sentences: 'The job of Financial Director requires people to reason in terms of numbers. Consequently, our procedure included a high level test which required you to abstract relevant financial information, determine a long-term trend in the information and to anticipate the likely consequences of that information. As it was a high level test, the items were very difficult even though ample time was allowed.' A written report would also give details of the norm group against which the scores were compared. For example, a comment might be: 'Your scores were compared with those of a large sample of graduate applicants. As the job is at a senior level, we used a fairly stringent level and we were looking for someone who attained a higher score than 70 per cent of graduate applicants.'

It is important to treat predictions of performance very carefully in written feedback. A typical comment might be, 'Your score suggests that selling direct to customers would not be an appropriate position.' In fact a series of comments are needed to cover eventualities of a very high prediction, a high prediction, an above average prediction, an acceptable prediction, a poor prediction and a very poor prediction. The latter categories need careful handling and should be expressed in a way which does not mislead a candidate into false action or misunderstanding (such as wasting effort applying for jobs where they are patently unsuitable) but which still allows him or her to maintain self-respect. Generally, it is better not to reveal numerical scores as they may be over-interpreted. Once the result has been stated, some indication of the confidence in the result and the predictions made is needed. For example, it might be necessary to write, 'It is fairly certain that if you took the test another day the same result would be obtained. There is, however, a one in eight chance that you would score in a higher category.' In other situations, it might be better to use verbal labels such as 'It is fairly certain that . . . ', 'It is likely that . . . ', or 'It is possible that . . . '. If there is a reason to believe that the candidate has some grasp of statistical jargon it may be permissible to write in terms of confidence limits and levels of probability.

Reports to organisations

Written reports to organisations are generally more succinct and may be more technical since the organisation's personnel probably have greater familiarity with the methods, procedures and jargon. However, it is still probably worth including an explanation of the technical aspects, either as an introduction or appendix.

Almost invariably there will be a need for a summary, probably at the start of the report. Where there is only one candidate, the summary should probably start with a recommendation for action and there are probably only three types of recommendation: hire without significant reservation; hire only if there is pressure to make an appointment; and do not hire. This limited range of possibilities is based on the assumption that a selection decision is being taken. If development, rather than selection, is the goal of assessment, the range of recommendations is much more varied. The subsequent sections in the report should then give the rationale for the decision. This rationale must be related to the test scores. It should also take into account the personnel specification: the more emphasis the personnel specification gives to an attribute measured by a test or other device, the less leeway there is to accept unsatisfactory scores. The rationale should also give an indication of the weights to be given to various items of evidence. In general, scores with higher reliabilities and proven validities should be given the highest weighting.

Where the results of several candidates are to be reported, it is usually better to use a tabular form of summary. Considerable ingenuity needs to be devoted to the design of the table. If possible, the visual arrangement should imply the conclusions and the weight to be placed on various items of information. For example, the list should probably start with the candidate with the best 'performance' (on the basis of the scores) and proceed to the candidate who has performed least well. Usually, the data justifying the greatest weight should be placed to the left of the page next to the candidate's name, so that it will be one of the first things to come to the attention of the reader. A well-designed format of this kind can be an invaluable aid in structuring the thought processes behind decisions and in highlighting inconsistencies. It is often useful to construct a table of this kind using a computer spreadsheet which allows the constant adjustment of the arrangement of rows and columns. If items are highly correlated, and therefore probably measuring the same thing, this can be signalled to the reader by giving both sets of information in the same column.

The body of the report should then contain a factual account of the data which would allow other people to reconstruct and independently evaluate the information. There should be a clear statement of the tests and scales used, the scores obtained and any norms applied. This is also the place to report any notable correlations between scales. The main report is also the place to indicate the significance of any differences between scores, although this can be implied by the fact that insignificant differences are ignored. One useful framework for the construction of the body of the report is the personnel specification, perhaps by starting and dealing in greatest depth with the items marked 'essential' on the personnel specification. Purists may insist that the body of the report also gives the standard errors, confidence limits of the group means and the test scores of the candidate. In practice, however, inclusion of these details in the main text makes a report almost unreadable and these details are often best placed in an appendix. A final point concerning reports is that care should be taken to exclude information which is unsystematic (such as corridor talk with just one candidate, personal likes or antipathies and the uninformed comments of others such as the observations of receptionists) or information which has been given on the agreed basis that it would not be reported.

Appendix I: Ordinates of the Normal Curve

Standard score Z	Selection ratio	Ordinate
2.33	1/100	0.027
2.05	1/50	0.048
1.64	1/20	0.103
1.28	1/10	0.176
1.15	1/8	0.206
1.06	1/7	0.228
0.97	1/6	0.248
0.84	1/5	0.280
0.67	1/4	0.319
0.43	1/3	0.364
0.00	1/2	0.399
−0.43	2/3	0.364
−0.67	3/4	0.318
−0.84	4/5	0.280
−1.28	9/10	0.176
−2.33	99/100	0.027

Appendix II: Standard Errors for Various Levels of Reliability

Reliability	Z	Quotient	T Score	Sten	Stannine
0.95	0.22	3.35	2.24	0.45	0.45
0.90	0.32	4.74	3.16	0.63	0.63
0.85	0.39	5.81	3.87	0.77	0.77
0.80	0.45	6.71	4.47	0.89	0.89
0.75	0.50	7.50	5.00	1.00	1.00
0.70	0.55	8.22	5.48	1.10	1.10
0.65	0.59	8.87	5.92	1.18	1.18
0.60	0.63	9.49	6.32	1.26	1.26
0.55	0.67	10.06	6.71	1.34	1.34
0.50	0.71	10.61	7.07	1.41	1.41

Notes on Use of Table

Step One: Establish level of reliability from test manual or other sources.
Step Two: Determine type of scale used.
Step Three: Read the standard error.
            For example, a test with a reliability of 0.90 using a quotient scale would have a standard error of 4.74.
            A test with a reliability of 0.60 using either stens or stannines would have a standard error of 1.26.

To establish *cutting scores* multiply the standard error of the Z score from the normal curve for the alpha level chosen (the tolerable margin of error). Typical values are shown in the next table.

Probability of score lying inside limits (α level)	verbal label	Z	half Z
0.50	as likely as not	0.00	0.67
0.33	twice as likely as not	0.43	0.97
0.10	9 times as likely as not	1.28	1.64
0.05	19 times as likely as not	1.64	1.96

To establish *confidence limits* multiply the standard error by Z for half the alpha (because the probability has to be distributed on *each* side of the mean).

Appendix III: Expectancy Tables

TABLE A: THEORETICAL EXPECTANCIES WHERE 30 PER CENT
ARE 'SUPERIOR'

	Predictor categories*				
r	A	B	C	D	E
0.15	38	35	33	32	30
0.20	40	37	34	32	30
0.25	43	39	36	33	30
0.30	46	40	37	33	30
0.35	49	42	38	34	30
0.40	51	44	39	34	30
0.45	55	46	40	35	30
0.50	58	48	41	35	30
0.55	61	50	42	36	30
0.60	64	52	43	36	30
0.65	68	54	44	37	30
0.70	72	57	46	37	30
0.75	76	59	47	37	30
0.80	80	62	48	37	30
0.85	85	65	49	37	30

*Predictor category code: institution expectancies, A – upper 20%; B – upper
40%; C – upper 60%; D – upper 80%, E – all.
Source: Lawshe *et al.* (1958). Used by permission.

Tables continue over

Appendix III

TABLE B: THEORETICAL EXPECTANCIES WHERE 40 PER CENT
ARE SUPERIOR

	Predictor categories*				
r	A	B	C	D	E
0.15	48	46	44	42	40
0.20	51	48	45	43	40
0.25	54	49	46	43	40
0.30	57	51	47	44	40
0.35	60	53	49	45	40
0.40	63	56	50	45	40
0.45	66	58	51	46	40
0.50	69	60	53	46	40
0.55	72	62	54	47	40
0.60	75	64	55	48	40
0.65	79	67	57	48	40
0.70	82	69	58	49	40
0.75	86	72	60	49	40
0.80	89	75	61	49	40
0.85	93	79	63	50	40

*Predictor catgeory code: institutional experiences, A – upper 20%; B – upper
40%; C – upper 60%; D – upper 80%; E – all.
Source: Lawshe *et al.* (1958). Used by permission.

TABLE C: THEORETICAL EXPECTANCIES WHERE 50 PER CENT
ARE 'SUPERIOR'

	Predictor categories*				
r	A	B	C	D	E
0.15	58	56	54	52	50
0.20	61	58	55	53	50
0.25	64	60	56	54	50
0.30	67	62	58	54	50
0.35	70	64	59	55	50
0.40	73	66	61	56	50
0.45	75	68	62	56	50

r	A	B	C	D	E
0.50	78	70	63	57	50
0.55	81	72	65	58	50
0.60	84	75	66	59	50
0.65	87	77	68	59	50
0.70	90	80	70	60	50
0.75	92	82	72	61	50
0.80	95	85	73	61	50
0.85	97	88	76	62	50

*Predictor catgeory code: institutional experiences, A – upper 20%; B – upper 40%; C – upper 60%; D – upper 80%; E – all.
Source: Lawshe *et al.* (1958). Used by permission.

TABLE D: THEORETICAL CATGORIES WHERE 60 PER CENT ARE 'SUPERIOR'

	*Predictor categories**				
r	A	B	C	D	E
0.15	68	66	64	62	60
0.20	71	67	65	63	60
0.25	73	69	66	63	60
0.30	76	71	68	64	60
0.35	78	73	69	65	60
0.40	81	75	70	66	60
0.45	83	77	72	66	60
0.50	86	79	73	67	60
0.55	88	81	75	68	60
0.60	90	83	76	69	60
0.65	92	85	78	70	60
0.70	94	87	80	71	60
0.75	96	90	81	71	60
0.80	98	92	83	72	60
0.85	100	97	88	74	60

*Predictor category code: institutional expectancies, A – upper 20%; B – upper 40%; C – upper 60%; D – upper 80%; E – all.
Source: Lawshe *et al.* (1958). Used by permission.

TABLE E: THEORETICAL CATGORIES WHERE 70 PER CENT ARE 'SUPERIOR'

	Predictor categories*				
r	A	B	C	D	E
0.15	77	75	73	72	70
0.20	79	77	75	73	70
0.25	81	78	76	73	70
0.30	84	80	77	74	70
0.35	86	82	76	75	70
0.40	88	83	79	75	70
0.45	90	85	91	76	70
0.50	91	87	82	77	70
0.55	93	88	83	78	70
0.60	95	90	85	79	70
0.65	96	92	86	80	70
0.70	97	93	88	80	70
0.75	98	95	89	81	70
0.80	99	97	91	82	70
0.85	100	98	93	84	70

*Predictor category code: institutional expectancies, A – upper 20%; B – upper 40%; C – upper 60%; D – upper 80%; E – all.
Source: Lawshe *et al.* (1958). Used by permission.

Appendix IV: Some Useful Formulae

FORMULAE FOR STANDARD DEVIATIONS

1.1
$$\sigma = \sqrt{\frac{\sum x^2}{Np}}$$
general formula for standard deviation of a population

1.2
$$\sigma = \sqrt{\frac{\sum x^2}{N-1}}$$
standard deviation of a population calculated from sample size N

where x = deviation from mean (i.e., $x_i - \bar{x}$)
N = sample size
Np = size of population

1.3
$$\sigma = \frac{1}{N}\sqrt{\sum x_i^2 - \left(\sum x_i\right)^2}$$
standard deviation computed without knowledge of deviations

where x_i = scores
N = sample size

FORMULAE FOR CORRELATIONS

2.1
$$r_{xy} = \frac{\sum XY}{N\sigma_x\sigma_y}$$
basic formula for product moment correlation

where X and Y are scores

2.2
$$xy = \frac{N\sum XY - \left(\sum X\right)\left(\sum Y\right)}{\sqrt{[N\sum X^2 - \left(\sum X\right)^2][N\sum Y^2 - \left(\sum Y\right)^2]}}$$
formula for computing product moment correlation from original data

where X and Y are original scores

2.3
$$\rho = 1 - \frac{6\sum D^2}{N(N^2-1)}$$
basic formula for rank order correlation

where D are differences in ranks

289

2.4
$$r_b = \frac{M_p - M_q}{\sigma_t} \times \frac{pq}{y}$$

bi-serial coeffcient used when one variable is reduced to two categories

where:

Mp = mean value for higher group
Mq = mean value for lower group
p = proportion of cases in higher group
q = proportion of cases in lower group
y = ordinate of normal curve at division p/q
σ_t = standard deviation of total sample

2.5
$$r_b = \frac{M_q - M_t}{\sigma_t} \times \frac{p}{y}$$

alternative bi-serial formulae

2.6
$$r_{pbi} = \frac{M_p - M_q}{\sigma_t} \sqrt{pq}$$

point bi-serial coefficient used when one of the variables is a genuine

2.7
$$r_{pbi} = \frac{M_p - M_t}{\sigma_t} \sqrt{\frac{p}{y}}$$

alternative point bi-serial formula

2.8
$$r_{cos-pi} = cos\left(\frac{180° \sqrt{bc}}{\sqrt{ad} + \sqrt{bc}}\right)$$

tetrachoric correlation used when both variables are reduced to a dichotomy

where a, b, c, d are respective frequencies in a 2×2 contingency table

2.9
$$r = \frac{t}{\sqrt{(t^2 + (N_t - 2)}}$$

estimation of point bi-serial correlation from t statistic

where:

N_t = total number in study

FORMULAE FOR ESTIMATING STANDARD ERRORS

3.1
$$se = sd \times \sqrt{1 - r_{xx}}$$

formula for estimating standard error from a reliabilty coefficient where:

se = standard error
sd = standard deviation of scale used
r_{xx} = reliabilty coefficient

3.2 $se_{comp} = \sqrt{se_1^2 + se_2^2 + 2r_{12}se_1se_2}$

formula for standard error of difference between two scores

where:

se_{comp} = standard error of composite
se_1 = standard error of measure 1
se_2 = standard error of measure 2
r_{12} = correlation between measures 1 and 2

3.3 $se_{diff} = \sqrt{se_1^2 + se_2^2 - 2r_{12}se_1se_2}$

formula for standard error of difference between two scores

notation as above but,

se_{diff} = standard error of the difference between two scores

FORMULAE FOR CORRECTING PRODUCT MOMENT CORRELATIONS

4.1 $r_{xy}\infty = \dfrac{r_{xy}}{\sqrt{r_{yy}}}$

where:

correction for attenuation of criterion

$r_{xy}\infty$ = corrected correlation
r_{xy} = original correlation
r_{yy} = reliabilty of criterion (or estimate of)

4.2 $r_n = \dfrac{2r_{hh}}{1 + r_{hh}}$

where:

Spearman-Brown correction for split-half reliability

r_n = corrected correlation
r_{hh} = original correlation based on half of the questions

4.3
$$r_c = \frac{r(\sum/\sigma)}{\sqrt{1 - r^2 + r^2(\sum^2/\sigma^2)}}$$

correlation for restriction of range of predictor (for example, test)

r_c = corrected correlation
r = original correlation
σ = standard deviation in restricted sample
$\sum$ = standard deviation in population

4.4
$$r_c = \sqrt{1 - \left(\frac{\sigma^2}{\sum^2}\right)(1 - r^2)}$$

correlation for restriction of range of criterion

same notation as 4.3.

4.5
$$cR^2 = 1 - (1 - R^2)\left(\frac{N-1}{n-m}\right)$$

formula for shrinkage of multiple correlation

where:

N = sample size
m = number of variables
R = unshrunk correlation
cR = corrected multiple correlation

FORMULAE FOR PROFILE MATCHING

5.1
$$r_p = \frac{4K - \sum w_j d_j^2}{4K + \sum d_j^2}$$

formula for comparing two group profiles where weights are attached to components

where:

K = median×square for number of scores in profile
w_j = weight to be given to a score (usually based on standard deviation of jth score)
d_j = difference between two groups in jth score

5.2
$$r_p = \frac{(4K + \sum D^2) - \sum d^2}{(4K - \sum D^2) - \sum D^2}$$

formula for comparing an individual profile with a group profile

where:

D = the difference between the group mean on a factor and the population mean

d = the difference between on individual score and group mean

FORMULAE FOR EVALUATING TEST UTILITY

6.1 $$k = \sqrt{1 - r^2}$$ coefficient of alienation (degree of lack of relationships)

6.2 $$E = 100(1 - \sqrt{1 - r^2})$$ index of forecasting efficiency (percentage reduction in error by prediction)

6.3 $$d = r^2 \times 100$$ coefficient of determination (percentage of variance accounted for)

6.4 $$\Delta u = (\Theta/p \times r \times SD_y \times N \times T) - c$$ utility of selection of N individuals over T years taking cost of selecting each individual into account

where p = proportion selected
Θ = ordinate of normal curve with probability of p
r = validity coefficient
SD_y = money value of one standard deviation in performance
N = number of people selected
T = average tenure
c = total selection costs including costs of those not offered employment

Bibliography

Abrahams, N. M. and Alf, E. (1972a) 'Pratfalls in moderator research', *Journal of Applied Psychology*, 56, 3, 245–51.

Abrahams, N. M. and Alf, E. (1972b) 'Reply to Dunnette's "Comments on Abrahams and Alf's 'Pratfalls in moderator research' " ' *Journal of Applied Psychology*, 56, 3, 257–61.

Ackerman, P. L. (1989) 'Within-task intercorrelations of skilled performance: implications for predicting individual differences?' (a comment on R. A. Henry and Hulin, 1987), *Journal of Applied Psychology*, 74, 2, 360–64.

Adkins, D. C. (1974) *Test Construction* (Columbus, Ohio: Merrill).

Albright, L. E., Glennon, J. R. and Smith, W. J. (1963) *The Use of Psychological Tests in Industry* (Copenhagen: Munksgaard).

Albright, L. E., Smith, W. J. and Glennon, J. R. (1959) 'A follow up on some "invalid" tests for selecting salesmen', *Personnel Psychology*, 12, 105–12.

Anastasi, A. (1982) *Psychological Testing* (New York: Macmillan).

Anderson, E. B. (1983) 'Analysing data using the Rasch model', in S.B.L. Anderson and H. S. Helmicle (eds), *An Educational Testing* (San Francisco: Jossey-Bass).

Anderson, N. and Shackleton, V. (1990) 'Decision making in the graduate selection interview: a field study', *Journal of Occupational Psychology*, 63, 63–76.

Anstey, E. (1977) 'A 30-year follow up of the CSSB procedure, with lessons for the future', *Journal of Occupational Psychology*, 50, 149–59.

APA (1954) *Technical Recommendations for Psychological Tests and Diagnostic Techniques* (Washington, DC: APA).

APA (1966) *Standards for Educational and Psychological Tests and Manuals* (Washington, DC: APS).

APA (1974) *Standards for Educational and Psychological Tests* (Washington, DC: APA: quoted by Anastasi, 1982).

APA (1981) 'Ethical principles of psychologists', *American Psychologist*, 36, 633–8.

Argyris, C. (1976) 'Problems and new directions for industrial psychology', in M. D. Dunnette (ed.), *Handbook of Industrial and Organizational Psychology* (Chicago: Rand McNally).

Arnold, J. D., Rauschenberger, J. M., Soubel, W. G. and Guion, R. M. (1982) 'Validation and utility of a strength test for selecting steelworkers', *Journal of Applied Psychology*, 67, 5, 588–604.

Arvey, R. D. (1979) *Fairness in Selecting Employees* (Reading, Mass.: Addison-Wesley).

Arvey, R. D. and Campion, J. E. (1982) 'The employment interview: a summary and review of recent literature', *Personnel Psychology*, 35, 281–322.

Ash, P. (1960) 'Validity information exchange, No. 13–07', *Personnel Psychology*, 13, 456.

Ash, R. A. (1980) 'Self assessments of five types of typing ability', *Personnel Psychology*, 33, 273–82.

Asher, J. J. (1972) 'The biographical item: can it be improved?' *Personnel Psychology*, 25, 251–69.

Asher, J. J. and Sciarrino, J. A. (1974) 'Realistic work sample tests: a review', *Personnel Psychology*, 27, 519–33.

Baehr, M. and Williams, G. B. (1967) 'Underlying dimensions of personal background data and their relationship to occupational classification', *Journal of Applied Psychology*, 51, 481–90.

Baier, D. E. and Dugan, R. D. (1956) 'Tests and performance in a sales organization', *Personnel Psychology*, 9, 17–26.

Bandura, A. (1977) *Social Learning Theory* (Englewood Cliffs, NJ: Prentice-Hall).

Bandura, A. (1986) *Social Foundations of Thought and Action.* (Englewood Cliffs, NJ: Prentice-Hall).

Bandura, A., Adams, N. and Beyer, J. (1977) 'Cognitive processes mediating behavioral change', *Journal of Personality and Social Psychology*, 35, 125–39.

Bandura, A. and Wood, R. (1989) 'Effect of perceived controllability and performance standards on self-regulation of complex decision making', *Journal of Personality and Social Psychology*, 56, 805–14.

Banks, M. H., Jackson, P. R., Stafford, E. M. and Warr, P. B. (1983) 'The job components inventory and the analysis of jobs requiring limited skill', *Personnel Psychology*, 36, 57–66.

Barlett, C. J. and O'Leary, B. S. (1969) 'A differential prediction model to moderate the effects of heterogeneous groups in personnel selection and classification', *Personnel Psychology*, 22, 1–17.

Barling, J. and Beattie, R. (1983) 'Self-efficacy beliefs and sales performance', *Journal of Organizational Behavior Management*, 5, 41–51.

Barrick, M. R. and Mount, M. K. (1991) 'The big five personality dimensions and job performance: a meta analysis', *Personnel Psychology*, 44, 1–26.

Bass, B. M. (1952) 'Ultimate criteria of organizational worth', *Personnel Psychology*, 5, 157–74.

Bass, B. M. (1954) 'The leaderless group discussion', *Psychological Bulletin*, 51, 456–92.

Bass, B. M. (1957) 'The reducing leniency in merit ratings', *Personnel Psychology*, 9, 359–69.

Bass, B. M. (1962) 'Further evidence on the dynamic character of criteria', *Personnel Psychology*, 15, 93–7.

Bechtoldt, H. P. (1959) 'Construct validity: a critique', *American Psychologist*, 619–29.

Beck, J. E. and Cox, C. J. (1980) *Advances in Management Education* (Chichester: John Wiley).

Behrend, H. (1953) 'Absence and turnover in a changing economic climate', *Occupational Psychology*, 27, 69–79.

Bem, D. J. (1972) 'Self perception theory', in L. Berkowitz (ed.) *Advances in Experimental Social Psychology*, vol. 6 (New York: Academic Press).

Bender, J. M. (1973) 'What is typical of assessment centres', *Personnel Psychology*, July/August, 50–7.

Bennett, G. K., Seashore, H. G. and Wesman, A. (1974) *Differential Aptitude Tests* (New York: Psychological Corporation).

Ben-Shakhar, G. (1989) 'Non-conventional methods in personnel selection', in P.Herriot (ed.) *Assessment and Selection in Organizations* (Chichester: John Wiley).

Ben-Shakhar, G., Bar-Hillel, M., Bille, Y., Ben-Abba, E. and Flug, A. (1986) 'Can graphology predict occupational success? Two empirical studies and some methodological ruminations', *Journal of Applied Psychology*, 71, 645–53.

Bentler, P. M. (1989) *EQS Structural Equations Program Manual* (Los Angeles: BMDP Statistical Software).

Berdie, F. S. (1971) 'What test questions are likely to offend the general public', *Journal of Educational and Psychological Measurement*, 8, 2, 87–93.

Berk, R. A. (ed.) (1984) *A Guide to Criterion Reference Test Construction* (Baltimore: Johns Hopkins University Press).

Berndadin, H. J., Albarase, K. M. and Cranny, C. J. (1976), 'A recomparison of behavioural expectation scales to summated scales', *Journal of Applied Psychology*, 61, 564–70.

Betz, N. E. and Weiss, D. J. (1975) *Simulation Studies of Two Stage Ability Testing*, (Research report 74–4 psychometric methods program (Minneapolis: University of Minnesota).

Bickel, P. J., Hammel, E. A. and O'Connel, J. W. (1975) 'Sex bias in graduate admissions: data from Berkeley', *Science*, 187, 398–404.

Bilodeau, E. A. (1966) Acquisition of Skill (London: Academic Press).

Binning, J. F., Goldstein, M. A., Garcia, M. F. and Scattaregia, J. H. (1988) 'Effects of pre-interview impressions on questioning strategies in same and opposite-sex employment interviews', *Journal of Applied Psychology*, 73, 30–7.

Blum, M. L. and Naylor, J. C. (1968) *Industrial Psychology: Its Theoretical and Social Foundation* (New York: Harper & Row).

Boam, R. and Sparrow, P. (eds) (1992) *Designing and Achieving Competency* (London: McGraw-Hill).

Boem, V. R. (1972) 'Negro–white differences in validity of employment and training selection procedure', *Journal of Applied Pyschology*, 56, 33–9.

Bolsher, B. T. and Springbett, B. M. (1961) 'The reaction of interviewers to favorable and unfavorable information', *Journal of Applied Psychology*, 45, 95–103.

Boshoff, A. B. (1969) 'A comparison of three methods for the evaluation of managerial positions', *Psychologica Africana*, 12, 212–21.

Boudreau, J. W. and Rynes, S. L. (1985) 'The role of recruitment in staffing utility analysis', *Journal of Applied Psychology*, 70, 354–66.

Bourgeois, R. P., Leim, M. A., Slivinski, L. W. and Grant, K. W. (1975). 'Evaluation of an assessment centre in terms of acceptibility', *Canadian Personnel and Industrial Relations Journal*, 17–20.

BPS (1974) *Code of Professional Conduct* (Division of Occupational Psychology: Leicester).

BPS (1980a) 'Notes for guidance in planning short courses in psychological testing', *Bulletin of the British Psychological Society*, 33, 244–9.

BPS (1980b) 'Technical recommendations for psychological tests', *Bulletin of the British Psychological Society*, 33, 161–4.

Brass, D. J. and Oldham, G. R. (1976) 'Validating an in-basket test using an alternative set of leadership scoring dimensions', *Journal of Applied Psychology*, 61, 652–57.

Brannick, M T., Michaels, C. E. and Baker, D. P. (1989) 'Construct validity of in-basket scores', Journal of Applied Psychology, 74, 957–63.

Bray, D. W. and Campbell, R. J. (1968) 'Selection of salesmen by means of an assessment centre', *Journal of Applied Psychology*, 52, 36–41.

Bray, D. W. and Grant, D. L. (1966) 'The assessment center in the measurement of potential for business management', *Psychological Monographs*, 625, 1–27.

Bray, D. W. and Moses, J. L. (1972) 'Personnel selection', *Annual Review of Psychology*, 23, 545–76.

British Institute of Management and Institute of Personnel Management (1980) *Selecting Managers: How British Industry Recruits* (London: BIM/IPM).

Browning, R. C. (1968) 'Validity of reference ratings from previous employers', *Personnel Psychology*, 21, 389–93.

Buckley, M. R. and Eder, R. W. (1988) 'B. M. Springbett and the notion of the "snap decision" in the interview', *Journal of Management*, 14, 59–69.

Burke, M. J. (1984) 'Validity of generalization: a review and critique of the correlation model', *Journal of Applied Psychology*, 37, 93–115.

Burns, T. (1957) 'Management in action', *Operational Research Quarterly*, 8, 45–60.

Byham, W. C. (1971) 'The assessment centre as an aid in managerial development', *Training and Development Journal*, 25, 10–22.

Byham, W. C. (1977) 'Application of the assessment center method', in J. L. Moses and W. C. Byham *Applying the Assessment Center Method* (New York: Pergamon).

Callender, J. C. and Osburn, H. G. (1982) 'Another view of progress in validity generalization: reply to Schmidt, Hunter, and Pearlman', *Journal of Applied Psychology*, 67, 846–52.

Campbell, C. P. (1977) *Handbook for the Strong Vocational Interest Blank* (Stanford, CA: Stanford University Press).

Campbell, D. T. and Fiske, D. W. (1959) 'Convergent and discriminant validation by the multitrait-multimethod matrix', *Psychological Bulletin*, 56, 81–105.

Campbell, J. P. (1976) 'Psychological Theory', in M. D. Dunnette (ed.), *Handbook of Industrial and Organisational Psychology* (Chicago: Rand McNally).

Campbell, J. T., Crooks, L. A., Mahoney, A. M. and Rock, D. A. (1973) *An Investigation of Sources of Bias in the Prediction of Job Performance – A Six Year Study*, ETS report PR-73-37 (Princeton, NJ: Educational Testing Service).

Campion, J. E. (1972) 'Work sampling for personnel selection', *Journal of Applied Psychology*, 56, 40–4.

Campion, M. A., Pursell, E. D. and Brown, B. K. (1988) 'Structured interviewing: raising the psychometric properties of the employment interview', *Personnel Psychology*, 41, 25–42.

Carlson, R. E. (1967) 'Selection interview decisions: the relative influence of appearance and factual written information on an interviewer's final rating', *Journal of Applied Psychology*, 51, 461–8.

Carlson, R. E., Thayer, P. W., Mayfield, E. C. and Peterson, D. A. (1971) 'Improvement in the selection interview', *Personnel Journal*, 50, 268–75.

Carroll, J. B. (1959) 'Review of the DAT', in O.D. Buros (ed.), *Fifth Mental Measurement Yearbook* (Highland Park, NJ: Gryphon Press).

Carroll, S. J. and Nash, A. N. (1972) 'Effectiveness of a forced choice reference check', *Personnel Adminstrative*, March–April, 42–6.

Cascio, W. F. and Phillips, N. F. (1979) 'Performance testing: a rose among thorns?' *Personnel Psychology*, 322, 751–66.

Cattel, R. B. (1957) *Personality and Motivation Structure and Measurement* (New York: Harcourt, Brace & World).

Cattell, R. B., Eber, H. W. and Tatsuoka, H. M. (1970) *Handbook for the Sixteen Personality Factor Questionnaire* (National Foundation for Educational Research).

Cattell, R. B., Horn, J. L., Sweeny, A. B. & Radcliff, J. A. (1959) *The Motivation Test* (Champagne, Ill: Institute of Personality Testing).

Cederblom, D. and Lounsbury, J. W. (1980) 'An investigation of user acceptance of peer evaluation', *Personnel Psychology*, 33, 567–79.

Champagne, J. E. and McCormick, E. K. (1964) *An Investigation of the Use of Worker-Oriented Job Variables in Job Evaluation* (Lafayette: Occupational Research Centre, Purdue University).

Christal, R. E. (1969) 'Collecting analysing and reporting information describing jobs and occupations', Comments by the Chairman and Proceedings of 19 Division of Military Psychology Symposium (Washington, DC: APA).

Christal, R. E. (1974) 'The United States Air Force occupational research project', *Journal Supplement Abstract Service Catalogue of Selected Documents in Psychology*, 4, 61.

Cleary, T. A. and Hilton, T. L. (1968) ' An investigation of item bias', *Educational and Psychological Measurement*, 28, 61–75.

Cohen, J. (1988) *Statistical Power Analysis for the Behavioral Sciences.* (Hillsdale, NJ: Lawrence Erlbaum).

Cole, N. S. (1973) 'Bias in Selection', *Journal of Educational Measurement*, 10, 237–55.

Cole, N. S. (1981) 'Bias in testing', *American Psychologist*, 36, 10, 1067–77.

Coombs, C. H. and Salter, G. A. (1949) 'A factorial approach to job families', *Psychometrika*, 14, 33–42.

Cooper, H. (1984) *The Integrative Research Review. A Systematic Approach* (Beverly Hills, CA: Sage).

Cornelius, E. T. and Hakel, M. D. (1978) A Study to Develop an Improved Enlisted Performance Evaluation System For The US Coast Guard (Washington, DC: US Department of Transport).

Costa, P. T. and McCrae, R. R. (1989) NEO P1/FFFI Manual Supplement (Odessa, FT: Psychological Assessment Resources).

Cox, J. W. (undated) *Cox Mechanical Test M1* (Altrincham, Cheshire: Human Factors).

Cranny, C. J. and Doherty, M. E. (1988) 'Importance ratings in job analysis: note on the misinterpretation of factor analyses', *Journal of Applied Psychology*, 73, 2, 320–2.

Cronbach, L. J. (1951) 'Coefficient alpha and the internal structure of tests', *Psychometrika*, 16, 297–334.

Cronbach, L. J. (1970) *Essentials of Psychological Testing* (New York: Harper & Row).

Cronbach, L. J. and Glesser, G. C. (1965) *Psychological Tests and Personnel Decisions* (Urbana: University of Illinois Press).

Cronbach, L J. and Meehl, P. E. (1955) 'Construct validity in psychological tests', *Psychological Bulletin*, 52, 4, 281–302.

Crooks, L. A. (1977) 'The selection and development of assessment center techniques', in Moses and Byham (1977).

Cunningham, J. W., Boese, R. R., Neeb, R. W. and Pass, J. J. (1983) 'Systematically derived work dimensions: factor analysis of the Occupational Analysis Inventory', *Journal of Applied Psychology*, 68, 232–52.

Cureton, E. E. (1971) 'The stability coefficient', *Educational and Psychological Measurement*, 31, 45–55.

Cureton, E. E., Cook, J. A., Fischer, R. T., Laser, S. A., Rockwell, N. J. and Simmons, J. W. (1973) 'Length of test and standard error of measurement', *Educational and Psychological Measurement*, 33, 63–8.

Daniels, A. W. and Otis, J. L. (1950) 'A method for analysing employment interviews', *Personnel Psychology*, 3, 425–44.

Davey, D. M. and Harris, M. (1982) *Judging People* (London: McGraw-Hill).

Dean, R. A. and Wanous, J. P. (1984) 'Effects of realistic job previews on hiring bank tellers', *Journal of Applied Psychology*, 69, 61–8.

Decker, P. J. (1982) 'The enhancement of behaviour modeling training of supervisory skills by the inclusion of retention processes', *Personnel Psychology*, 35, 323–32.

De Nisi, A. S. and Shaw, J. B. (1977) 'Investigations of the use of self reports of abilities', *Journal of Applied Psychology*, 62, 642–4.

Deubert, L. W., Smith, M. C., Downs, S., Jenkins, L. C. B. and Berry, D. C. (1975) 'The selection of dental students: a pilot study of an assessment of manual ability by practical tests', *British Dental Journal*, 139, 357–61.

Development Dimensions (1975) *Catalogue of Assessment and Development Exercises* (Pittsburgh, PA: Development Dimension).

De Witte, K. (1989) 'Recruiting and Advertising', in P. Herriot, *Assessment and Selection in Organisations* (Chichester: John Wiley).

Digman, J. M. (1990) 'Personality structure: the emergence of the five factor model', *Annual Review of Psychology*, 41, 417–40.

Dipboye, R. L. and Macan, T. (1988) 'A process view of the selection/recruitment interviews', in R. S. Schuler, S. A. Youngblood, and V. L. Huber (eds), *Readings in Personnel and Human Resource Management* (St Paul, MN: West Publishing).

Dipboye, R. L., Fontenelle, G. A. and Garner, K. (1984) 'Effects of previewing the application on interview process and outcomes', *Journal of Applied Psychology*, 69, 118–28.

Dipboye, R. L., Stramler, C. S. and Fontenelle, G. A. (1984) 'The effects of the application on recall of information from the interview', *Academy of Management Journal*, 27, 561–75.

Division of Occupational Psychology (1983) 'Code of professional conduct', in *Register of Members of the Division of Occupational Psychology of the British Psychological Society* (Leicester: BPS).

Dobson, P. (1989) 'Reference reports', in P.Herriot (ed.), *Assessment and Selection in Organizations* (Chichester: John Wiley).

Dodd, W. E. (1977) 'Attitudes towards assessment center programs', in Moses and Byham (1977).

Dougherty, T. W., Ebert, R. J. and Callender, J. C. (1986) 'Policy capturing in the employment interview', *Journal of Applied Psychology*, 71, 9–15.

Downey, J. E. (1919) *Graphology and the Psychology of Handwriting* (Baltimore: Warwick & Yorke).

Downs, S. (1968) 'Selecting the older trainee: a pilot study of trainability tests', *National Institute of Industrial Psychology Bulletin*, 19–26.

Downs, S. (1973) 'Trainability assessments: sewing machinists', *Research Paper SL6* (Cambridge, England: Industrial Training Research Unit).

Downs, S. (1977) 'Trainability testing: a practical approach to selection', *Training Information Paper No. 11* (London: Her Majesty's Stationery Office).

Downs, S., Farr, R. M. and Colbeck, L. (1978) 'Self appraisal: A convergence of selection and guidance', *Journal of Occupational Psychology*, 51, 271–8.

Drakely, R. J. (1989) 'Biographical data', in P.Herriot (ed.), *Assessment and Selection in Organizations* (Chichester: John Wiley).

Drakely, R. J., Herriot, P. and Jones, A. (1988) 'Biographical data, training success and turnover', *Journal of Occupational Psychology*, 61, 145–52.

Dreger, R. M. and Miller, K. S. (1968) 'Comparative psychological studies of whites and negroes in the United States: 1959–65', *Psychological Bulletin Monograph Supplement*, part 2 (September, 1–58).

Dreher, G. F., Ash, R. A. and Hancock, P. (1988) 'The role of the traditional research design in underestimating the validity of the employment interview', *Personnel Psychology*, 41, 315–27.

Dreher, G. F. and Sackett, P. R. (1983) *Perspectives on Employee Staffing and Selection: Readings and Commentary* (Homewood, Ill: Irwin).

Dulewicz, V. and Fletcher, C. (1982) 'The relationship between previous experience, intelligence and background characteristics of participants and their performance in an assessment centre', *Journal of Occupational Psychology*, 55, 197–207.

Dunnette, M. D, (1962) 'Personnel management', *Annual Review of Psychology*, 13, 285–314.

Dunnette, M. D. (1963a) 'A modified model for selection research', *Journal of Applied Psychology*, 47, 317–23.

Dunnette, M. D. (1963b) 'A note on the criterion', *Journal of Applied Psychology*, 47, 251–4.

Dunnette, M. D. (1972) 'Comments on Abrahams and Alf's "Pratfalls in moderator research"', *Journal of Applied Psychology*, 56, 3, 252–6.

Eberhardt, B. J. and Muchinsky, P. M. (1982) 'An empirical investigation of the factor stability of Owen's Biographical Questionnaire', *Journal of Applied Psychology*, 67, 138–45.

Edwards, A. L. (1957) *Techniques of Attitude Scale Construction* (New York: Appleton-Century Crofts).

Edwards, B. J. (1975) 'Application forms', in B. Ungerson (ed.), *Recruitment Handbook* (Aldershot: Gower).

Ekpo-Ufot, A. (1979) 'Self-perceived task relevant abilities, rated job performance and complaining behaviour of junior employees in a government ministry', *Journal of Applied Psychology*, 64, 429–34.

Elliot, A. G. P. (1981) 'Some implicators of lie scale scores in real-life selection', *Journal of Occupational Psychology*, 54, 9–16.

Equal Employment Opportunity Commission (1978) *Uniform Guidelines for Employee Selection Procedures* (Washington, DC: Equal Employment Opportunity Commission).

Eysenck, H. J. (1970) *The Structure of Human Personality* (London: Routledge & Kegan Paul).

Eysenck, H. J. and Nias, D. K. B. (1982) *Astrology: Science or Superstition?* (London: Temple Smith).

Eysenck, S. B. G. and Eysenck, H. J. (1963) 'An experimental investigation of desirability response set in a personality questionnaire', *Life Sciences*, 5, 343–55.

Faby, R. H. and Frogatt, K. L. (1987) 'A longitudinal examination of the membership patterns of minorities and women in referral union', *Journal of Labour Research*, 8, 1, 93–101.

Fahr, J. L., Werbel, J. D. and Bedeian, A. G. (1988) 'An empirical investigation of self appraisal-based performance evaluation', *Personnel Psychology*, 41, 141–56.

Fay, C. H. and Latham, G. P. (1982) 'Effects of training and rating scales on rating errors', *Personnel Psychology*, 35, 105–16.

Feltham, R. (1987) 'Validity of a police assessment centre: a 1–19-year follow up', *Journal of Occupational Psychology*, 61, 129–52.

Fine, S. A. (1986) 'Job analysis', in R. Buk, *Performance Assessment* (Baltimore: Johns Hopkins University Press).

Fine, S. A. and Elsner, E. J. (1980) *Performance Appraisal in the Department of Housing and Urban Development: A Functional Job Analysis Approach* (Washington, DC: Advanced Resources Research Organization).

Fine, S. A. and Wiley, W. W. (1977) *An Introduction to Job Analysis* (Kalamazoo, Michigan: Upjohn Institute for Employment Research).

Flanagan, J. C. (1954) 'The critical incident technique', *Psychological Bulletin*, 52, 327–58.

Flanagan, J. C. (1960) *Flanagan Industrial Tests* (Chicago: Science Research Associates).

Flanagan, J. C. and Burns, R. K. (1955) 'The employee performance record: a new appraisal and development tool', *Harvard Business Review*, 33, 5, 95–102.

Fleishman, E. A. (1966) 'Human abilities and the acquisition of skill', in Bilodeau (1966).

Fleishman, E. A. (1975) 'Toward a taxonomy of human performance', *American Psychologist*, 37, 1–14.

Fleishman, E. A. and Hogan, J. C. (1978) *A Taxonomic Method for Assessing the Physical Requirements of Jobs: The Physical Abilities Analysis Approach* (Washington, DC: Advanced Resources Organization).

Fleishman, E. A. and Quaintance, M. K. (1984) *Taxomonies of Human Performance* (London: Academic Press).

Fletcher, C. (1983) 'Sex of interviewer as an influence on interviewee perceptions', *British Journal of Social Psychology*, 22, 169–70.

Fletcher, C. and Spencer, A. (1984) 'Sex of candidate and sex of interviewer as determinants of self-presentation orientation in interviews: an experimental study', *International Review of Applied Psychology*, 33, 305–13.

Fletcher, C. and Williams, R. (1976) 'The influence of performance feedback in appraisal interviews', *Journal of Occupational Psychology*, 49, 75–83.

Foley, P. P. (1971) *Validity of the Officer Qualification Test for Minority Group Applicants to Officer Candidate School* (Washington, DC: Naval Personnel Research and Development Laboratory).

Forbes, R. J. and Jackson, P. R. (1980) 'Non-verbal behaviour and the outcome of selection interviews', *Journal of Occupational Psychology*, 53, 65–72.

Fordham, K. G. (1975) 'Job advertising', in B. Ungerson (ed.), *Recruitment Handbook* (Aldershot: Gower).

Fox, G. and Dinur, Y. (1988) 'Validity of self-assessment: a field evaluation', *Personnel Psychology*, 41, 581–92.

Fox, J. B. and Scott, J. R. (1943) 'Absenteeism: management's problem', *Business Research Studies*, Harvard University, Bureau of Business Research.

Frank, F. D. and Whipple, D. (1978) 'An assessor certificate program: based on simulation of the assessor job', *Journal of Assessment Center Technology*, 1 (Spring).

Frayne, C. A. and Latham, G. P. (1987) 'Application of social learning theory to employee self-management of attendance', *Journal of Applied Psychology*, 72, 387–92.

Frederiksen, N. and Gilbert, A. C. F. (1960) 'Replication of a study of differential predictability', *Educational and Psychological Measurement*, 20, 4, 759–67.

Frederiksen, N. and Melville, D. S. (1954) 'Differential predictability in the use of test scores', *Educational and Psychological Measurement*, 14, 647–56.

Frederiksen, N., Saunders, D. R. and Wand, B. (1957) 'The "in-basket test"', *Psychological Monographs: General and Applied*, 71, whole no. 483.

Funder, D. C. and Ozer, D. J. (1983) 'Behaviour as a function of the situation', *Journal of Personality and Social Psychology*, 44, 107–12.

Gael, S. and Grant, D. L. (1972) 'Employment test validation for minority and non-minority telephone company service representatives', *Journal of Applied Psychology*, 56, 2, 135–9.

Gardner, K. E. and Williams, A. P. O. (1973) 'A twenty-five year follow-up of an extended interview procedure in the Royal Navy: Part 1', *Occupational Psychology*, 47, 1–13.

Gatewood, R., Thornton, G. C. and Hennessey, H. W. (1990) 'Reliability of exercise ratings in the leaderless group discussion', *Journal of Occupational Psychology*, 63, 331–42.

Gaugler, B., Rosenthal, D. B., Thornton, G. C. and Bentson, C. (1987) 'Meta-analysis of assessment center validity', *Journal of Applied Psychology*, 72, 493–511.

Gaugler, B. B. and Thornton, G. C. (1989) 'Number of assessment center dimensions as a determinant of assessor accuracy', *Journal of Applied Psychology*, 74, 611–18.

Gauquelin, M. (1978) *Cosmic Influences on Human Behavior*, 2nd edn (New York: ASI).

Gauquelin, M. (1980) *Spheres of Destiny* (London: Dent).

Gauquelin, M., Gauquelin, F. and Eysenck, S. B. G. (1979) 'Personality and position of the planets at birth: an empirical study', *British Journal of Social and Clinical Psychology*, 18, 71–5.

George, D. I. and Smith, M. C. (1988) 'Self assessment in personnel selection: An investigation using seasonal workers', *Applied Psychology: An International Review*, 37, 337–50.

Getzels, J. W. and Jackson, P. W. (1962) *Creativity and Intelligence* (Chichester: John Wiley).

Ghiselli, E. E. (1956) 'Dimensional problems of criteria', *Journal of Applied Psychology*, 40, 1–4.

Ghiselli, E. E. (1960) 'The prediction of predictablility', *Educational and Psychological Measurement*, 20, 1, 3–8.

Ghiselli, E. E. (1966) *The Validity of Occupational Aptitude Tests* (New York: Wiley).

Ghiselli, E. E. (1973) 'The validity of aptitude tests in personnel selection', *Personnel Psychology*, 26, 461–77.

Ghiselli, E. E. and Brown, C. W. (1955) *Personnel and Industrial Psychology* (New York: McGraw-Hill).

Gifford, R., Ng, C. F. and Wilkinson, M. (1985) 'Non verbal cues in the employment interview: links between applicant qualities and interviewer judgements', *Journal of Applied Psychology*, 70, 729–36.

Gill, R. W. T. (1979) 'The in-tray (in-basket) exercise as a measure of management potential', *Journal of Occupational Psychology*, 52, 185–97.

Gill, D., Ungerson, B. and Thakur, M. (1973) *Performance Appraisal in Perspective: A Survey of Current Practice* (London: Institute of Personnel Management).

Glass, G. V. (1976) 'Primary, secondary and meta-analysis of research', *Educational Researcher*, 5, 3–8.

Glass, G. V., McGaw, B. and Smith, M. L. (1981) Meta-Analysis in Social Research (Beverly Hills, CA: Sage).

Glickman, A. S. (1956) 'The naval knowledge test', *Journal of Applied Psychology*, 40, 389–92.

Goldstein, A. P. and Sorcher, M. (1974) *Changing Supervisory Behaviour* (New York: Pergamon Press).

Goldstein, I. L. (1971) 'The application blank: how honest are the responses?' *Journal of Applied Psychology*, 55, 491–2.

Gordon, M. E. and Cohen, S. L. (1973) 'Training behavior as a predictor of trainability', *Personnel Psychology*, 26, 261–72.

Gordon, M. E. and Kleiman, L. S. (1976) 'The prediction of trainability using a work-sample test and an aptitude test: a direct comparison', *Personnel Psychology*, 29, 243–53.

Grant, D. L. and Bray, D. W. (1966) 'The assessment center in the measurement of potential for business management', *Psychological Monographs*, 80, whole no. 625.

Grigg, A. E. (1948) 'A farm knowledge test', *Journal of Applied Psychology*, 32, 425–35.

Guilford, J. P. (1959) *Personality* (New York: McGraw-Hill).

Guilford, J. P. and Fruchter, B. (1978) *Fundamental Statistics in Psychology and Education* (New York: McGraw-Hill).

Guinn, M., Tupes, E. C. and Aley, W. E. (1970) *Cultural Subgroup and Differences in the Relationships between Air Force Aptitude Composites and Training Criteria*, Technical Report no. 70-35 (Brooks Air Force Base, Texas: Air Force Human Resources Laboratory).

Guion, R. M. (1965) *Personnel Testing* (New York: McGraw-Hill).

Guion, R. M. (1977) 'Content validity – the source of my discontent', *Applied Psychological Measurement*, 1, 1, 1–10.

Guion, R. M. (1978) ' "Content validity" in moderation', *Personnel Psychology*, 31, 205–13.

Gulliksen, H. (1950) *Theory of Mental Tests* (New York: Wiley).

Guzzo, R. A., Jackson, S. E. and Katzell, R. A. (1986) 'Meta-analysis', in L. L. Cummings and B. M. Staw (eds), *Research in Organizational Behavior*, 9 (Greenwich, CT: JAI Press).

Haefner, J. E. (1977) 'Race, age, sex and competence as factors in employer selection of the disadvantaged', *Journal of Applied Psychology*, 62, 2, 199–202.

Hahn, D. C. and Dipboye, R. L. (1988) 'Effects of training and information on the accuracy and reliability of job evaluations', *Journal of Applied Psychology*, 73, 2, 146–53.

Hambleton, R. K., Swaminathan, H., Cook, L. L. , Eignor, D. R. and Gifford, J. A. (1978) 'Developments in latent trait theory: models, technical issues, and applications', *Review of Educational Research*, 48, 4, 467–510.

Hakel, P. M., Dobmay, J. and Dunnette, M. D. (1970) *Checklists for Describing Job Applicants* (Minnesota: University of Minnesota Industrial Relations Center).

Harris, M. M. (1989) 'Reconsidering the employment interview: a review of recent literature and suggestions for future research', *Personnel Psychology*, 42, 691–726.

Harris, M. M. and Fink, L. S. (1987) 'A field study of applicant reactions to employment opportunities: does the recruiter make a difference?', *Personnel Psychology*, 40, 765–84.

Harris, M. M. and Schaubroeck, J. (1988) 'A meta-analysis of self-supervisor, self-peer, and peer–supervisor ratings', *Personnel Psychology*, 41.

Hartley, C., Brecht, M., Pagerey, P., Weeks, G., Chapanis, A. and Hoecker, D. (1977) 'Subjective time estimates of work tasks by office workers', *Journal of Occupational Psychology*, 50, 23–36.

Harvey, O. L. (1934) 'The measurement of handwriting considered as a form of expressive movement', *Character and Personality*, 2, 310–21.

Harvey, R. J. and Hayes, T. L. (1986) 'Monte Carlo baselines for inter-rater reliability correlations using the Position Analysis Questionnaire', *Personnel Psychology*, 39, 345–57.

Harvey, R. J., Friedman, L., Hakel, M. D. and Cornelius, E. T. (1988) 'Dimensionality of the Job Element Inventory, simplified worker-oriented job analysis questionnaire', Journal of Applied Psychology, 73, 4, 639–646.

Harvey, R. J. and Lozada-Larsen, S. R. (1988) 'Influence of amount of job descriptive information on job analysis rating accuracy', *Journal of Applied Psychology*, 73, 3, 457–61.

Heilman, M. E. (1980) 'The impact of situation factors on personnel decisions concerning women. Varying the sex composition of the applicant pool', *Organizational Behavior and Human Performance*, 26, 386–96.

Heilman, M. E. and Saruwatari, L. R. (1979) 'When beauty is beastly: the effects of appearance and sex on evaluations of job applicants for managerial and non managerial jobs', *Organizational Behavior and Human Performance*, 23, 360–72.

Heim, A. W. (1967) *AH4 Group Test of General Intelligence* (Slough: National Foundation for Educational Research).

Heim, A. W. (1968) *Manual for the A5 Group Test of High-Grade Intelligence* (Slough: National Foundation for Educational Research).

Heim, A. W., Watts, K. P. and Simmonds, V. (1970) *Manual for the AH6 Group Tests of High-Level Intelligence* (Slough: National Foundation for Educational Research).

Heneman, H. G. (1974) 'Comparisons of self and superior ratings of managerieral performance', *Journal of Applied Psychology*, 59, 638–42.

Henry, J. (ed.) (1967) *Criterion Conference* (Pinehurst: Richardson Foundation).

Henry, R. A. and Hulin, C. L. (1987) 'Stability of skilled performance across time; some generalisations and limitations on utilities', *Journal of Applied Psychology*, 72, 3, 457–62.

Henry, R. A. and Hulin, C. L. (1989) 'Changing validities: ability–performance relations and utilities', *Journal of Applied Psychology*, 74, 2, 365–7.

Herriot, P. (1981) 'Towards an attributional theory of the selection interview', *Journal of Occupational Psychology*, 54, 165–73.

Herriot, P. (1989) 'Selection as a social process', in J. M. Smith and Robertson (1989).

Herriot, P. and Rothwell, C. (1981) 'Organzational choice and decision theory. Effects of employers' literature and selection interview', *Journal of Occupatinal Psychology*, 54, 17–31.

Hinricks, R. (1964) 'Communications activity of industrial research personnel', *Personnel Psychology*, 17, 193–204.

Hodgkiss, J. (1979) *Differential Aptitude Tests: British Manual* (Slough: National Foundation for Educational Research).

Hogan, R. (1986) *Hogan Personality Inventory* (Minneapolis: National Computer Systems).

Holland, J. L. (1978) *Manual for the Vocational Preference Inventory* (Palo Atton, CA: Consulting Psychologists Press).

Holdsworth, R. E. (1975) 'Identifying management potential', *British Institute of Management Survey Report No. 27* (London: BIM)

Holland, J. L. (1959) 'A theory of vocational choice', *Journal of Counselling Psychology*, 6, 35–44.

Hollandsworth, J. G., Kazelskis, R., Stevens, J. and Dressel, M. E. (1979) 'Relative contributions of verbal communication to employment decisions in the job interview setting', *Personnel Psychology*, 32, 359–67.

Hollingsworth, H. L. (1929) *Vocational Psychology and Character-Analysis* (New York: Appleton Century Crofts).

Horn, J. L. and Knapp, J. R. (1973) 'On the subjective character of the empirical base of the structure of intellect model', *Psychological Bulletin*, 80, 1, 33–43.

Hough, L. M. (1984) Development and evaluation of "The Accomplishment Record' method of selecting and promoting professionals", *Journal of Applied Psychology*, 69, 1, 135–46.

Howard, G. S. and Dailey, P. R. (1979) 'Response-shift bias: a source of contamination of self report measures', *Journal of Applied Psycholgy*, 62, 144–50.

Howard, G. S., Dailey, P. R. and Gulanick, N. A. (1979) 'The feasibility of informed pretests in attenuating response shift bias', *Applied Psychology Measurement*, 3, 481–94.

Huck, J. R. (1973) 'Assessment centers: a review of the external and internal validities', *Personnel Psycholgy*, 26, 191–212.

Huck, J. R. and Bray, D. W. (1976) 'Management assessment center evaluations and subsequent job performance of white and black females', *Personnel Psychology*, 29, 13–30.

Hulin, C. L. (1962) 'The measurement of executive success', *Journal of Applied Psychology*, 46, 303–6.

Humphreys, L. G. (1973) 'Statistical definitions of test validity for minority groups', *Journal of Applied Psychology*, 58, 1, 1–4.

Hunter, J. E. and Hirsh, H. R. (1987) 'Applications of meta-analysis', in C. L. Cooper and I. T. Robertson (eds), *International Review of Industrial and Organizational Psychology* (Chichester: John Wiley).

Hunter, J. E. and Hunter, R. F. (1984) 'Validity and utility of alternative predictors of job performance', *Psychological Bulletin*, 96, 72–98.

Hunter, J. E. and Schmidt, F. L. (1976) 'A critical analysis of the statistical and ethical implications of various definitions of "test bias"', *Psychological Bulletin*, 83, 1053–71.

Hunter, J. E. and Schmidt, F. L. (1978) 'Differential and single group validity of employment tests by race: a critical analysis of three recent studies', *Journal of Applied Psychology*, 63, 1, 1–11.

Hunter, J. E. and Schmidt, F. L. (1982) 'Fitting people to jobs: the impact of personnel selection on rational productivity' in M. D. Dunnette and E. Fleishman (eds), *Human Performance and Productivity* (Hillsdale, NJ: Lawrence Erlbaum).

Hunter, J. E. and Schmidt, F. L. (1990) *Methods of Meta-analysis: Correcting error and bias in research findings* (London Sage).

Hunter, J. E. and Schmidt, F. L. (1990) 'Dichotomizing continuous variables: the implications for meta-analysis'. *Journal of Applied Psychology*.

Hunter, J. E., Schmidt, F. L. and Hunter, R. (1979) 'Differential validity of employment tests by race: a comprehensive review and analysis', *Psychological Bulletin*, 86, 4, 721–35.

Hunter, J. E., Schmidt, F. L. and Jackson, G. B. (1982) *Meta-Analysis: Cumulating Research Findings across Studies* (Beverly Hills, CA: Sage).

Ilgen, D. R. and Seely, W. (1974) 'Realistic expectations as an aid in reducing voluntary resignations', *Journal of Applied Psychology*, 59, 452–5.

Ilgen, D. R., Fisher, C. D. and Taylor, M. S. (1979) 'Consequences of individual feedback on behavior in organizations', *Journal of Applied Psychology*, 64, 349–71.

Jansen, A. (1973) *Validation of Graphological Judgements* (Paris: Mouton).

Janz, T. (1982) 'Initial comparisons of patterned behavior description interviews versus structured interviews', *Journal of Applied Psychology*, 67, 577–80.

Janz, T. (1989) 'The patterned behavior description interview: the best prophet of the future in the past', in R. W., Eder and G. R. Ferris (eds), *The Employment Interview: Theory, Research and Practice* (Beverly Hills, C.A.: Sage).

Jarratt, R. F. (1948) 'Percent increase in output of selected personnel as an index of test efficiency', *Journal of Applied Psychology*, 32, 135–45.

Jenkins, J. G. (1946) 'Validity for what?' *Journal of Consulting Psychology*, 10, 93–8.

Jensen, A. R. (1974) 'How biased are culture-loaded tests?', *Genetic Psychology Monographs*, 90, 185–244.

Jensen, A. R, (1977) 'An examination of culture bias in the Wonderlic Personnel test', *Intelligence*, 1, 51–64.

Jensen, A. R. (1980) *Bias in Mental Testing* (London: Methuen).

Jeswald, T. A. (1977) 'Issues in establishing an assessment center', in Moses and Byham (1977).

Jones, A. (1981) 'Inter-rater reliability in the assessment of group exercises at a UK assessment centre', *Journal of Occupational Psychology*, 54, 79–86.

Jones, M. H. (1950) 'The adequacy of employee selection reports', *Journal of Applied Psychology*, 34, 219–24.

Joreskog, K. G. (1969) 'A general approach to confirmatory maximum likelihood factor analysis', *Psychometika*, 34, 183–202.

Joreskog, K. G. and Sorbom, D. (1988) LISREL 7, *A Guide to the Program and Application* (Chicago: SPSS).

Kagan, J. and Lesser, G. S. (eds) (1961) *Contemporary Issues in Thematic Apperception Methods* (Springfield, Ill.: Charles C. Thomas).

Kane, J. J. and Lawler, E. E. (1978) 'Methods of peer assessment', *Psychological Bulletin*, 85, 555–86.

Kelley, H. H. and Michela, J. L. (1980) 'Attribution theory and research', *Annual Review of Psychology*, 31, 457–501.

Kelly, G. A. (1955) *The Psychology of Personal Constructs* (New York: Norton).

Keenan, A. (1976) 'Effects of non-verbal behaviour of interviews on candidates' performance', *Journal of Occupational Psychology*, 49, 171–6.

Keenan, A. and Wedderburn, A. A. I. (1980) 'Putting the boot on the other foot: candidates' descriptions of interviewers', *Journal of Occupational Psychology*, 53, 81–9.

Kesselman, G. A. and Lopez, F. E. (1979) 'The impact of job analysis on employment test validation for minority and non-minority accounting personnel', *Personnel Psychology*, 32, 91–108.

Kesselman, G., Lopez, F. M., Jr and Lopez, F. E. (1982) 'The development and validation of a self-report, scored in-basket test in an assessment centre setting', *Public Personnel Management*, 11, 228.

Kilcross, M. C. (1976) *A Review of Research in Tailored Testing*, Report no. 9/76 (Farnborough, Hants: APRE, Royal Aircraft Establishment).

Kleiman, L. S. and Faley, R. H. (1988) 'Voluntary affirmative actions and preferential treatment: Legal and research implications', *Personnel Psychology*, 41, 3, 481–96.

Klemmer, E. T. and Snyder, F. W, (1972) 'Measurement of time spent communicating', *Journal of Communication*, 22, 142–58.

Klien, S. P. and Owens, W. A. (1965) 'Faking of a scored life history blank as a function of criterion objectivity', *Journal of Applied Psychology*, 49, 452–4.

Klimoski, R. and Brickner, M. (1987) 'Why do assessment centers work? The puzzle of assessment center validity', *Personnel Psychology*, 40, 243–60.

Klimoski, R. J. and Rafaeli, A. (1983) 'Inferring personal qualities through handwriting analysis', *Journal of Occupational Psychology*, 56, 191–202.

Klimoski, R. J and Strickland, W. J. (1977) 'Assessment centres – valid or merely prescient?' *Personnel Psychology*, 30, 353–61.

Krug, R. E. (1961) 'Personnel selection', in B. von H. Gilmer (ed.), *Industrial Psychology* (New York: McGraw-Hill).

Kuder, G. F. (1960) *Administrators' Manual for the Kuder Preference Record* (Chicago: Science Research Associates).

Kuder, G. F. and Richardson, M. W. (1937) 'The theory of estimation of test reliability', *Psychometrika* 2, 151–60.

Landy, F. J. (1976) 'The validity of the interview in police officer selection', *Journal of Applied Psychology*, 61, 193–8.

Landy, F. J. and Trumbo, D. A. (1980) *Psychology of Work Behaviour* (Homewood, Ill.: Dorsey Press).

Landy, F. J. and Rastegary, H. (1989) 'Criteria for selection', in J. M., Smith and Robertson (1989).

Latham, G. P. and Saari, L. M. (1979) 'Application of social learning theory to trained supervisors through behavioural modeling', *Journal of Applied Psycholgy*, 64, 239–46.

Latham, G. P. and Saari, L. M. (1984) 'Do people do what they say? Further studies on the situational interview', *Journal of Applied Psychology*, 69, 569–73.

Latham, G. P., Sarri, L. M., Pursell, E. D. and Campion, M. A. (1980) 'The situational interview', *Journal of Applied Psycholgy*, 65, 422–47.

Latham, G. P. and Wexley, K. N. (1981) *Increasing Productivity through Performance Appraisal* (Reading, Mass.: Addison-Wesley).

Lawler, E. E. and Rhode, J. G. (1976) *Information and Control in Organizations* (Pacific Palisades: Goodyear).

Lawshe, C. H. (1952) 'What can industrial psychology do for small business employee selection?', *Personnel Psychology*, 5, 31–4.

Lawshe, C. H. and Bolda, R. A. (1958) 'Expectancy charts I: their use and empirical development', *Personnel Psychology*, 11, 353–65.

Lawshe, C. H. and Schucker, R. E. (1959) 'The relative efficiency of four weighting methods in multiple methods in multiple prediction', *Educational Psychology Measurement*, 19, 103–14.

Lawshe, C. H., Bolda, R. A., Brune, R. L. and Auclair, G. (1958) 'Expectancy charts II: their theoretical development', *Personnel Psychology*, 11, 545–60.

Ledvinka, J., Markos, V. H. and Ladd, R. T. (1982) 'Long-range impact of fair selection standards on minority employment', *Journal of Applied Psychology*, 67, 1, 18–36.

Lee, C. and Gillen, D. J. (1989) 'Relationship of Type A behaviour pattern, self-efficacy perceptions on sales performance', *Journal of Organizational Behaviour*, 10, 75–81.

Lefcourt, H. M. (1976) *Locus of Control: Current Trends in Theory and Research* (Hillsdale, NJ: Lawrence Erlbaum).

Lemke, E. A. and Kirchner, J. H. (1971) 'Multivariate study of handwriting, intelligence and personality correlates', *Journal of Personality Assessment*, 35, 584–92.

Lent, R. H., Auback, H. A. and Levin, L. S. (1971) 'Predictors, criteria, and significant results', *Personnel Psychology*, 24, 519–33.

Leonard, R. L. (1976) 'Cognitive complexity and the similarity–attraction paradigm', *Journal of Research in Personality*, 10, 83–8.

Levine, A. S. and Zachert, V. (1951) 'Use of biographical inventory in the Air Force classification program', *Journal of Applied Psychology*, 35, 241–4.

Levine, E. L. (1983) *Everything You Wanted to Know about Job Analysis* (Tampa, FL: Mariner).

Levine, E. L., Ash, R. A. and Bennet, A. (1980) 'Exploratory comparative study of four job analysis methods', *Journal of Applied Psychology*, 524–35, 65, 5.

Levine, E. L., Flory, A. and Ashe, R. A. (1977) 'Self assessment in personnel selection', *Journal of Applied Psychology*, 52, 428–35.

Lewin, A. Y. and Zwany A. (1976) 'Peer nominations: a model, a literature critique and paradigm for research', *Personnel Psychology*, 29, 423–47.

Lewis, C. (1980) 'Investigating the employment interview: a consideration of counselling skills', *Journal of Occupational Psychology*, 53, 111–16.

Likert, R. and Quasha, W. H. (1941) *Minnesota Paper Form Board* (New York: Psychological Corporation).

Linn, R. L. (1973) 'Fair test use in selection', *Review of Educational Research*, 43, 139–61.

Loewenthal, K. (1975) 'Handwriting and self-presentation', *Journal of Social Psychology*, 96, 267–70.

Loewenthal, K. (1982) 'Handwriting as a guide to character', in Davey and Harris (1982).

Lopez, F. L. (1988) 'Threshold traits analysis system', in S. Gael (ed.), *The Job Analysis Handbook* (New York: Wiley).

Lord, F. M. (1971) 'The self-scoring flexilevel test', *Journal of Educational Measurement*, 8, 147–51.

Lord, F. M. (1980) *Applications of Item Response Theory to Practical Testing Problems* (Hillsdale, NJ: Lawrence Erlbaum).

Lord, F. M. and Novick, M. R. (1968) *Statistical Theories of Mental Test Scores* (New York: Addison-Wesley).

Lumsden, J. (1976) 'Test theory', *Annual Review of Psychology*, 27, 254–80.

Luntz, C. (1962) *Vocational Guidance by Astrology* (Saint Paul, Minnesota: Llewellyn Public).

Mabe, P. A. and West, S. G. (1982) 'Validity of self-evaluation of ability: A review and meta-analysis', *Journal of Applied Psychology*, 67, 280–296.

Macau, T. H. and Dipboye, R. L. (1988) 'The effects of interviewers' initial impressions on information gathering', *Organizational Behavior and Human Decision Processes*, 42, 364–87.

McCall, M. W., Morrison, A. and Hannan, R. L. (1978) *Studies of Managerial Work: Results and Methods* (Greenboro, NC: Centre for Creative Leadership).

McClelland, D. C. (1963) *The Achievement Motive* (New York: Appleton-Century-Crofts).

McClelland, D. C. (1976) *The Achieving Society* (New York: Irvington).

McClelland, D. C. and Bradburn, N. M. (1957) 'N Achievement and Managerial Success', paper, Harvard (quoted in McClelland, 1976).

McClelland, J. N. and Rhodes, F. (1969) 'Prediction of job success for hospital aides and orderlies from MMPI scores and personal history data', *Journal of Applied Psychology*, 53, 49–54.

McCormick, E. H. and Asquith, R. H. (1960) *An Analysis of Work Patterns of CIC Personnel for CUA-59 Class Ships* (Washington, DC: The Clifton Corporation).

McCormick, E. H. and Tiffin, J. (1974) *Industrial Psychology* (Englewood Cliffs, NJ: Prentice-Hall).

McCormick, E. J. (1959) 'The development of processes for indirect or synthetic validity, III. Application of job analysis to indirect validity', *Personnel Psychology*, 12, 402–13.

McCormick, E. J. (1976) 'Job and task analysis', in M. D. Dunnette (ed.), *Handbook of Industrial and Organizational Psychology* (Chicago: Rand McNally).

McCormick, E. J., Cunningham, J. W. and Gordon, G. C. (1967) 'Job dimensions based on fictional analysis of worker oriented job variables', *Personnel Psychology*, 20, 417–30.

McCormick, E. J., Cunningham, J. W. and Thornton, G. C. (1972) 'The prediction of job requirements by a structured job analysis procedure', *Personnel Psychology*, 26, 431–40.

McCormick, E. J., Jeanneret, P. R. and Mecham, R. C. (1972) 'A study of job characteristics and job dimensions based on the Position Analysis Questionnaire (PAQ)', *Journal of Applied Psychology*, 56, 347–68.

McDaniel, M. A, and Jones, J. W. (1986) 'A meta analysis of the validity of the employee attitude inventory theft scales', *Journal of Business and Psychology*, 1, 1, 31–50.

McDonald, T. and Hakel, M. D. (1985) Effects of applicant race, sex, suitability and answers on interviewer's questioning strategy and ratings. *Personnel Psychology*, 38, 321–334.

McEvoy, G. M. and Buller, P. F. (1987) 'User acceptance of peer appraisals in an industrial setting', *Personnel Psychology* 40, 4, 785–97.

McIntyre, S., Moberg, D. J. and Posner, B. Z. (1980) 'Preferential treatment in pre selection decisions according to sex and race', *Academy of Management Journal*, 23, 4, 738–49.

McKerracher, D. W. and Watson, R. A. (1968) 'The Eysenck Personality Inventory in male and female subnormal psychopaths in a special security hospital', *British Journal of Social and Clinical Psychology*, 7, 295–302.

Macleod, S. (1982) 'Applied astrology: an intuitive approach', in Davey and Harris (1982).

McLoughlin, C. S. and Koh, T. H. (1982) 'Testing intelligence: a decision suitable for the psychologist', *Bulletin of the British Psychological Society*, 35, 308–11.

Makin, P. J. and Robertson, I. T. (1983) 'Self assessment, realistic job previews and occupational decisions', *Personnel Review*, 12, 21–5.

Marquardt, L. D. and McCormick, E. J. (1972) *Attribute Rating Profiles of the Job Elements of the Position Analysis Questionnaire* (Lafayette, Ind.: Department of Psychological Sciences, Purdue University), Contract NR 151 231.

Marquardt, L. D. and McCormick, E. J. (1974) *The Utility of Job Dimensions based on Form B of the Position Analysis Questionnaire in a Job Component Validation Model* (Lafayette, Ind.: Occuaptional Research Centre, Department of Psychological Sciences, Purdue University), Report no. 5.

Marshall, G. (1964) *Predicting Executive Achievement* (unpublished DBA thesis, Harvard).

Maurer, S. D. and Fay, C. (1988) 'Effect of situational interviews, conventional structured interviews and training on interview rating agreement: an experimental analysis', *Personnel Psychology*, 41, 329–44.

Mayfield, E. C., Brown, S. H. and Hamstra, B. W. (1980) 'Selection interviewing in the life insurance industry: an update of research and practice', *Personnel Psychology*, 33, 725–39.

Mayo, J., White, O. and Eysenck, H. J. (1977) 'An empirical study of the relation between astrological factors and personality', *Journal of Social Psychology*, 105, 229–36.

Mecham, R. C. (1970) 'The Synthetic Prediction of Personnel Test Requirements and Job Evaluation Points using the Position Analysis Questionnaire', PhD thesis, Lafayette, Ind.: Purdue University.

Mecham, R. C. and McCormick, E. J. (1969) *The Rated Attribute Requirements of Job Elements in the Position Analysis Questionnaire* (Lafayette, Ind.: Occupational Research Centre, Purdue University), Report no. 1.

Meehl, P. E. (1954) *Clinical vs. Statistical Prediction* (Minneapolis: University of Minnesota Press).

Mehrabian, A. (1965) 'Communication length as an index of communicator attitude', *Psychology Reports*, 17, 519–22.

Messick, S. (1974) *The Standard Problem: Meaning and Values in Measurement and Evaluation*, Presidential address to Division of Measurement and Evaluation, APA, New Orleans, August 1974, reported by Guion (1977).

Meyer, H. H. (1961) 'An Exploratory Study of the Executive Position Description Questionnaire in the Jewel Tea Company Inc.', Conference on executive study (quoted by Prien and Ronan, 1971).

Meyer, H. H. (1970) 'The validity of the in-basket test as a measure of managerial performance', *Personnel Psychology*, 23, 297–307.

Meyer, H. H. and Bertotti, J. M. (1956) 'Uses and misuses of tests in selecting key personnel', *Personnel*, 277–85.

Miele, F. (1979) 'Cultural bias in the WISC', *Intelligence*, 3, 149–64.

Meyerson, P., Prien, E. and Vick, T. (1965) 'Differentiating positions using an executive position questionnaire', *Journal of Industrial Psychology*, 3, 3, 19–23.

Mintz, A. and Blum, M. L. (1949) 'A re-examination of accident proneness concept', *Journal of Applied Psychology*, 33, 195–211.

Mintzberg, H. H., (1973) *The Nature of Managerial Work* (New York: Harper & Row).

Mischel, W. (1968) *Personality Assessment* (New York: Wiley).

Mischel, W. (1977) 'Self control and the self', in T. Mischel (ed.), *The Self Psychological and Philosophical Issues* (Totowa, NJ: Rowman & Littlefield).

Mitchell, T. W. and Klimoski, P. M. (1982) 'Is it rational to be empirical? A test of methods of scoring biographical data', *Journal of Applied Psychology*, 71, 311–17.

Moe, K. O. and Zeiss, A. M. (1982) 'Measuring self-efficacy expectations for social skills: a methodological enquiry', *Cognitive Therapy and Research*, 6, 191–205.

Monahan, C. J. and Muchinsky, P. M. (1983) 'Three decades of personnel selection research', *Journal of Occupational Psychology*, 56, 3, 215–25.

Morrisby, J. R. (1955) *Manual for the Differential Test Battery* (Slough: National Foundation for Educational Research).

Morse, J. E. and Archer, W. B. (1967) *Procedural Guide for Conducting Occuaptional Surveys in the United States Air Force* PRL-TR-67–11 (Lackland Air Force Base: Personnel Research Laboratory, Aerospace Division).

Mosel, J. N. and Cozan, L. W. (1952) 'The accuracy of application blank work histories', *Journal of Applied Psychology*, 36, 365–9.

Mosel, J. N. and Goheen, H. W. (1959) 'The employment recommendation questionnaire: III validity of different types of references', *Personnel Psychology*, 12, 469–77.

Moses, J. L. and Byham, W. C. (1977) *Applying the Assessment Center Method* (New York: Pergamon).

Moss, D. (1984) 'In-basket performance and cognitive complexity', Unpublished MSc dissertation, University of Manchester Institute of Science and Technology.

Mossholder, K. W. and Arvey, R. D. (1984) 'Synthetic validity: a conceptual and comparative review', *Journal of Applied Psychology*, 69, 322–33.

Muchinsky, P. M. (1979) 'The use of reference reports in personnel selection: a review and evaluation', *Journal of Occupational Psychology*, 52, 287–97.

Mumford, M. D., Stokes, G. S., Owens, W. A. and Sparks, C. P. (1991) 'Development determinants of individual action: theory and practice in the application of background data measures', in M. D. Dunnette (ed.), *Handbook of Industrial and Organizational Psychology*, 2nd edn (Orlando, FL: Consulting Psychologist Press).

Munroe Frazer, J. (1966) *Employment Interviewing* (London: Macdonald & Evans).

Murphy, K. R. (1986) 'When your top choice turns you down: effects of rejected offers on the utility of selection tests', *Psychological Bulletin*, 99, 133–8.

Murray, H. A. (1938) *Explorations in Personality* (Oxford University Press).

Naylor, J. C. and Shine, L. C. (1965) 'A table for determining the increase in mean criterion score obtained by using a selection device', *Journal of Industrial Psychology*, 3, 33–42.

Neidig, R. D. and Neidig, P. J. (1984) 'Multiple assessment center exercises and job relatedness', *Journal of Applied Psychology*, 69, 182–6.

Neiner, A. G. and Owens, W. A. (1982) 'Relationships between two sets of biodata with 7 years separation', *Journal of Applied Psychology*, 67, 146–50.

Nevo, B. (1988) 'Yes, graphology can predict occupational success: rejoinder to Ben-Shakhar, *et al.*', *Perceptual and Motor Skills*, 66, 92–4.

Newman, J. M. (1978) 'Discrimination recruitment: an empirical analysis', *Industrial and Labour Relations Review*, 32, 15–23.

Nias, D. K. B. (1982) 'Astrology: fact or fiction?' in Davey and Harris (1982).

Noe, R. A. and Schmitt, N. (1986) 'The influence of trainee attitudes on training effectiveness: test of a model', *Personnel Psychology*, 39, 497–523.

Noe, R. A. and Steffy, B. D. (1987) 'The influence of individual characteristics and assessment center evaluation on career exploration and job involvement', *Journal of Vocational Behavior*, 30, 187–302.

Orpen, C. (1985) 'Patterned behavior description interviews versus unstructured interviews: a comparative validity study', *Journal of Applied Psychology*, 70, 774–6.

Orr, D. B. (1960) 'A new method of clustering jobs', *Journal of Applied Psychology*, 44, 44–9.

Owens, W. A. (1971) 'A quasi-actuarial basis for individual assessment', *American Psychologist*, 26, 992–9.

Owens, W. A. (1976) 'Background data', in M. D. Dunnette (ed.), *Handbook of Industrial and Organizational Psychology* (Chicago: Rand McNally).

Owens, W. A. and Schoenfeldt, L. F. (1979) 'Towards a classification of persons', *Journal of Applied Psychology*, 64, 569–607.

Pace, L. A. and Schoenfeldt, L. F. (1977) 'Legal concerns in the use of weighted applications', *Personnel Psychology*, 30, 159–66.

Palmer, G. J. and McCormick, E. J. A. (1961) 'A factor analysis of job activities', *Journal of Applied Psychology*, 45, 289–94.

Palormo, J. M. (1973) *Computer Programmer Aptitude Battery* (Chicago: Science Research Associates).

Parker, D. and Parker, J. (1975) *The Compleat Astrologer* (London: Mitchell Beazley).

Parry, M. E. (1968) 'Ability of psychologists to estimate validities of personnel tests', *Personnel Psychology*, 21, 139–47.

Parsons, C. K. and Liden, R. C. (1984) 'Interviewer perceptions of applicant qualifications: a multivariate field study of demographic characteristics and non verbal cues', *Journal of Applied Psychology*, 69, 557–68.

Patterson, J. (1976) *Interpreting Handwriting* (New York: McKay).

Pearlman, K. (1980a) 'Job families: a review and discussion of their implications for personnel selection', *Psychological Bulletin*, 87, 1–28.

Pearlman, K. (1980b) 'Seeing the whole picture: application of cumulated validity data to issues in clerical selection', in V. J. Benz (Chair), *Methodological Implications of Large-Scale Validity Studies Of Clerical Occupations*, Symposium presented at the meeting of the APA, Montreal.

Pearlman, K., Schmidt, F. L. and Hunter, J. E. (1980) 'Validity generalization results for tests used to predict job proficiency and training success in clerical occupations', *Journal of Applied Psychology*, 65, 373–406.

Pearn, M. A. (undated) *The Fair Use of Selection Tests* (Slough: National Foundation for Educational Research).

Pervin, L. A. (1980) *Personality: Theory Assessment and Research*, 3rd edn (Chichester: John Wiley).

Phares, E. J. (1976) *Locus of Control and Personality* (Morristown, NJ: General Learning Press).

Pollock, J. and Lake, T. (1983) *What Do You Want to Know about Job Candidates* (London: Centre of Professional Employment Counselling, 37 Jermyn Street).

Popovich, P. and Wanous, J. P. (1982) 'The realistic job preview as persuasive communication', *Academy of Management* Review, 7, 570–8.

Powell, G. N. (1984) 'Effects of job attributes and recruiting practices on applicant decisions: a comparison', *Personnel Psychology*, 37, 721–32.

Prien, E. P. (1977) 'The function of job analysis in content validation', *Personnel Psychology*, 30, 167–74.

Prien, E. P., Barrett, G. V. and Suwtlik, B. (1965) 'Use of questionnaires in job evaluation', *Journal of Industrial Psychology*, 3, 91–4.

Prien, E. P. and Ronan, W. W. (1971) 'Job analysis: a review of research findings', *Personnel Psychology*, 24, 371–96.

Primoff, E. S. (1975) *How to Prepare and Conduct Job Element Examinations*, GPO No. 029–000–00131–6 (Washington, DC: US Government Printing Office).

Primoff, E. S. (1980) 'The use of self assessments in examining', *Personnel Psychology*, 33, 283–290.

Psychological Corporation (1944) *General Clerical Test* (New York: Psychological Corporation).

Putz-Osterloh, W. (in press) 'Complex problem solving as a diagnostic tool', in H. Schuler, J. L. Farr and J. M. Smith, *Personnel Selection and Assessment: Individual and Organisational Perspectives* (Hillsdale, NJ: Lawrence Erlbaum).

Rafaeli, A. and Klimoski, R. J. (1983) 'Predicting sales success through handwriting analysis: an evaluation of the effects of training and handwritten sample content', *Journal of Applied Psychology*, 68, 212–17.

Rand, T. M. and Wexley, K. M. (1975) 'Demonstration of the effect "similar to me" in simulated employment interviews', *Psychological Reports*, 36, 535–44.

Rasch, G. (1966) 'An individualistic approach to item analysis', in P. F. Lazarsfeld and N. W. Henry, (eds), *Reading in Mathematical Social Sciences* (Cambridge MA: MIT Press).

Raven, J. L. (1960) *Guide to the Standard Progressive Matrices* (London: H. K. Lewis).

Rawls, D. and Rawls, J. R. (1968) 'Personality characteristics and personal history data of successful and less successful executives', *Psychological Reports*, 23, 1032–4.

Reilly, R. R., Blood, M. R., Brown, B. M. and Maletsa, C. A. (1981) 'The effects of realistic job previews: a study and discussion of the literature', *Personnel Psychology*, 34, 823–4.

Reilly, R. R. and Chao, G. T. (1982) 'Validity and fairness of some alternative employee selection procedures', *Personnel Psychology*, 35, 1–62.

Reilly, R. R., Henry, S. and Smither, J. W. (1990) 'An examination of the effects of using behavior checklists on the construct validity of assessment center dimensions', *Personnel Psychology*, 43, 71–84.

Richards, S. A. and Jafee, C. L. (1972) 'Blacks supervising whites: a study of interracial difficulties in working together in a simulated organisation', *Journal of Applied Psychology*, 56, 234–40.

Ritchie, R. J. and Moses, J. L. (1983) 'Assessment center correlates of women's advancement into middle management: a 7-year longitudinal analysis', *Journal of Applied Psychology*, 68, 227–31.

Robertson, I. T. (1989) 'Construct validity in managerial selection and assessment', in B. J. Fallon, H. P. Pfister and J. Brebner (eds), *Advances in Industrial Organizational Psychology* (Amsterdam: Elsevier).

Robertson, I. T. and Downs, S. (1979) 'Learning and the prediction of performance: development of trainability testing in the United Kingdom', *Journal of Applied Psychology*, 64, 42–50.

Robertson, I. T. and Downs, S. (1989) 'Work sample tests of trainability: a meta-analysis', *Journal of Applied Psychology*, 74, 402–10.

Robertson, I. T. and Kandola, R. S. (1982) 'Work sample tests: validity, adverse impact and applicant reaction', *Journal of Occupational Psychology*, 55, 171–83.

Robertson, I. T. and Makin, P. J. (1986) 'Management selection in Britain: a survey and critique', *Journal of Occupational Psychology* 59, 1, 45–57.

Robertson, I. T. and Mindel, R. M. (1980) 'A study of trainability testing', *Journal of Occupational Psychology*, 53, 131–8.

Robertson, I. T., Gratton, L. and Rout, U. (1990) 'The validity of situational interviews for administrative jobs', *Journal of Organizational Behavior*, 11, 69–76.

Robertson, I. T., Gratton, L. and Sharpley, D. (1987) 'The psychometric properties and design of assessment centres: dimensions into exercises won't go', *Journal of Occupational Psychology*, 60, 187–95.

Robertson, I. T., Iles, P. A., Gratton, L. and Sharpley, D. S. (1991) 'The psychological impact of personnel selection methods on candidates', *Human Relations* 44, 963–82.

Robertson, I. T. and Smith, J. M. (1989) 'Personnel selection', in J. M. Smith and I. T. Robertson (eds), *Advances in Selection and Assessment* (Chichester: John Wiley).

Robinson, D. D. (1981) 'Content oriented personnel selection in a small business setting', *Personnel Psychology*, 34, 77–87.

Rodger, A. (1953) *The Seven Point Plan* (London: National Institute of Industrial Psychology).

Rosen, B. and Jerdee, T. H. (1976) 'The nature of job-related age stereotypes', *Journal of Applied Psychology*, 61, 2, 180–3.

Rosen, B. and Merich, M. F. (1979) 'Influence of strong vs weak fair employment policies and applicants' sex on selection and salary recommendations in management simulations', *Journal of Applied Psychology*, 64, 435–9.

Rosenthal, D. and Lines, R. (1972) 'Handwriting as a correlate of extraversion', *Journal of Personality Assessment*, 42, 45–8.

Rosenthal, R. (1984) *Meta-Analysis Procedures for Social Research* (Beverly Hills, CA: Sage).

Ross, L. (1977) 'The intuitive psychologist and his short comings: distortion in the attribution process', *Advances in Experimental Social Psychology*, 10, 174–220.

Rothstein, M. and Jackson, D. N. (1980) 'Decision making in the employment interview: An experimental approach', *Journal of Applied Psychology*, 65, 271–83.

Rotter, J. B. (1960) 'Some implications of a social learning theory for the predicition of goal directed behaviour from testing procedures', *Pscyological Review*, 67, 301–16.

Rotter, J. B. (1966) 'Generalised expectancies for internal versus external control of reinforcement', *Psychological Monographs*, 80, 1, 609.

Rowe, P. M. (1989) 'Unfavorable information and interview decisions', in R. W. Eder, and G. R. Ferris (eds), *The Employment Interview: Theory, Research and Practice* (Beverly Hills, CA: Sage), 77–89.

Ruch, W. W. (1972) 'A reanalysis of published differential validity studies', Paper presented at American Psychological Association meeting Honolulu, September, quoted by Jensen (1980).

Rundquist, E. A. (1969) 'The prediction ceiling', *Personnel Psychology*, 22, 109–16.

Runnymede Trust (BPS Joint Working Party on Employment Assessment and Racial Discrimination) (1980) *Discriminating Fairly: A Guide to Fair Selection* (London: Runnymede Trust/BPS).

Rusmore, J. T. (1967) 'Identification of aptitudes associated with two criteria of management. Success for twenty theorectically defined jobs', in J. Henry (1967), quoted in Prien (1977).

Russell, C. J., Mattson, J., Devlin, S. E. and Atwates, D. (1990) 'Predictive validity of biodata items generated from retrospective life experience essays', *Journal of Applied Psychology*, 75, 569–80.

Russell, J. S., Wexley, K. E. and Hunter, J. E. (1984). 'Questioning the effectiveness of behaviour modeling training in an industrial setting', *Personnel Psychology*, 37, 465–81.

Sackett, P. R. (1982) 'The interviewer as hypothesis tests: the effects of impressions of an applicant on interview questioning strategy', *Personnel Psychology*, 35, 789–803.

Sackett, P. R. and Dreher, F. F. (1982) 'Constructs and assessment center dimensions: Some troubling empirical findings', *Journal of Applied Psychology*, 67, 401–10.

Sackett, P. R. and Dreher, G. F. (1984) 'Situation specificity of behaviour and assessment center validation strategies: a rejoinder to Neidig and Neidig', *Journal of Applied Psychology*, 69, 187–90.

Sackett, P. R. and Harris, M. M. (1984) 'Honesty testing for personnel selection: a review and critique', *Personnel Psychology*, 37, 221–46.

Sackett, P. R., Schmitt, N., Tenopyr, M. L., Kehoe, J. and Zedeck, S. (1985) 'Commentary on forty questions about validity generalization and meta-analysis', *Personnel Psychology*, 38, 697–798.

Sackett, P. R., Zedeck, S. and Fogli, L. (1988) 'Relations between measure of typical and maximal job performance', *Journal of Applied Psychology*, 73, 482–6.

Sanchez, J. I. and Levin, E. L. (1989) 'Determining important tasks within jobs: a policy-capturing approach', *Journal of Applied Psychology*, 74, 2, 336–42.

Sandoval, J. and Miille, M. P. W. (1980) 'Accuracy of judgements of WISC-R item difficulty for minority groups', *Journal of Consulting and Clinical Psychology*, 48, 2, 249–53.

Saville, P. and Holdsworth, R. (1983) *Management Interest Inventory* (Esher, Surrey: Saville-Holdsworth).

Saville, P. and Holdsworth, R. (1984) *Occupational Personality Questionnaire* (Esher, Surrey: Saville-Holdsworth).

Saville-Holdsworth Ltd (1988) WPS Manual (Esher, Surrey: Saville-Holdsworth).

Saville-Holdsworth Ltd (1989) *Word Processing Aptitude Battery* (Esher, Surrey: Saville-Holdsworth).

Sawyer, J. (1966) 'Measurement and predicition, clinical and statistical', *Psychological Bulletin*, 66, 178–200.

Schmidt, F. L., Berner, J. G. and Hunter, J. E. (1973) 'Racial differences in validity of employment tests', *Journal of Applied Psychology*, 58, 1, 5–9.

Schmidt, F. L., Greenthal, A. C., Hunter, J. E., Berner, J. G. and Seaton, F. W. (1977) 'Job samples vs paper and pencil trades and technical tests: adverse impact and examine attitudes', *Personnel Psychology*, 30, 187–97.

Schmidt, F. L. and Hunter, J. E. (1977) 'Development of a general solution to the problem of validity generalization', *Journal of Applied Psychology*, 62, 529–40.

Schmidt, F. L. and Hunter, J. E. (1978) 'Moderator research and the law of small numbers', *Personnel Psychology*, 31, 215–29.

Schmidt, F. L., Hunter, J. E. and Caplan, J. R. (1981) 'Validity generalization results for two groups in the petroleum industry', *Journal of Applied Psychology*, 66, 261–73.

Schmidt, F. L., Hunter, J. E. and Pearlman, K. (1981) 'Task differences as moderators of aptitude test validity in selection: a red herring', *Journal of Applied Psychology*, 66, 2, 166–85.

Schmidt, F. L., Hunter, J. E. and Pearlman, K. (1982) 'Assessing the economic impact of personnel programs on workforce productivity', *Journal of Applied Psychology*, 35, 333–47.

Schmidt, F. L., Hunter, J. E., Pearlman, K. and Hirsh, H. R. (1985) 'Forty questions about validity generalization and meta-analysis', *Personnel Psychology*, 38, 697–798.

Schmidt, F. L., Hunter, J. E. and Urry, V. W, (1976) 'Statistical power in criterion-related validation studies', *Journal of Applied Psychology*, 61, 4, 473–85.

Schmitt, N. (1976) 'Social and situational determinants of interview decisions: implications for the employment interview', *Personnel Psychology*, 29, 79–101.

Schmitt, N. and Coyle, B. W. (1976) 'Applicant decisions in the employment interview', *Journal of Applied Psychology*, 61, 184–92.

Schmitt, N. and Fine, S. A. (1983) 'Inter-rater reliability of judgements of functional levels and skill requirements of jobs based on written task statements', *Journal of Occupational Psychology*, 56, 121–7.

Schmitt, N., Ford, J. K. and Stutts, D. M. (1986) 'Changes in self perceived ability as a function of performance in an assessment centre', *Journal of Occupational Psychology*, 59, 4, 327–35.

Schmitt, N., Gooding, R. Z., Noe, R. A. and Kirsch, M. (1984) 'Meta-analyses of validity studies published between 1964 and 1982 and the investigation of study characteristics', *Personnel Psychology*, 37, 407–22.

Schmitt, N., Mellon, P. M. and Bylenga, C. (1978) 'Sex differences in validity for academic and employment criteria', *Journal of Applied Psychology*, 63, 2, 145–50.

Schmitt, N. and Ostroff, C. (1986) 'Operationalizing the "behavioral consistency" approach: selection test development based on a content-oriented strategy', *Personnel Psychology*, 39, 91–108.

Schmitt, N. and Robertson, I. T. (1990) 'Personnel selection', *Annual Review of Psychology*, 41, 289–319.

Schmitt, N., Schneider, J. R. and Cohen, S. A. (1990) 'Factors affecting validity of a regionally administered assessment center', *Personnel Psychology*, 43.

Schrader, A. D. and Osburn, H. G. (1977) 'Biodata taking: effects of induced subtlety and position specificity', *Personnel Psychology*, 30, 395–404.

Schuler, H. (in press) 'Social validity of selection situations', in H. Schuler, J. L. Farr and J. M. Smith (eds), *Personnel Selection and Performance Appraisal: Organisations and Individual Perspectives* (Hillsdale, NJ: Lawrence Erlbaum).

Schwab, D. P. and Heneman, H. G. (1969) 'Relationships between interview structure and interview relability in an employment situation', *Journal of Applied Psychology*, 53, 214–17.

Schwab, D. P., Heneman, H. G. and DeCottis (1975) 'Behaviorally anchored rating scales: a review of the literature', *Personnel Psychology*, 28, 549–62.

Science Research Associates (1980) *Catalogue of Tests for Business and Industry* (Chicago: Science Research Associates).

Seashore, H. G. (1962) 'Women are more predictable than men', *Journal of Counselling Psychology*, 9, 261–70.

Shackleton, V. J. and Newell, S. (1991) 'A comparative survey of methods used in top British and French companies', *Journal of Occupational Psychology*, 64, 23–36.

Sharma, J. M. and Vardhan (1975) 'Graphology – what handwriting can tell you about an applicant', *Personnel*, 52, 57–63.

Shaw, J. B. and McCormick, E. J. (1976) *The Prediction of Job Ability Requirements Using Attribute Data Based upon the Position Analysis Questionnaire*, Report prepared for USA Office of Naval Research (Purdue: Department of Psychological Sciences, Purdue University), contract no. N000 14 76 CO274.

Siegal, A. I. (1983) 'The miniature job training and evaluation approach: additional findings', *Personnel Psychology*, 36, 41–56.

Siegel, A. I. and Bergman, B. A. (1975) 'A job learning approach to performance prediction', *Personnel Psychology*, 28, 325–39.

Simas, K. and McCarrey, M. (1979) 'Impact of recruiter authoritarianism and applicant sex on evaluation and selection decisions in a recruitment interview analogue study', *Journal of Applied Psychology*, 64, 483–91.

Simpson, D. and Saville, P. (1975) *British Reliability and Validity Data on the Computer Programmer Aptitude Battery* (Slough: National Foundation for Educational Research).

Smith, J. M. (1980) 'Applicants and uses of repertory grids in management education', in Beck and Cox (1980).

Smith, J. M. (1981) 'Are There Four Fatal Flaws in the 30 year CSSB follow up?' Paper read at the Annual Occupational Psychology Conference of the BPS, University of Sussex.

Smith, J. M. (1982) 'Selection interviewing: a four-step approach', in G. Breakwell, H. Foot and R. Gilmour (eds), *Social Psychology: A Practical Manual* (London: BPS and Macmillan Press).

Smith, J. M. (1984) *Survey Item Bank* (Bradford: MCB Publications).
Smith, J. M. and Abrahamsen, M. (1992) 'Patterns of selection in six countries', *The Psychologist*, May, 205–7.
Smith, J. M., Hartley, J. and Stewart, B. J. M. (1978) 'A case study of repertory grids used in vocational guidance', *Journal of Occupational Psychology*, 51, 1, 97–104.
Smith, J. M. and Stewart, B. J. M. (1977) 'Repertory grids: a flexible tool for establishing the content and structure of a manager's thoughts', in D. Ashton (ed.), *Management Bibliographies and Reviews*, vol. 3 (Bradford: MCB Publications).
Smith, J. M. and Robertson, I. T. (1989) *Advances in Selection and Assessment* (Chichester: Wiley).
Smith, P. L. (1976) 'The problem of criteria', in M. D. Dunnette (ed.), *Handbook of Industrial and Organizational Psychology* (Chicago: Rand McNally).
Smith, P. L. and Kendall, L. M. (1963) 'Retranslation of expectations: an approach to the construction of unambiguous anchors for rating scales', *Journal of Applied Psychology*, 47, 149–55.
Sneath, F., Tahkur, M. and Medjuck, B. (1976) *Testing People at Work* (London: Institute of Personnel Management).
Sonneman, U. and Kerman, J. P. (1962) 'Handwriting analysis – a valid selection tool?', *Personnel Psychology*, 39, 8–14.
Sparks, C. P. (1970) 'Validity of psychological tests', *Personnel Psychology*, 23, 39–46.
Sparrow, J., Patrick, J., Spurgeon, P. and Barwell, F. (1982) 'The use of job component analysis related aptitudes in personnel selection', *Journal of Occupational Psychology*, 53, 3, 157–64.
Spearman, C. (1927) *The Abilities of Man* (London: Macmillan).
Spector, P. E., Brannick, M. T. and Coovert, M. D. (1989) 'Job analysis', in C. L. Cooper, and I. T. Robertson (eds), *International Review of Industrial and Organisational Psychology 1989* (Chichester: John Wiley).
Springbett, B. M. (1958) 'Factors affecting the final decision in an employment interview', *Canadian Journal of Psychology*, 12, 13–22.
Stanley, J. C. (1967) 'Further evidence via analysis of variance that women are more predictable academically than men', *Ontario Journal of Educational Research*, 10, 49–56.
Stark, S. (1959) 'Research criteria of executive success', *Journal of Business*, 32, 1–14.
Stewart, R. (1967) *Managers and their Jobs* (London: Macmillan).
Stone, C. L. and Sawatzki, B. (1980) 'Hiring bias and the disabled interview: effects of manipulating work history and disability information of the disabled job applicant', *Journal of Vocational Behavior*, 16, 96–104.
Strauss, G. and Sayles, L. R. (1980) *Personnel: The Human Problems of Management* (Englewood Cliffs, NJ: Prentice-Hall).
Strong, E. K. (1951) 'Permanence of interest scores over 22 years', *Journal of Applied Psychology*, 35, 89–92.
Stumpf, S. A., Brief, A. P. and Hartman, K. (1987) 'Self-efficacy expectations and coping with career-related events', *Journal of Vocational Behavior*, 31, 91–108.

Tavernier, G. (1973) *Design of Personnel Systems and Records* (Aldershot: Gower).

Taylor, J. B. (1968) 'Rating scales as measures of clinical judgement: a method for increasing scale reliability and sensitivity', *Educational Psychological Measurement*, 28, 747–66.

Taylor, M. S. and Bergmann, T. J. (1987) 'Organizational recruitment activities and applicants' reactions at different stages of the recruitment process', *Personnel Psychology*, 40, 261–85.

Teel, K. S. and Dubois, H. (1983) 'Participants' reactions to assessment centres', *Personnel Administrator* (March), 85–91.

Tenopyr, M. L. (1977) 'Content–construct confusion', *Personnel Psychology*, 30, 47–54.

Tenopyr, M. L. and Oeltjen, P. D. (1982) 'Personnel selection and classification', *Annual Review of Psychology*, 33, 582–618.

Tett, R. P. and Jackson, D. N. (1990) 'Organization and personality correlates of participative behaviours using an in-basket exercise', *Journal of Occupational Psychology*, 63, 175–88.

Tett, R. P., Jackson, D. N. and Rothstein, M. (1991) 'Personality measures as predictors of job performance: a meta analytic review', *Personnel Psychology*, 44, 703–42.

Thomas, P. J. (1975) *Racial Differences in the Prediction of Class 'A' School Grades*, Technical Bulletin NPRDC-TR-75-39 (San Diego, CA: Navy Personnel Research and Development Center).

Thompson, H. A. (1970) 'Comparison of predictor and criterion judgements of managerial performance using the multi-trait multi-method approach', *Journal of Applied Psychology*, 54, 496–502.

Thorndike, R. L. (1949) *Personnel Selection: Test and Measurement Techniques* (New York: Wiley).

Thorndike, R. L. (1971) 'Concepts of culture fairness', *Journal of Educational Measurement*, 8, 2, 63–70.

Thornton, G. C. (in press) 'The effect of selection practices on applicants' perceptions of organisational characteristics', in H. Schuler, J. L. Farr and J. M. Smith, *Personnel Selection and Performance Appraisal: Individual and Organizational Perspectives* (Hillsdale, NJ: Lawrence Erlbaum).

Thornton, G. C. III (1980) 'Psychometric properties of self appraisals of job performance', *Personnel Psychology*, 33, 263–71.

Thornton, G. C. and Byham, W. C. (1982) *Assessment Centers and Managerial Performance* (New York: Academic Press).

Thurstone, L. L. (1938) *Primary Mental Abilities* (University of Chicago Press).

Thurstone, L. L. and Thurstone, T. G. (1941) *Factorial Studies of Intelligence* (Chicago: University of Chicago Press).

Thurstone, T. G. and Thurstone, L. L. (1952) *Thurstone Test of Mental Alertness* (Henley on Thames: Science Research Associates).

Tiffin, J. and Phelan, R. F. (1953) 'Use of the Kuder Preference Record to predict turnover in an industrial plant', *Personnel Psychology*, 6, 195–204.

Tomkins, S. S. (1961) Discussion of Dr Murstein's paper in J. Kagan and G. S. Lesser (eds.) *Contemporary Issues in Thematic Apperception Methods* (Springfield, Ill.: Charles C. Thomas).

Torrow, W. W. and Pinter, P. R. (1976) 'The development of a managerial job taxonomy: a system for classifying and evaluating executive positions', *Journal of Applied Psychology*, 61, 4, 410–18.

Trattner, M. H. (1963) 'Comparison of three methods for assembling aptitude test batteries', *Personnel Psychology*, 16, 221–32.

Trattner, M. H., Fine, S. A. and Kubis, J. F. (1955) 'A comparison of worker requirement ratings made by reading job descriptions and by direct observation', *Personnel Psychology*, 8, 183–94.

Trattner, M. H. and O'Leary, B. S. (1980) 'Sample sizes for specified statistical power in testing for differential validity', *Journal of Applied Psychology*, 65, 2, 127–34.

Tuller, W. L. and Barrett, G. V. (1976) 'The future autobiography as a predictor of sales success', *Journal of Applied Psychology*, 61, 3, 371–3.

Uhrbrock, R. S. (1961) '2000 scaled items', *Personnel Psychology*, 3, 285–316.

Ulrich, L. and Trumbo, D. (1965) 'The selection interview since 1949', *Psychological Bulletin*, 53, 100–16.

Ungerson, B. (1974) 'Assessment centres – a review of research findings', *Personnel Review*, 3, 4–13.

Urry, V. W. (1977) 'Tailored testing: a successful application of latent trait theory', *Journal of Educational Measurement*, 14, 2, 181–96.

USA Government (1978) *Uniform Guidelines on Employee Selection Procedures*, Federal Register, 43, no. 166, 38296–38309.

Valenzi, E. and Andrews, I. R. (1973) 'Individual differences in the decision process of employment interviewers', *Journal of Applied Psychology*, 58, 49–53.

Vernon, P. E. (1960) *The Structure of Human Abilities* (London: Methuen).

Vernon, P. E. (1969) *Intelligence and Cultural Environment* (London: Methuen).

Vincent, M. D. (1974) *Vincent Mechanical Diagrams Test* (Slough: National Foundation for Educational Research).

Wainer, H. and Thissen, D. (1981) 'Graphical data analysis', *Annual Review of Psychology*, 32, 191–241.

Wallace, S. R. (1974) 'How high the validity', *Personnel Psychology*, 27, 397–407.

Walner, T. (1975) 'Hypotheses of handwriting and their verification', *Professional Psychology*, 6, 8–16.

Wanous, J. P. (1977) 'Organizational entry: newcomers moving from outside to inside', *Psychological Bulletin*, 84, 601–18.

Wechsler, D. (1955) *Wechsler Adult Intelligence Scale* (New York: Psychological Corporation).

Weekley, J. A. and Gier, J. A. (1987) 'Reliability and validity of the situational interview for a sales position', *Journal of Applied Psychology*, 72, 484–87.

Weisner, W. H. and Cronshaw, S. F. (1988) 'A meta-analytic investigation of the impact of interview format and degree of structure on the validity of the employment interview', *Journal of Occupational Psychology*, 61, 4, 275–90.

Weiss, D. J. and Davis, R. V. (1960) 'An objective validation of factual interview data', *Journal of Applied Psychology*, 44, 381–5.

Wernimont, P. F. and Campbell, J. P. (1968) 'Signs, samples and criteria', *Journal of Applied Psychology*, 52, 372–6.

West, L. and Bolanovich, D. J. (1963) 'Evaluation of typewriting proficiency: preliminary test development', *Journal of Applied Psychology*, 47, 403–7.

Wexley, K. N. and Nemeroff, H. F. W. (1974) 'The effects of racial prejudice, race of applicant and biographical similarity on interviewer evaluations of job applicants', *Journal of Social and Behavioral Sciences*, 20, 66–78.

Wexley, K. N. and Silverman, S. B. (1978) 'An examination of differences between managerial effectiveness and response patterns on a structured job analysis questionnaire', *Journal of Applied Psychology*, 63, 5, 646–9.

Whitener, E. M. (1990) 'Confusion of confidence intervals and credibility intervals in meta-analysis', *Journal of Applied Psychology*, 75, 315–21.

Whitlock, G. H., Clouse, R. J. and Spencer, W. F. (1963) 'Predicting accident proneness', *Personnel Psychology*, 16, 35–44.

Wiens, A. N., Jackson, R. H., Manaugh, T. S. and Matarazzo, J. D. (1969) 'Communication length as an index of communicator attitude: a replication', *Journal of Applied Psychology*, 53, 264–6.

Wietz, J. and Nuckols, R. C. (1953) 'A validation study of "How Supervise"', *Journal of Applied Psychology*, 37, 7–8.

Wing, A. M. and Baddely, A. D. (1978) 'A simple measure of handwriting as an index of stress', *Bulletin of the Psychonomic Society*, II, 245–6.

Winter, D. G. and Stewart, A. J. (1977) 'Power motive reliability as a function of retest instructions', *Journal of Consulting Clinical Psychology*, 45, 436–40.

Wollowick, H. B. and McNamara, W. J. (1969) 'Relationships of the components of an assessment center to management success', *Journal of Applied Psychology*, 53, 348–52.

Wonderlic, E. F. (1959) *Wonderlic Personnel Test* (PO Box 7, Northfield, Illinois: E. F. Wonderlic).

Woodruffe, C. (1990) *Assessment Centres* (London: Institute of Personnel Management).

Wright, P. M., Lichenfels, P. A. and Pursell, E. D. (1989) 'The structured interview: Additional studies and a meta-analysis', *Journal of Occupational Psychology*, 62, 191–9.

Young, I. P. and Heneman, J. G. (1986) 'Predictors of interviewee reactions to selection interview', *Journal of Research and Development in Education*, 19, 2, 29–36.

Youngman, R., Ostoby, J. D., Monk, J. D. and Heywood, J. (1978) *Analysing Jobs* (Aldershot: Gower Press).

Zalinski, J. S. and Abrahams, N. M. (1979) 'The effects of item context in faking personnel selection inventories', *Personnel Psychology*, 32, 161–6.

Zdep, S. M. and Weaver, H. B. (1967) 'The graphoanalytic approach to selecting life insurance salesmen', *Journal of Applied Psychology*, 51, 295–9.

Zedeck, S., Tziner, A. and Middlestat, S. E. (1983) 'Interviewing validity and reliability: an individual analysis approach', *Personnel Psychology*, 36, 335–70.

Zepp, M., Belenky, A. and Rosen, T. (1977) *Reliability of Functional Job Analysis Statements* (Washington, DC: Sidney Fine Associates).

Index

Centre
for Public and
Volunt   Sector